AMERICA'S RANKING AMONG NATIONS

A GLOBAL PERSPECTIVE OF THE UNITED STATES IN GRAPHIC DETAIL

MICHAEL D. DULBERGER

Donated
By

Elaine Hinshaw

Published in the United States of America
by Bernan Press, a wholly owned subsidiary of
The Rowman & Littlefield Publishing Group, Inc.
4501 Forbes Boulevard, Suite 200
Lanham, Maryland 20706

Bernan Press
800-865-3457
customercare@bernan.com
www.bernan.com

ISBN-13: 978-1-59888-603-0

~ <u>Contents</u> ~

Chapter 3: U.S. Education in Relation to the World

Chapter 4: U.S. Education

Chapter 5: The U.S. Economy in Relation to the World

Chapter 6: U.S. Economy

Chapter 7: The U.S. Role in International Trade

Chapter 8: U.S. Employment in Relation to the World

Chapter 9: U.S. Employment

Chapter 10: U.S. Energy in Relation to the World

Chapter 11: U.S. Energy

Chapter 12: U.S. Health in Relation to the World

Chapter 13: U.S. Innovation in Relation to the World

Chapter 14: U.S. National Defense in Relation to the World

Appendices

Index

America's Ranking Among Nations
A Global Perspective of the United States in Graphic Detail

We've all heard the expression: *You are entitled to your own opinions but not your own facts.* Have you ever considered exactly how you learn the "facts"?

In recent years, there has been a great deal of public discourse and shouting about America's decline in everything from economic, military, and environmental matters to the collapse of the American family unit, while the world changes around us at accelerating speed. We read about China's incredible economic growth, the European debt crisis, the Arab Awakening and the increasing polarization between wealthy and poor in America. To grasp the essence of these changes, and to judge their implications, it is essential that we first acquire a broad foundation of knowledge obtained from unbiased sources. With a strong foundation we become more capable of assimilating new information, assessing both its credibility and relevance, from which we can build our own points of view.

This book was created to spare the reader the effort of seeking out and vetting validated informational resources and to provide key metrics, in graphic format, about the United States and how the United States compares with other nations. All the information presented includes the attributed sources to enable verification or augmentation of the data. The author's objective is to deliver maximum knowledge with minimum effort on the part of the reader. Unlike most books written on social-economic-global matters, this book presents facts without opinions, enabling the reader to literally see the United States' ranking vis-á-vis all the world's nations. The data used to create the charts have been distilled from extensive data sources to focus on comparing the U.S. against the most economically powerful countries and also against those countries that are in the top ten position—regardless of economic status. Many of the charts extend over a 50–60 year period making trends visually obvious and easy for the reader to extrapolate as he/she chooses. Collectively these charts provide a compendium of revealing information about America's position among the world's nations, presented in a nonsensational, objective manner.

Most people rely on the news media to stay informed about national and global events; however consider for a moment the news reporters' information sources. Those sources are often political leaders who have their own agenda and provide only supporting facts. It's not that the information is wrong but rather that it is selective. It is also unusual to receive a broad perspective on a topic from the media, which focuses on immediate issues rather than providing educational background data. Despite these informational handicaps, each of us has somehow created opinions on most topics, since our brains are trained to force-fit information we receive into the framework of our existing beliefs. These beliefs tend to become reinforced with time since we subconsciously filter new information to fit our established thought paradigms.

Many of our "facts" may actually be dogma, so entrenched in our thinking that we are not even aware that we lack objectivity. We often develop personal positions on important issues without a solid foundation of supporting information. If asked to explain our views we most likely repeat political party rhetoric we've become comfortable with and have learned to align with.

The critical criteria in determining the value of any informational resource are its pedigree, i.e., how reliable the source is, and the ease with which one can extract the specific information being sought. There are many organizations and individuals providing "facts" so one must view all sources with healthy skepticism. Ulterior motives are sometimes obvious (please donate to ...) but some are more insidious, designed to influence public opinion as do many politically motivated websites and blogs. The late-night comedy shows you watch may have more influence on your attitudes about current events through their subliminal messages than your favorite newspapers.

Fortunately, establishing a credible information baseline is much easier to achieve today than it would have been just a decade ago, thanks to universal access to high-speed Internet and hundreds of public databases now available just keystrokes away to anyone who takes the time to seek them out.

You can now access thousands of characteristics about the residents and government of virtually any of the 193 sovereign nations on the planet. You can compare military manpower, obesity prevalence, infant mortality, national debt, crude oil imports, and even the number of cell phone subscriptions. Many databases extend back in time 50 years or more, and when graphically displayed can help you develop your own sense of change and what it portends for the future.

It may not surprise you to learn that the United States Census Bureau publishes massive amounts of data, but did you know they publish *international* data, as does the Federal Reserve, Internal Revenue Service, United States Department of Energy, Congressional Budget Office, Bureau of Economic Analysis, Energy Information Administration and many other government agencies. Even the Central Intelligence Agency publishes extensive volumes comparing all the world's countries, and the results are readily available to the general public. In addition to the U.S. government resources there are also highly credible international organizations with accessible databases, including The World Bank, the World Health Organization and the United Nations, to name a few. (See Appendix V for the complete listing of information resources used in creating this book.)

Ironically, a major digital-information age dilemma has become the overabundance of information. It's like having a fire hose when you only need a sip of water. Just try googling "U.S. ranking in the world for ...." (fill in the blanks) and you'll find millions of results!

This book will enable you to see for yourself America's standing relative to other nations in each of hundreds of metrics. The author is confident you will readily learn facts that will stimulate your thinking and may change the lens through which you view the world, regardless of your political persuasion. Perhaps you may even change some of your opinions! The more people in our democratic republic are exposed to global reality checks, the better will be the solutions debated around the family room and in the halls of Congress. The author is also confident that when you finish this book you'll return to it, again and again, as a refresher of the facts.

~

Chapter 1: U.S. Demographics in Relation to the World

Overview

The United States, China, and Canada are approximately the same geographic size, each occupying 7.1 percent of the world's land area, compared with Russia, the largest country in the world, occupying 12.6 percent. In 2011, 312 million people out of the world's 6.97 billion inhabitants called the United States home, the third most populated country, with approximately one-quarter of the number of people that live in China or India. While the United States' portion of the world's population declined from 6.0 percent to 4.5 percent over the past fifty years, India's portion has increased from 14.0 percent to 17.1 percent.

In 2011, India had 12 times the population density (persons per square mile) as the United States.

One-half of the U.S. population was above age 36.9 years (median age) whereas the world's median age was 28.4 years and 13.9 percent of the U.S. population was over age 64 compared with the world's average of 7.6 percent.

Approximately 1-in-5 working-age residents in the United States were over age 64, compared with approximately 1-in-7 in 1960.

The world's average number of live births per woman has continuously declined over the past 50 years and in 2011 was approximately 2.5 births. The U.S. live birth rate has stabilized over the past two decades at 2.1, considered to be the population replacement level. However, the U.S. population level continues to grow due to a net migration of approximately one million persons per year, which is the largest net migration of any country.

In 2007, 14 percent of all persons in the United States were born elsewhere, an increase from 9 percent in 1988, ranking fifth among developed countries after Luxembourg (43 percent), Australia (25 percent), Switzerland (21 percent) and Canada (20 percent).

~

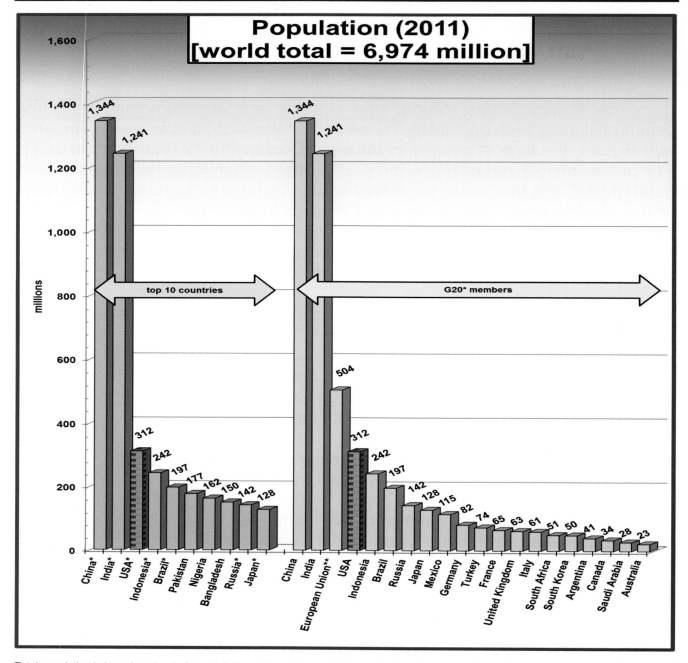

Population (2011)
[world total = 6,974 million]

Total population is based on the de facto definition of population, which counts all residents regardless of legal status or citizenship—except for refugees not permanently settled in the country of asylum, who are generally considered part of the population of their country of origin. The 2011 world total population was 6.97 billion, compared with 3.03 billion in 1960.

SOURCE: World Bank. (1) United Nations, Department of Economic and Social Affairs (advanced Excel tables). (2) Census reports and other statistical publications from national statistical offices, (3) Eurostat: Demographic Statistics, (4) Secretariat of the Pacific Community: Statistics and Demography Programme, (5) U.S. Census Bureau: International Database, and (6) World Bank estimates. 2011 database accessed September 2012.

http://data.worldbank.org/data-catalog/world-development-indicators?cid=GPD_WDI and http://data.worldbank.org/indicator/all

*G20 Members (see Appendix I): Argentina, Australia, Brazil, Canada, China, France, Germany, India, Indonesia, Italy, Japan, South Korea, Mexico, Russian Federation, Saudi Arabia, South Africa, Turkey, United Kingdom, United States and the European Union**

**European Union (see Appendix II): Austria, Belgium, Bulgaria, Cyprus, Czech Rep., Denmark, Estonia, Finland, France, Germany, Greece, Hungary, Ireland, Italy, Latvia, Lithuania, Luxembourg, Malta, Netherlands, Poland, Portugal, Romania, Slovakia, Slovenia, Spain, Sweden, and the United Kingdom

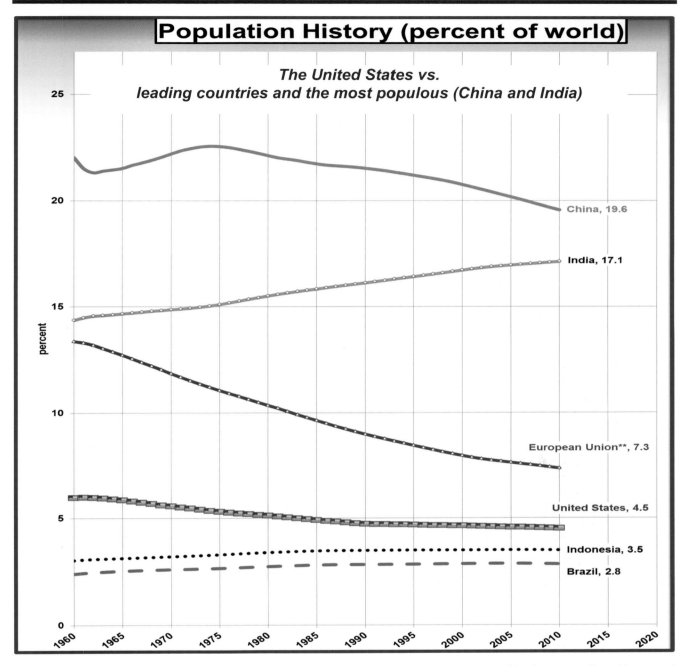

Population History (percent of world)

The United States vs.
leading countries and the most populous (China and India)

China, 19.6
India, 17.1
European Union**, 7.3
United States, 4.5
Indonesia, 3.5
Brazil, 2.8

percent

Total population is based on the de facto definition of population, which counts all residents regardless of legal status or citizenship—except for refugees not permanently settled in the country of asylum, who are generally considered part of the population of their country of origin. The 2011 world total population was 6.97 billion compared with 3.03 billion in 1960.

SOURCE: World Bank. (1) United Nations, Department of Economic and Social Affairs (advanced Excel tables). (2) Census reports and other statistical publications from national statistical offices, (3) Eurostat: Demographic Statistics, (4) Secretariat of the Pacific Community: Statistics and Demography Programme, (5) U.S. Census Bureau: International Database, and (6) World Bank estimates. 2010 database accessed March 2012.

http://data.worldbank.org/data-catalog/world-development-indicators?cid=GPD_WDI and http://data.worldbank.org/indicator/all

**European Union (see Appendix II): Austria, Belgium, Bulgaria, Cyprus, Czech Rep., Denmark, Estonia, Finland, France, Germany, Greece, Hungary, Ireland, Italy, Latvia, Lithuania, Luxembourg, Malta, Netherlands, Poland, Portugal, Romania, Slovakia, Slovenia, Spain, Sweden, and the United Kingdom

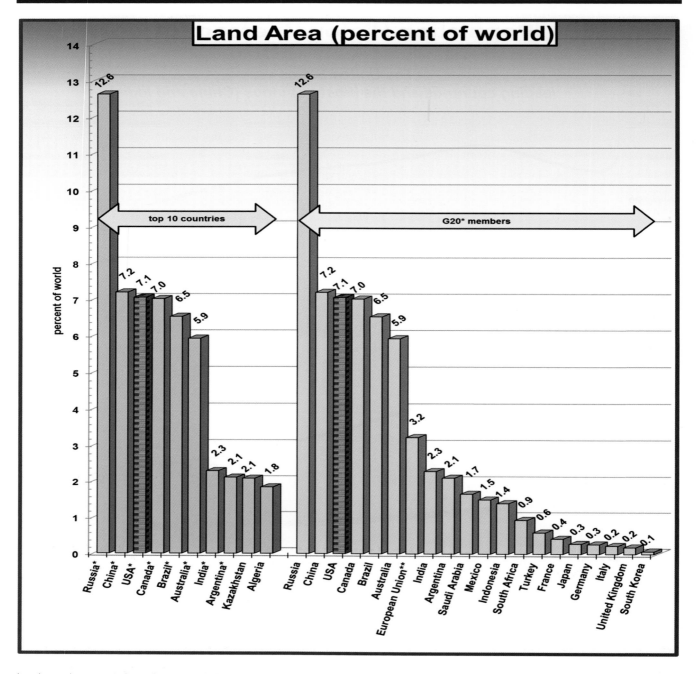

Land area is a country's total area, excluding area under inland water bodies, national claims to continental shelf, and exclusive economic zones.

SOURCE: World Bank. Food and Agriculture Organization, electronic files and web site; 2010 database accessed April 2012.

http://data.worldbank.org/data-catalog/world-development-indicators?cid=GPD_WDI.

*G20 Members (see Appendix I): Argentina, Australia, Brazil, Canada, China, France, Germany, India, Indonesia, Italy, Japan, South Korea, Mexico, Russian Federation, Saudi Arabia, South Africa, Turkey, United Kingdom, United States and the European Union**

**European Union (see Appendix II): Austria, Belgium, Bulgaria, Cyprus, Czech Rep., Denmark, Estonia, Finland, France, Germany, Greece, Hungary, Ireland, Italy, Latvia, Lithuania, Luxembourg, Malta, Netherlands, Poland, Portugal, Romania, Slovakia, Slovenia, Spain, Sweden, and the United Kingdom

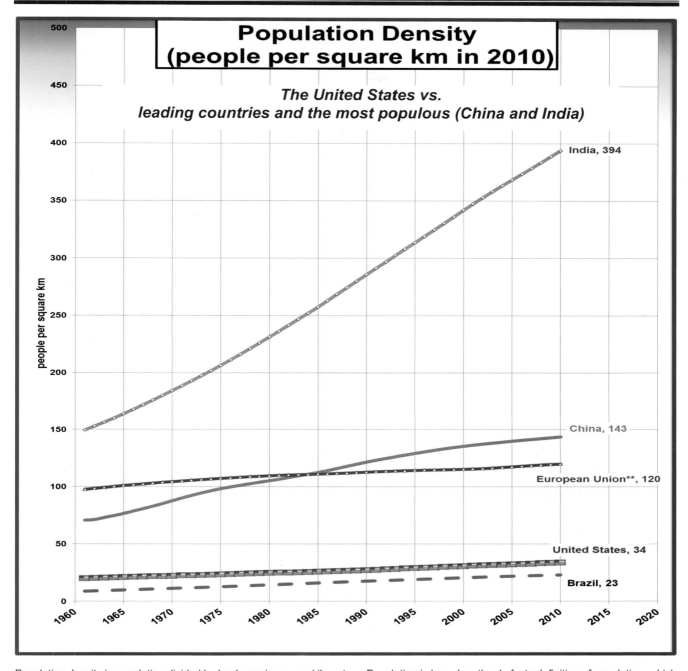

Population density is population divided by land area in square kilometers. Population is based on the de facto definition of population, which counts all residents regardless of legal status or citizenship—except for refugees not permanently settled in the country of asylum, who are generally considered part of the population of their country of origin.

SOURCE: World Bank. Food and Agriculture Organization, electronic files and web site; 2010 database accessed April 2012.

http://data.worldbank.org/data-catalog/world-development-indicators?cid=GPD_WDI.

*G20 Members (see Appendix I): Argentina, Australia, Brazil, Canada, China, France, Germany, India, Indonesia, Italy, Japan, South Korea, Mexico, Russian Federation, Saudi Arabia, South Africa, Turkey, United Kingdom, United States and the European Union**

**European Union (see Appendix II): Austria, Belgium, Bulgaria, Cyprus, Czech Rep., Denmark, Estonia, Finland, France, Germany, Greece, Hungary, Ireland, Italy, Latvia, Lithuania, Luxembourg, Malta, Netherlands, Poland, Portugal, Romania, Slovakia, Slovenia, Spain, Sweden, and the United Kingdom

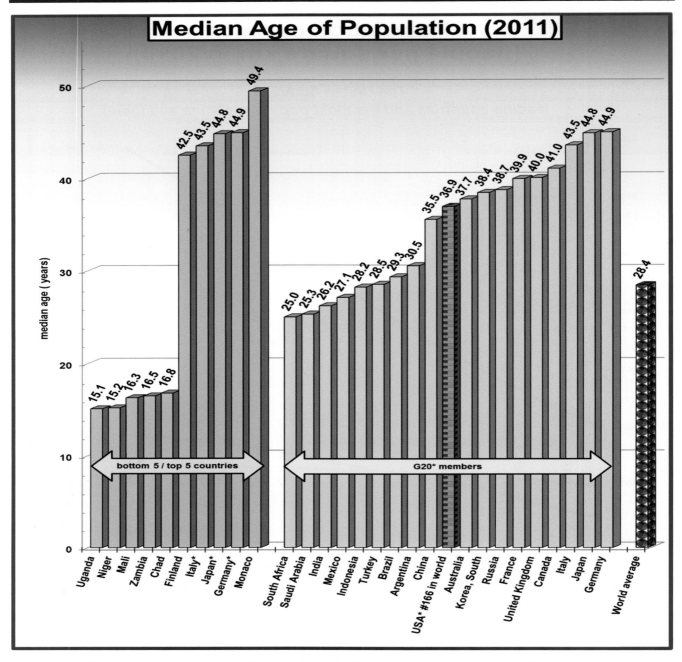

Median Age of Population (2011)

median age (years)

bottom 5 / top 5 countries

G20* members

Uganda 15.1, Niger 15.2, Mali 16.3, Zambia 16.5, Chad 16.8, Finland 42.5, Italy* 43.5, Japan* 44.8, Germany* 44.9, Monaco 49.4

South Africa 25.0, Saudi Arabia 25.3, India 26.2, Mexico 27.1, Indonesia 28.2, Turkey 28.5, Brazil 29.3, Argentina 30.5, China 35.5, USA* #166 in world 36.9, Australia 37.7, Korea, South 38.4, Russia 38.7, France 39.9, United Kingdom 40.0, Canada 41.0, Italy 43.5, Japan 44.8, Germany 44.9

World average 28.4

Median age divides a population into two numerically equal groups; that is, half the people are younger than this age and half are older. It is a single index that summarizes the age distribution of a population; 2011 database.

SOURCE: Central Intelligence Agency

https://www.cia.gov/library/publications/the-world-factbook/fields/2177.html

*G20 Members (see Appendix I): Argentina, Australia, Brazil, Canada, China, France, Germany, India, Indonesia, Italy, Japan, South Korea, Mexico, Russian Federation, Saudi Arabia, South Africa, Turkey, United Kingdom, United States and the European Union**

**European Union (see Appendix II): Austria, Belgium, Bulgaria, Cyprus, Czech Rep., Denmark, Estonia, Finland, France, Germany, Greece, Hungary, Ireland, Italy, Latvia, Lithuania, Luxembourg, Malta, Netherlands, Poland, Portugal, Romania, Slovakia, Slovenia, Spain, Sweden, and the United Kingdom

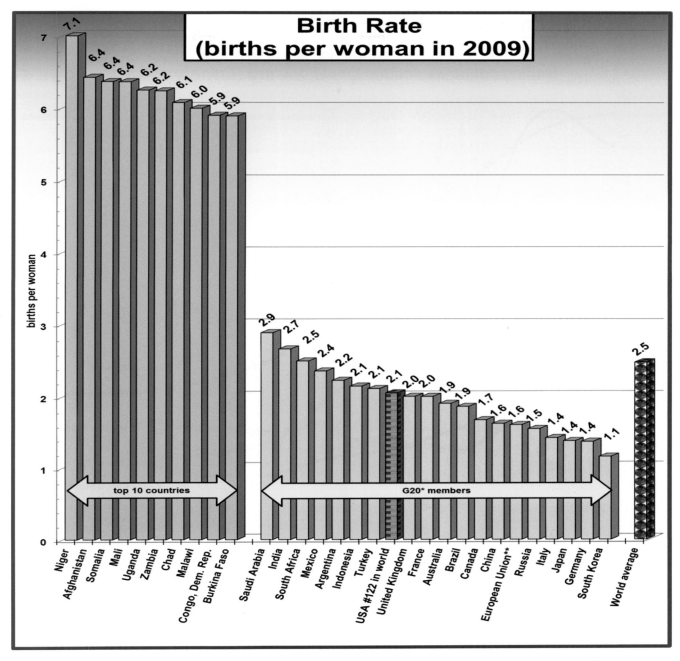

**Birth Rate
(births per woman in 2009)**

Birth (fertility) rate represents the number of children that would be born to a woman if she were to live to the end of her childbearing years and bear children in accordance with current age-specific fertility rates.

SOURCE: World Bank. (1) United Nations Population Division. World Population Prospects. New York, United Nations, Department of Economic and Social Affairs (advanced Excel tables). Available at http://esa.un.org/unpd/wpp2008/index.htm. (2) Census reports and other statistical publications from national statistical offices, (3) Eurostat: Demographic Statistics, (4) Secretariat of the Pacific Community: Statistics and Demography Programme, (5) U.S. Census Bureau: International Database, and (6) household surveys conducted by national agencies, Macro International, and the U.S. Centers for Disease Control and Prevention.

http://data.worldbank.org/data-catalog/world-development-indicators?cid=GPD_WDI

*G20 Members (see Appendix I): Argentina, Australia, Brazil, Canada, China, France, Germany, India, Indonesia, Italy, Japan, South Korea, Mexico, Russian Federation, Saudi Arabia, South Africa, Turkey, United Kingdom, United States and the European Union**

**European Union (see Appendix II): Austria, Belgium, Bulgaria, Cyprus, Czech Rep., Denmark, Estonia, Finland, France, Germany, Greece, Hungary, Ireland, Italy, Latvia, Lithuania, Luxembourg, Malta, Netherlands, Poland, Portugal, Romania, Slovakia, Slovenia, Spain, Sweden, and the United Kingdom

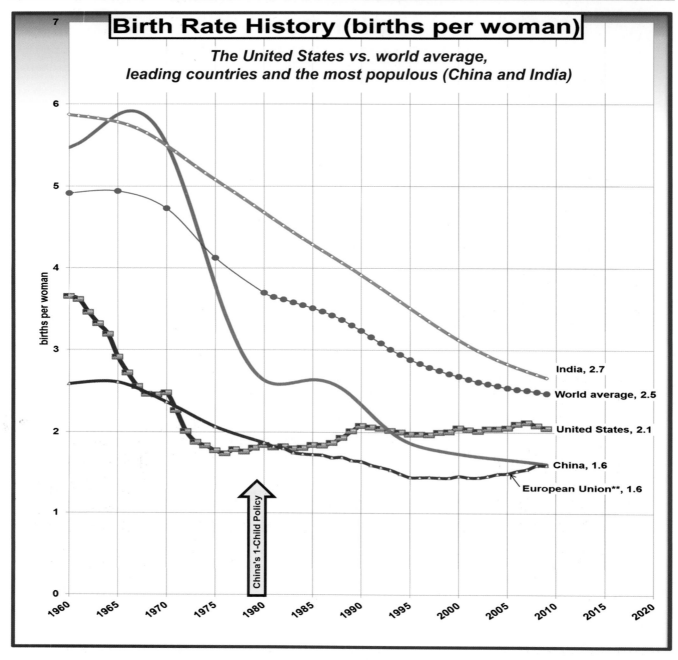

Birth Rate History (births per woman)

The United States vs. world average, leading countries and the most populous (China and India)

(y-axis: births per woman, ranging 0 to 7)

India, 2.7
World average, 2.5
United States, 2.1
China, 1.6
European Union**, 1.6

China's 1-Child Policy

(x-axis years: 1960, 1965, 1970, 1975, 1980, 1985, 1990, 1995, 2000, 2005, 2010, 2015, 2020)

Total birth rate (also referred to as fertility rate) represents the number of children that would be born to a woman if she were to live to the end of her childbearing years and bear children in accordance with current age-specific fertility rates.

SOURCE: World Bank. (1) United Nations Population Division. World Population Prospects. New York, United Nations, Department of Economic and Social Affairs (advanced Excel tables). Available at http://esa.un.org/unpd/wpp2008/index.htm. (2) Census reports and other statistical publications from national statistical offices, (3) Eurostat: Demographic Statistics, (4) Secretariat of the Pacific Community: Statistics and Demography Programme, (5) U.S. Census Bureau: International Database, and (6) household surveys conducted by national agencies, Macro International, and the U.S. Centers for Disease Control and Prevention.

http://data.worldbank.org/data-catalog/world-development-indicators?cid=GPD_WDI

**European Union (see Appendix II): Austria, Belgium, Bulgaria, Cyprus, Czech Rep., Denmark, Estonia, Finland, France, Germany, Greece, Hungary, Ireland, Italy, Latvia, Lithuania, Luxembourg, Malta, Netherlands, Poland, Portugal, Romania, Slovakia, Slovenia, Spain, Sweden, and the United Kingdom

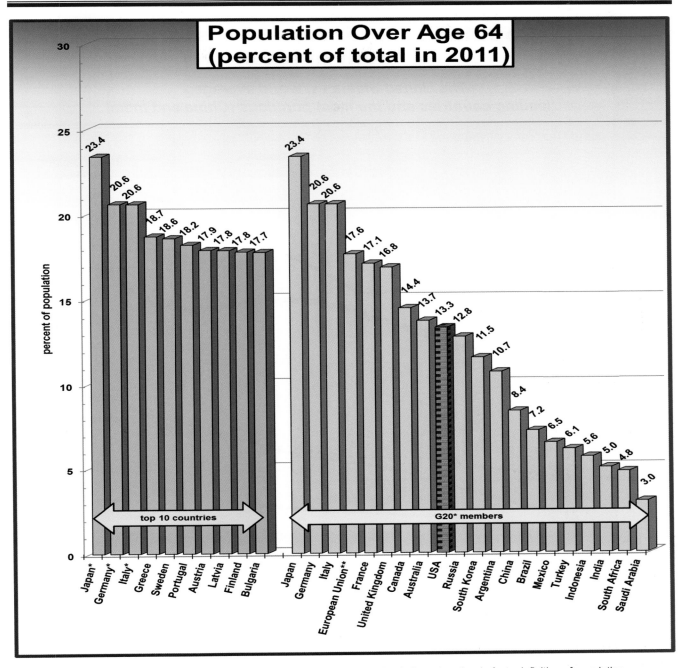

Population Over Age 64 (percent of total in 2011)

top 10 countries: Japan* 23.4, Germany* 20.6, Italy* 20.6, Greece 18.7, Sweden 18.6, Portugal 18.2, Austria 17.9, Latvia 17.8, Finland 17.8, Bulgaria 17.7

G20* members: Japan 23.4, Germany 20.6, Italy 20.6, European Union** 17.6, France 17.1, United Kingdom 16.8, Canada 14.4, Australia 13.7, USA 13.3, Russia 12.8, South Korea 11.5, Argentina 10.7, China 8.4, Brazil 7.2, Mexico 6.5, Turkey 6.1, Indonesia 5.6, India 5.0, South Africa 4.8, Saudi Arabia 3.0

Population ages 65 and above as a percentage of the total population. Population is based on the de facto definition of population.

SOURCE: World Bank staff estimates from various sources including census reports, the United Nations Population Division's World Population Prospects, national statistical offices, household surveys conducted by national agencies, and Macro International.

http://data.worldbank.org/data-catalog/world-development-indicators?cid=GPD_WDI

*G20 Members (see Appendix I): Argentina, Australia, Brazil, Canada, China, France, Germany, India, Indonesia, Italy, Japan, South Korea, Mexico, Russian Federation, Saudi Arabia, South Africa, Turkey, United Kingdom, United States and the European Union**

**European Union (see Appendix II): Austria, Belgium, Bulgaria, Cyprus, Czech Rep., Denmark, Estonia, Finland, France, Germany, Greece, Hungary, Ireland, Italy, Latvia, Lithuania, Luxembourg, Malta, Netherlands, Poland, Portugal, Romania, Slovakia, Slovenia, Spain, Sweden, and the United Kingdom

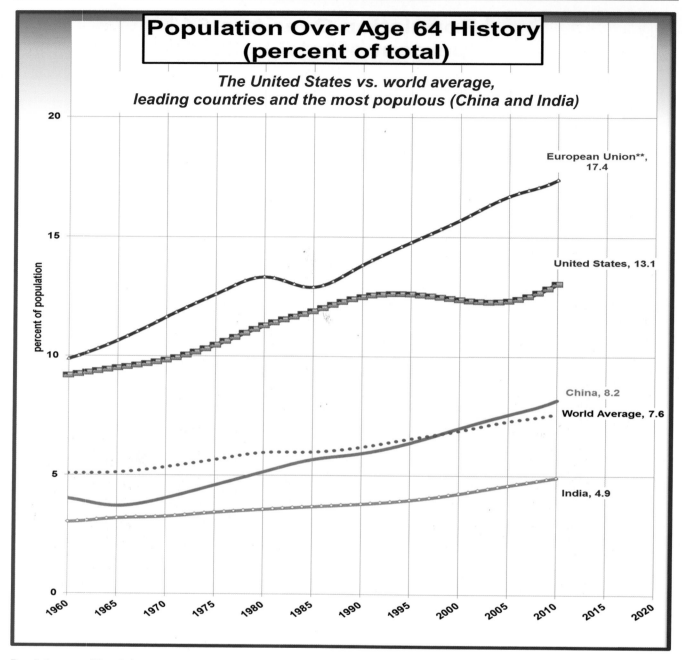

Population Over Age 64 History (percent of total)

The United States vs. world average, leading countries and the most populous (China and India)

European Union**, 17.4

United States, 13.1

China, 8.2

World Average, 7.6

India, 4.9

Population ages 65 and above as a percentage of the total population. Population is based on the de facto definition of population.

SOURCE: World Bank staff estimates from various sources including census reports, the United Nations Population Division's World Population Prospects, national statistical offices, household surveys conducted by national agencies, and Macro International.

http://data.worldbank.org/data-catalog/world-development-indicators?cid=GPD_WDI

*G20 Members (see Appendix I): Argentina, Australia, Brazil, Canada, China, France, Germany, India, Indonesia, Italy, Japan, South Korea, Mexico, Russian Federation, Saudi Arabia, South Africa, Turkey, United Kingdom, United States and the European Union**

**European Union (see Appendix II): Austria, Belgium, Bulgaria, Cyprus, Czech Rep., Denmark, Estonia, Finland, France, Germany, Greece, Hungary, Ireland, Italy, Latvia, Lithuania, Luxembourg, Malta, Netherlands, Poland, Portugal, Romania, Slovakia, Slovenia, Spain, Sweden, and the United Kingdom

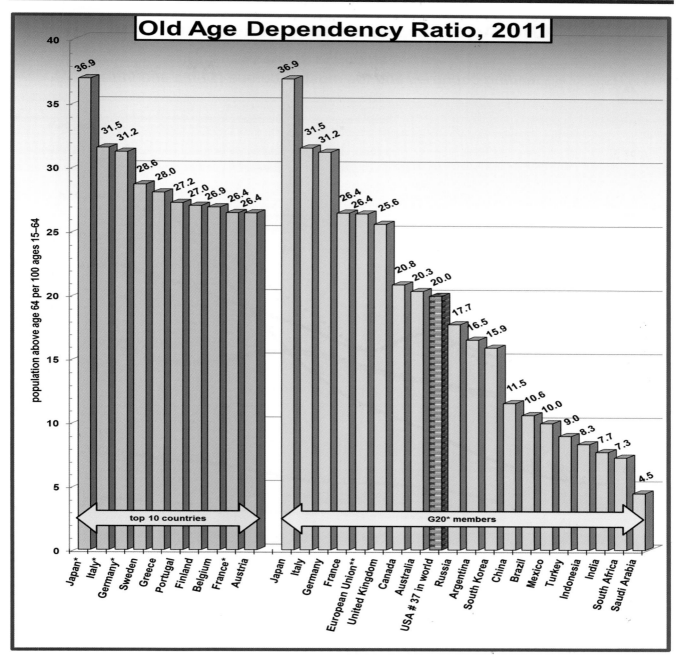

Old Age Dependency Ratio, 2011

population above age 64 per 100 ages 15–64

top 10 countries: Japan* 36.9, Italy* 31.5, Germany* 31.2, Sweden 28.6, Greece 28.0, Portugal 27.2, Finland 27.0, Belgium 26.9, France* 26.4, Austria 26.4

G20* members: Japan 36.9, Italy 31.5, Germany 31.2, France 26.4, European Union** 26.4, United Kingdom 25.6, Canada 20.8, Australia 20.3, USA #37 in world 20.0, Russia 17.7, Argentina 16.5, South Korea 15.9, China 11.5, Brazil 10.6, Mexico 10.0, Turkey 9.0, Indonesia 8.3, India 7.7, South Africa 7.3, Saudi Arabia 4.5

Old age dependency ratio is the ratio of the number of older dependents—people older than 64—to the working-age number of persons—those ages 15–64. Data are shown as the proportion of dependents per 100 working-age population.

SOURCE: World Bank staff estimates from various sources including census reports, the United Nations Population Division's World Population Prospects, national statistical offices, household surveys conducted by national agencies, and Macro International; 2011 database accessed September 2012.

http://data.worldbank.org/data-catalog/world-development-indicators?cid=GPD_WDI and http://data.worldbank.org/indicator/all

*G20 Members (see Appendix I): Argentina, Australia, Brazil, Canada, China, France, Germany, India, Indonesia, Italy, Japan, South Korea, Mexico, Russian Federation, Saudi Arabia, South Africa, Turkey, United Kingdom, United States and the European Union**

**European Union (see Appendix II): Austria, Belgium, Bulgaria, Cyprus, Czech Rep., Denmark, Estonia, Finland, France, Germany, Greece, Hungary, Ireland, Italy, Latvia, Lithuania, Luxembourg, Malta, Netherlands, Poland, Portugal, Romania, Slovakia, Slovenia, Spain, Sweden, and the United Kingdom

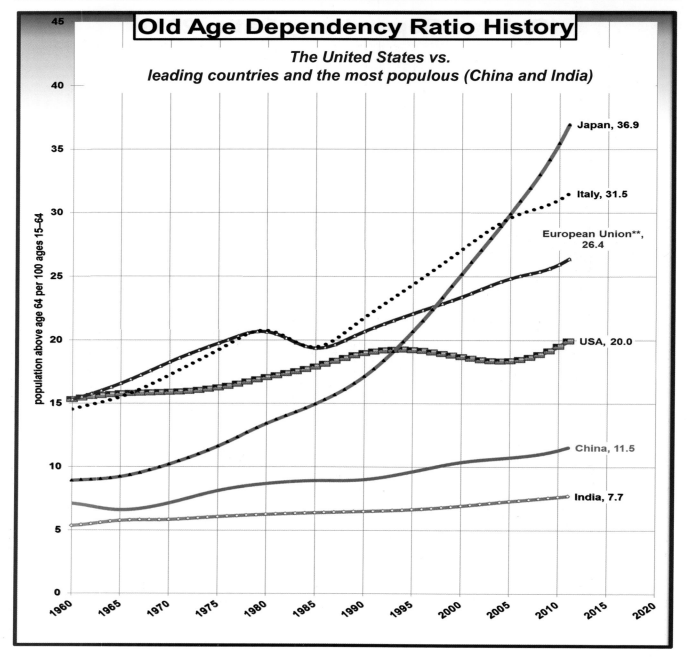

Old Age Dependency Ratio History

The United States vs.
leading countries and the most populous (China and India)

Japan, 36.9

Italy, 31.5

European Union**, 26.4

USA, 20.0

China, 11.5

India, 7.7

Old age dependency ratio is the ratio of the number of older dependents—people older than 64—to the working-age number of persons—those ages 15–64. Data are shown as the proportion of dependents per 100 working-age population.

SOURCE: World Bank staff estimates from various sources including census reports, the United Nations Population Division's World Population Prospects, national statistical offices, household surveys conducted by national agencies, and Macro International; 2011 database accessed September 2012.

http://data.worldbank.org/data-catalog/world-development-indicators?cid=GPD_WDI and http://data.worldbank.org/indicator/all

**European Union (see Appendix II): Austria, Belgium, Bulgaria, Cyprus, Czech Rep., Denmark, Estonia, Finland, France, Germany, Greece, Hungary, Ireland, Italy, Latvia, Lithuania, Luxembourg, Malta, Netherlands, Poland, Portugal, Romania, Slovakia, Slovenia, Spain, Sweden, and the United Kingdom

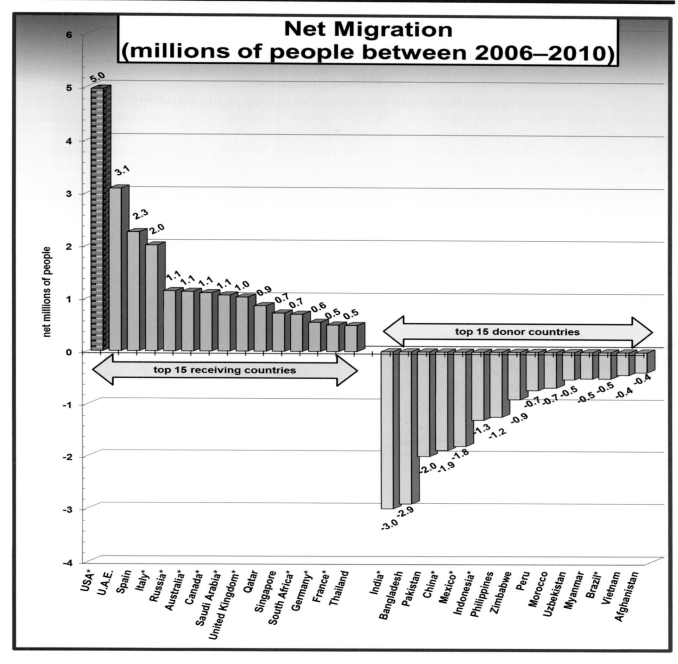

Net Migration (millions of people between 2006–2010)

Net migration is the net total of migrants during the period, that is, the total number of immigrants less the annual number of emigrants, including both citizens and noncitizens. Data are five-year estimates. To derive estimates of net migration, the United Nations Population Division takes into account the past migration history of a country or area, the migration policy of a country, and the influx of refugees in recent periods. The data to calculate these official estimates come from a variety of sources, including border statistics, administrative records, surveys, and censuses.

SOURCE: World Bank. United Nations Population Division, World Population Prospects; 2010 database accessed April 2012.

http://data.worldbank.org/data-catalog/world-development-indicators?cid=GPD_WDI and http://data.worldbank.org/indicator/all

*G20 Members (see Appendix I): Argentina, Australia, Brazil, Canada, China, France, Germany, India, Indonesia, Italy, Japan, South Korea, Mexico, Russian Federation, Saudi Arabia, South Africa, Turkey, United Kingdom, United States and the European Union**

**European Union (see Appendix II): Austria, Belgium, Bulgaria, Cyprus, Czech Rep., Denmark, Estonia, Finland, France, Germany, Greece, Hungary, Ireland, Italy, Latvia, Lithuania, Luxembourg, Malta, Netherlands, Poland, Portugal, Romania, Slovakia, Slovenia, Spain, Sweden, and the United Kingdom

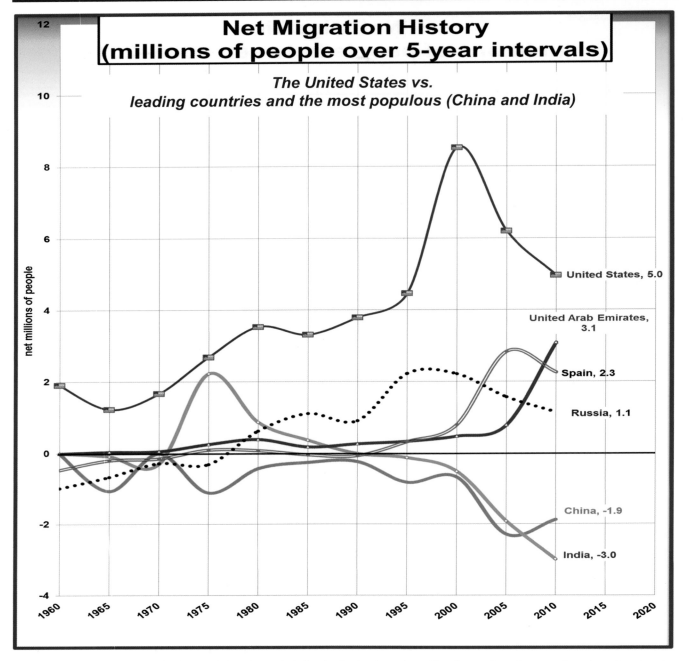

Net Migration History (millions of people over 5-year intervals)

The United States vs. leading countries and the most populous (China and India)

United States, 5.0
United Arab Emirates, 3.1
Spain, 2.3
Russia, 1.1
China, -1.9
India, -3.0

Net migration is the net total of migrants during the period, that is, the total number of immigrants less the annual number of emigrants, including both citizens and noncitizens. Data are five-year estimates. To derive estimates of net migration, the United Nations Population Division takes into account the past migration history of a country or area, the migration policy of a country, and the influx of refugees in recent periods. The data to calculate these official estimates come from a variety of sources, including border statistics, administrative records, surveys, and censuses.

SOURCE: World Bank. United Nations Population Division, World Population Prospects; 2010 database accessed April 2012.

http://data.worldbank.org/data-catalog/world-development-indicators?cid=GPD_WDI and http://data.worldbank.org/indicator/all

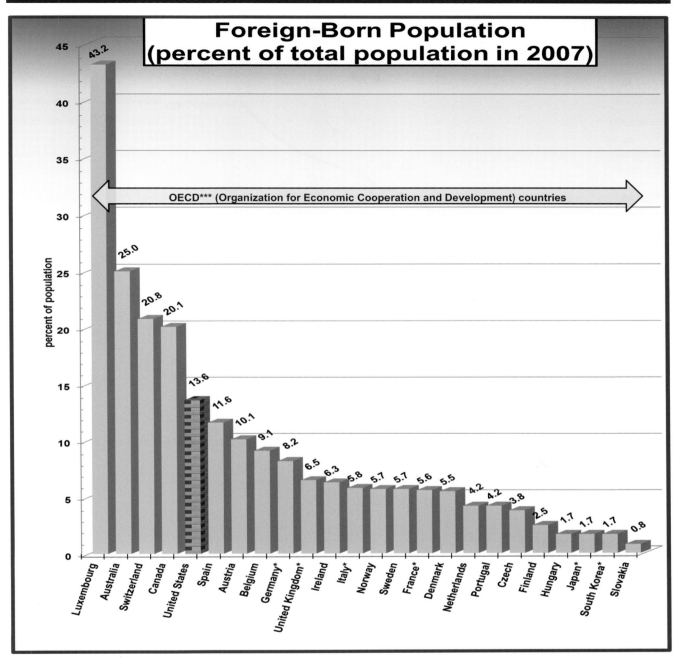

Foreign-Born Population (percent of total population in 2007)

In Australia, Canada, and the United States the foreign-born data refer to people present in the country who are foreign born. In the European countries and Japan they generally refer to foreigners and represent the nationalities of residents; as a result, persons born in these countries may be counted among the foreign population, whereas others, who are foreign born, may have acquired the host-country nationality. Data are from censuses for Australia, Canada, France, Mexico, New Zealand, and the United States, and from population registers for the other countries.

SOURCE: U.S. Census Bureau

http://www.census.gov/econ/susb/methodology.html

*G20 Members (see Appendix I): Argentina, Australia, Brazil, Canada, China, France, Germany, India, Indonesia, Italy, Japan, South Korea, Mexico, Russian Federation, Saudi Arabia, South Africa, Turkey, United Kingdom, United States and the European Union**

**European Union (see Appendix II): Austria, Belgium, Bulgaria, Cyprus, Czech Rep., Denmark, Estonia, Finland, France, Germany, Greece, Hungary, Ireland, Italy, Latvia, Lithuania, Luxembourg, Malta, Netherlands, Poland, Portugal, Romania, Slovakia, Slovenia, Spain, Sweden, and the United Kingdom

***OECD (see appendix III for members)

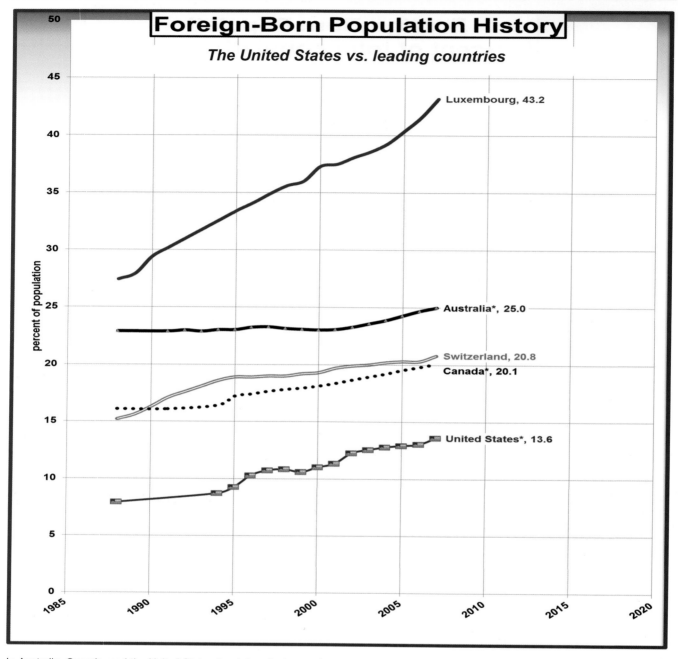

Foreign-Born Population History
The United States vs. leading countries

Luxembourg, 43.2

Australia*, 25.0

Switzerland, 20.8

Canada*, 20.1

United States*, 13.6

percent of population

In Australia, Canada, and the United States the data refer to people present in the country who are foreign born. In the European countries and Japan they generally refer to foreigners and represent the nationalities of residents; as a result, persons born in these countries may be counted among the foreign population, whereas others, who are foreign born, may have acquired the host-country nationality. Data are from censuses for Australia, Canada, France, Mexico, New Zealand, and the United States, and from population registers for the other countries.

SOURCE: U.S. Census Bureau

http://www.census.gov/econ/susb/methodology.html

*G20 Members (see Appendix I): Argentina, Australia, Brazil, Canada, China, France, Germany, India, Indonesia, Italy, Japan, South Korea, Mexico, Russian Federation, Saudi Arabia, South Africa, Turkey, United Kingdom, United States and the European Union**

Chapter 2: U.S. Demographics

Overview

There were 117.5 million households in the United States in 2009 with an average of 2.6 members each, 60 percent with only one or two members. Between 1967 and 2009 the portion of non-white households increased from 8.9 percent to 18.7 percent of all U.S. households.

In 2008, 41 percent of all women who gave birth in the United States were unmarried, an increase from 28 percent in 1990.

In 2010, U.S. prisons and jails held 2.3 million people, in addition to 5 million on parole or probation. Since 1982, the number of adults under correctional supervision increased by a factor of 3.3.

Of the total U.S. black male population, 9.9 percent, ages 30–34, were incarcerated.

One-third of all federal imprisonments were for the crime of drug trafficking.

One million aliens were sent back to their country of origin, including 128,000 criminals removed by court order.

Of the total U.S. population, 76 percent were Christian and 13 percent professed no religion.

Of all adults, 58 percent voted in the 2008 presidential election; 32 percent of Hispanic adults voted, and 73 percent of college graduates with bachelor's degrees or higher voted.

~

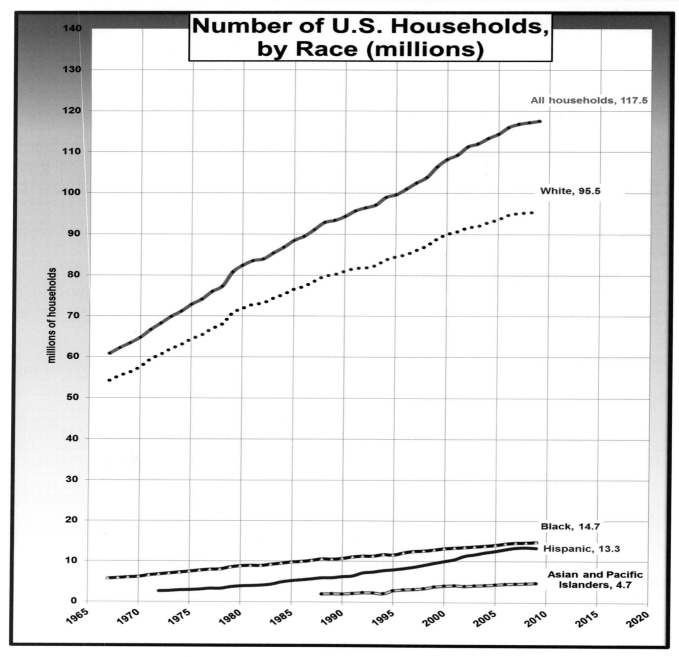

Number of U.S. Households, by Race (millions)

All households, 117.5

White, 95.5

Black, 14.7

Hispanic, 13.3

Asian and Pacific Islanders, 4.7

millions of households

U.S. Households. Note that commencing in 2003 the questionnaire permitted respondents to select more than 1 race and therefore the sum of individual races exceeds the total number of households.

SOURCE: U.S. Census Bureau

http://www.census.gov/hhes/www/income/data/historical/history.html

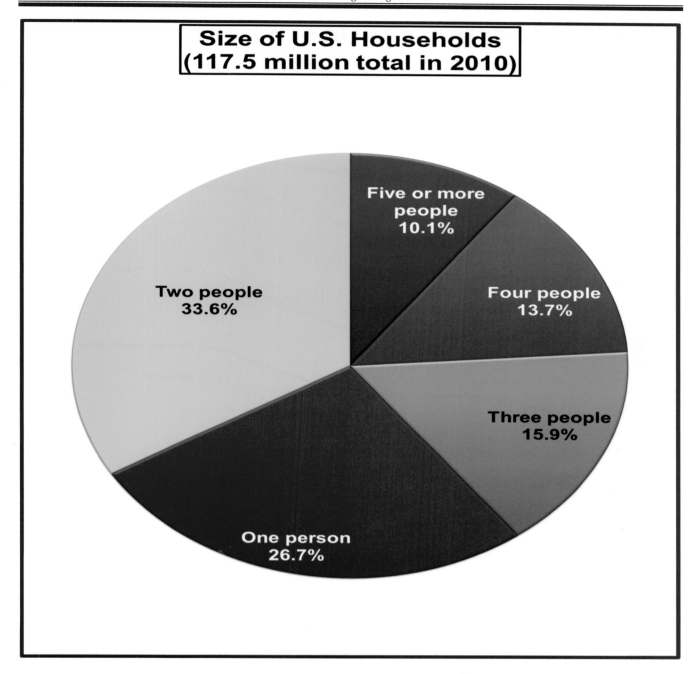

Size of U.S. Households
(117.5 million total in 2010)

Five or more people 10.1%

Four people 13.7%

Two people 33.6%

Three people 15.9%

One person 26.7%

U.S. Households. [117.5 million total U.S. households in 2010.]

SOURCE: U.S. Census Bureau

http://www.census.gov/hhes/www/income/data/historical/history.html

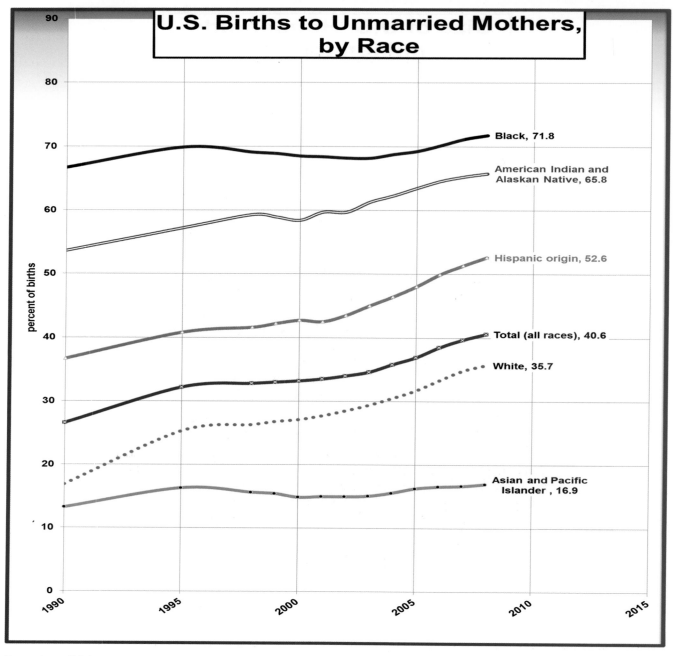

U.S. Births to Unmarried Mothers, by Race

Black, 71.8

American Indian and Alaskan Native, 65.8

Hispanic origin, 52.6

Total (all races), 40.6

White, 35.7

Asian and Pacific Islander , 16.9

Percentage of births to unmarried mothers represents registered births. Excludes births to nonresidents of the United States. Data are based on race and Hispanic origin of mother.

SOURCE: U.S. Census Bureau. U.S. National Center for Health Statistics, National Vital Statistics Reports (NVSR), Births: Final Data for 2008, Volume 59, No.1, December 2010

http://www.census.gov/econ/susb/methodology.html

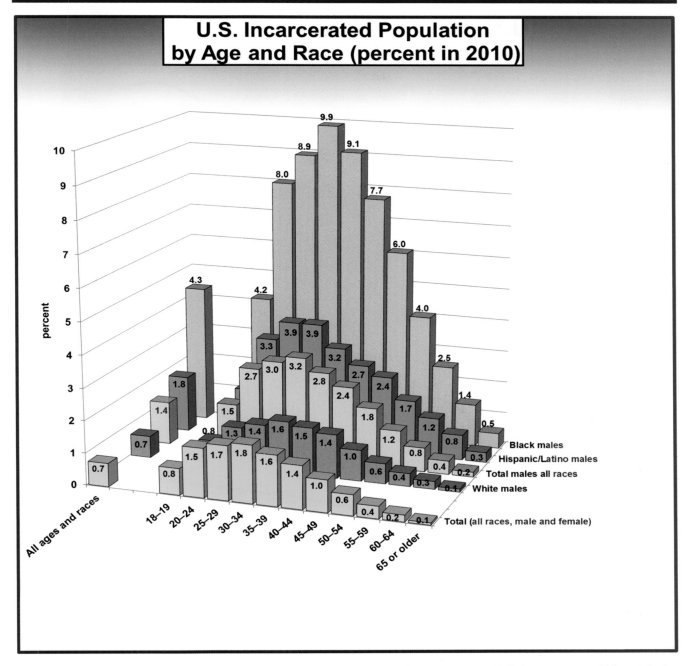

U.S. Incarcerated Population by Age and Race (percent in 2010)

Estimated percentage of U.S. resident population held in custody in state or federal prisons or in local jails by sex, race, and Hispanic/Latino origin, and age, June 30, 2010. Based on the total incarcerated population on June 30, 2010, and the U.S. resident population estimates for July 1, 2010, by sex, race, and Hispanic/Latino origin, and age. Total includes American Indians, Alaska Natives, Asians, Native Hawaiians, other Pacific Islanders, and persons identifying two or more races.

SOURCE: 2010 database from Bureau of Justice Statistics

askbjs@usdoj.gov

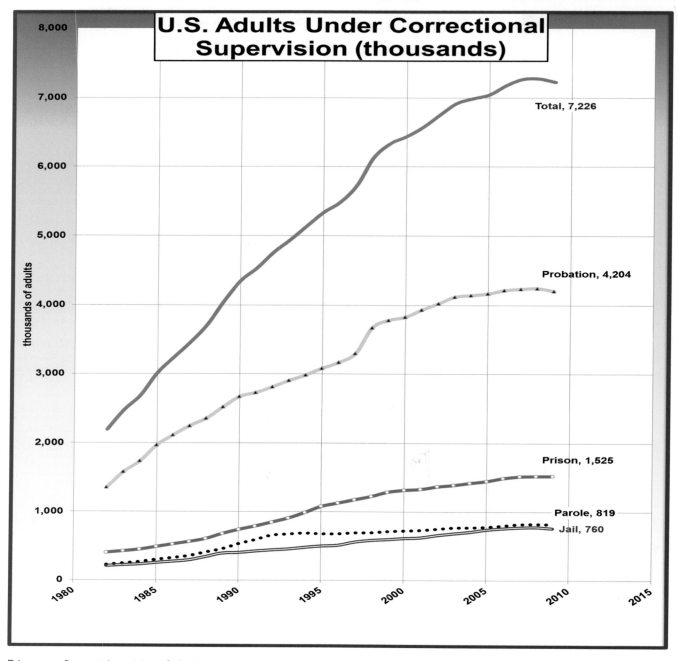

U.S. Adults Under Correctional Supervision (thousands)

Total, 7,226

Probation, 4,204

Prison, 1,525

Parole, 819

Jail, 760

thousands of adults

1980 1985 1990 1995 2000 2005 2010 2015

Prison - confinement in a state or federal correctional facility to serve a sentence of more than 1 year.

Jail - confinement in a local jail while pending trial, awaiting sentencing, serving a sentence that is usually less than 1 year, or awaiting transfer to other facilities after conviction.

Probation - court ordered community supervision of convicted offenders by a probation agency.

Parole - community supervision after a period of incarceration.

SOURCE: U.S. Census Bureau. U.S. Department of Justice, Bureau of Justice Statistics (BJS), Correctional Populations in the United States, 2009; Prisoners in 2009; Jail inmates at Midyear 2009—Statistical Tables; Probation and Parole in the United States, 2009.

http://bjs.ojp.usdoj.gov/index.cfm?ty=tp&tid=1

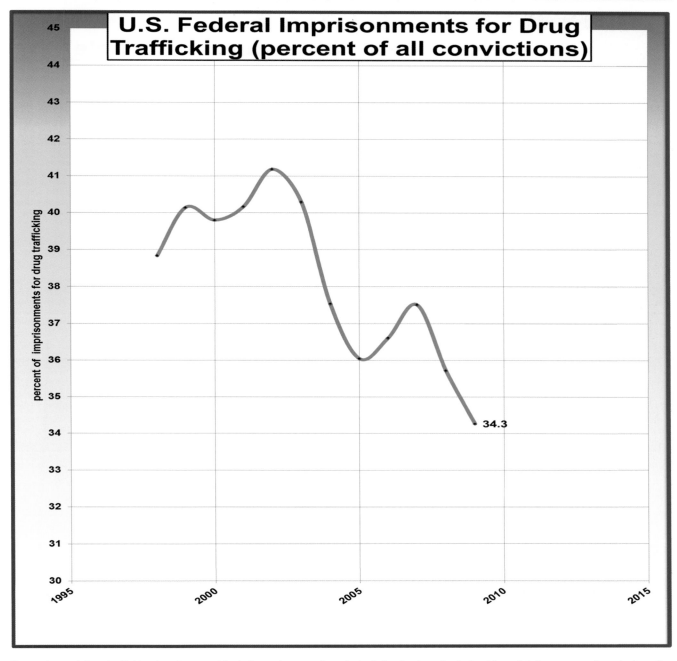

U.S. Federal Imprisonments for Drug Trafficking (percent of all convictions)

34.3

Percentage of drug trafficking imprisonment includes only commitments to federal prison for federal law violations; commitments from the District of Columbia Superior Court are excluded.

SOURCE: BJS' Federal Justice Statistics Program

http://bjs.ojp.usdoj.gov/fjsrc/

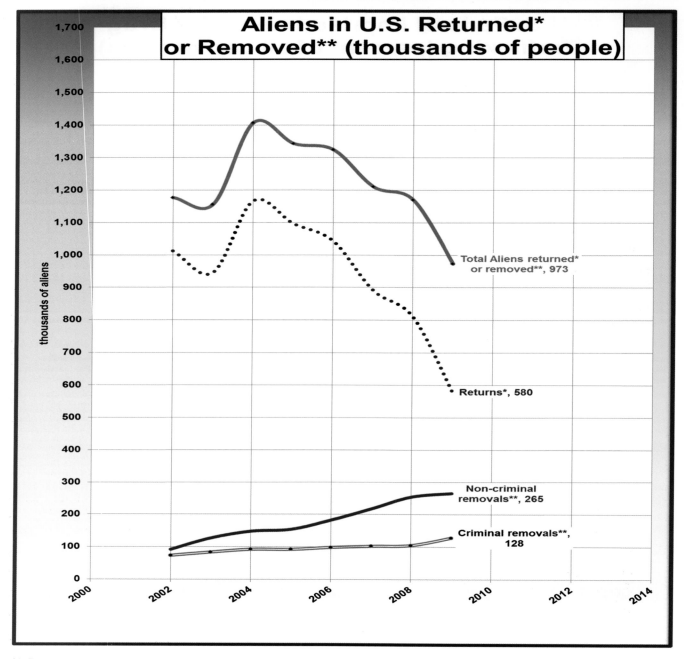

Aliens in U.S. Returned* or Removed** (thousands of people)

Total Aliens returned* or removed**, 973

Returns*, 580

Non-criminal removals**, 265

Criminal removals**, 128

*A Return is the confirmed movement of an inadmissible or deportable alien out of the United States that is not based on an order of removal. Most are Mexican nationals who have been apprehended by the U.S. Border Patrol and are returned to Mexico.

**Removals are the compulsory and confirmed movement of an inadmissible or deportable alien out of the United States based on an order of removal.

SOURCE: U.S. Census Bureau; U.S. Department of Homeland Security, Office of Immigration Statistics, Yearbook of Immigration Statistics, 2009.

http://www.dhs.gov/files/statistics/publications

http://www.census.gov/compendia/statab/cats/international_statistics/vital_statistics_health_education.html

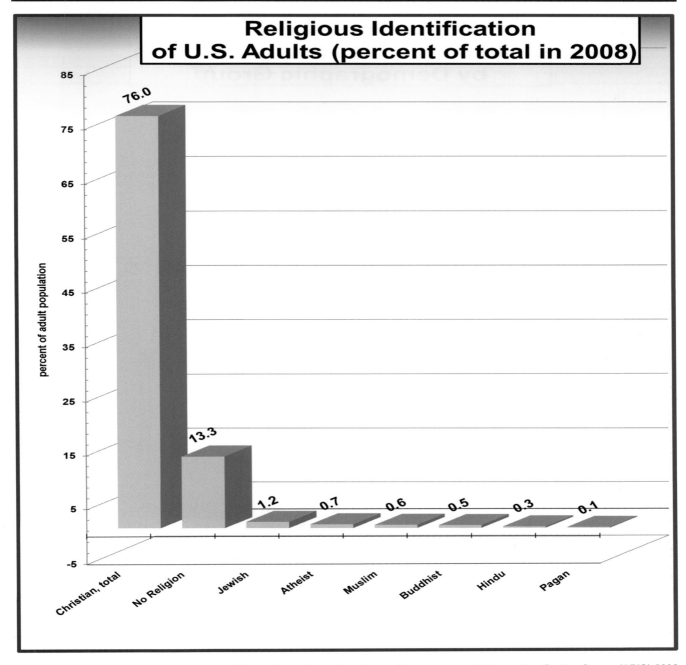

Religious Identification of U.S. Adults (percent of total in 2008)

percent of adult population

- Christian, total: 76.0
- No Religion: 13.3
- Jewish: 1.2
- Atheist: 0.7
- Muslim: 0.6
- Buddhist: 0.5
- Hindu: 0.3
- Pagan: 0.1

Self-Described Religious Identification of Adult Population: The methodology of the American Religious Identification Survey (ARIS) 2008 replicated that used in previous surveys. The three surveys are based on random-digit-dialing telephone surveys of residential households in the continental U.S.A (48 states): 54,461 interviews in 2008, 50,281 in 2001, and 113,723 in 1990. Respondents were asked to describe themselves in terms of religion with an open-ended question. Interviewers did not prompt or offer a suggested list of potential answers. Moreover, the self-description of respondents was not based on whether established religious bodies, institutions, churches, mosques or synagogues considered them to be members. Instead, the surveys sought to determine whether the respondents regarded themselves as adherents of a religious community.

SOURCE: U.S. Census Bureau

http://www.census.gov/compendia/statab/cats/international_statistics/vital_statistics_health_education.html

http://www.trincoll.edu/Academics/centers/ISSSC/Pages/ARIS-Data-Archive.aspx

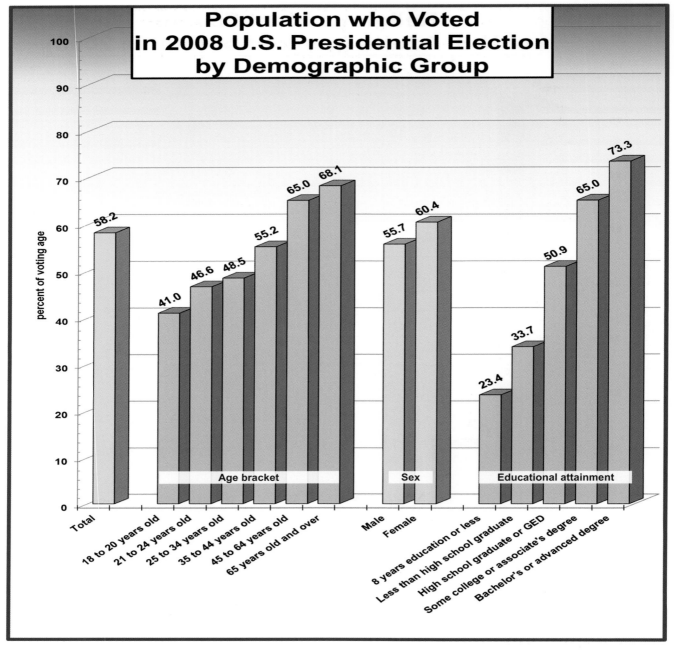

Population who Voted in 2008 U.S. Presidential Election by Demographic Group

percent of voting age

Total — 58.2

Age bracket
- 18 to 20 years old — 41.0
- 21 to 24 years old — 46.6
- 25 to 34 years old — 48.5
- 35 to 44 years old — 55.2
- 45 to 64 years old — 65.0
- 65 years old and over — 68.1

Sex
- Male — 55.7
- Female — 60.4

Educational attainment
- 8 years education or less — 23.4
- Less than high school graduate — 33.7
- High school graduate or GED — 50.9
- Some college or associate's degree — 65.0
- Bachelor's or advanced degree — 73.3

Percent of civilian non-institutional population 18 years old and over, including aliens, reporting they voted in the 2008 presidential election.

SOURCE: U.S. Census Bureau, Voting and Registration in the Election of November 2010, Current Population Reports, P20-423, P20-442, P20-552, P20-556, P20-557, P20-562 and earlier reports; and unpublished data

http://www.census.gov/compendia/statab/cats/international_statistics/vital_statistics_health_education.html

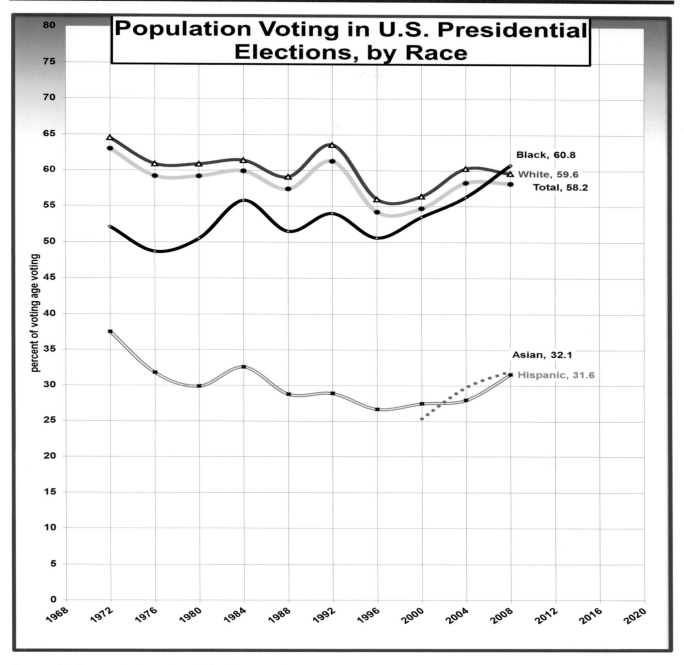

Population Voting in U.S. Presidential Elections, by Race

Black, 60.8
White, 59.6
Total, 58.2

Asian, 32.1
Hispanic, 31.6

Percent of civilian non-institutional population 18 years old and over, including aliens, reporting they voted in presidential elections.

SOURCE: U.S. Census Bureau, Voting and Registration in the Election of November 2010, Current Population Reports, P20-423, P20-442, P20-552, P20-556, P20-557, P20-562 and earlier reports; and unpublished data

http://www.census.gov/compendia/statab/cats/international_statistics/vital_statistics_health_education.html

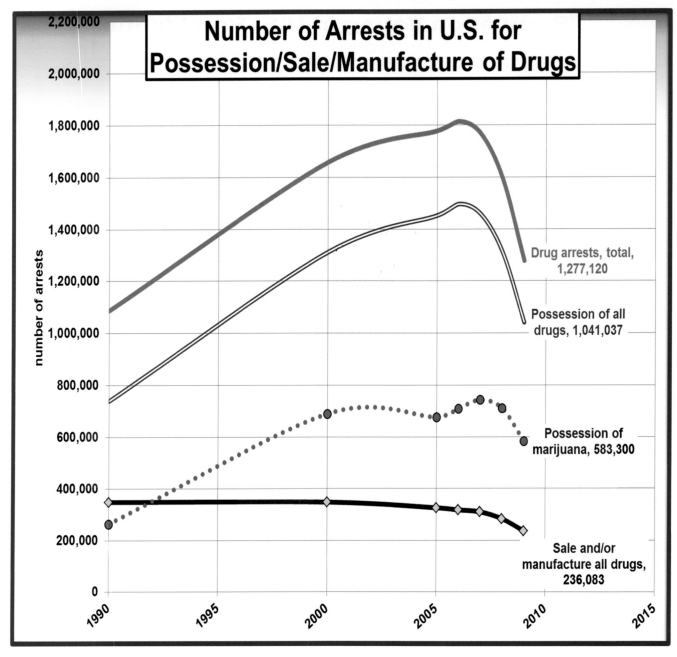

Number of Arrests in U.S. for Possession/Sale/Manufacture of Drugs

Drug arrests, total, 1,277,120

Possession of all drugs, 1,041,037

Possession of marijuana, 583,300

Sale and/or manufacture all drugs, 236,083

The FBI's Uniform Crime Reporting (UCR) Program counts one arrest for each separate instance in which a person is arrested, cited, or summoned for an offense. The UCR Program collects arrest data on 29 offenses, as described in offense definitions. Because a person may be arrested multiple times during a year, the UCR arrest figures do not reflect the number of individuals who have been arrested. Rather, the arrest data show the number of times that persons are arrested, as reported by law enforcement agencies to the UCR Program.

SOURCE: U.S. Census Bureau / U.S. Department of Justice, Federal Bureau of Investigation, Uniform Crime Reports Arrests Master Files

http://www.census.gov/compendia/statab/cats/law_enforcement_courts_prisons/arrests.html

Chapter 3: U.S. Education in Relation to the World

Overview

The United States spends 5.5 percent of GDP* on public education, about the same as England, France and Saudi Arabia, the most of the G20** members, whereas Japan spends one third less. Despite these expenditures, the United States ranks below the average of 30 developed countries in math literacy of 15 year-olds. Japan's students are near the top performers in math literacy as they also are in science and reading while U.S. students rank average in these categories.

Thirty-two percent of U.S. adults have attained a tertiary education compared with an average of 21 percent among developed nations. Tertiary education includes all education leading to bachelor's or master's degrees, or advance research programs.

~

*GDP = Gross Domestic Product = private consumption + gross private investment + government consumption (exclusive of transfer payments such as Social Security) + [exports − imports].

G20 Members (see Appendix I): Argentina, Australia, Brazil, Canada, China, France, Germany, India, Indonesia, Italy, Japan, South Korea, Mexico, Russian Federation, Saudi Arabia, South Africa, Turkey, United Kingdom, United States and the European Union*

***European Union (see Appendix II): Austria, Belgium, Bulgaria, Cyprus, Czech Rep., Denmark, Estonia, Finland, France, Germany, Greece, Hungary, Ireland, Italy, Latvia, Lithuania, Luxembourg, Malta, Netherlands, Poland, Portugal, Romania, Slovakia, Slovenia, Spain, Sweden, and the United Kingdom

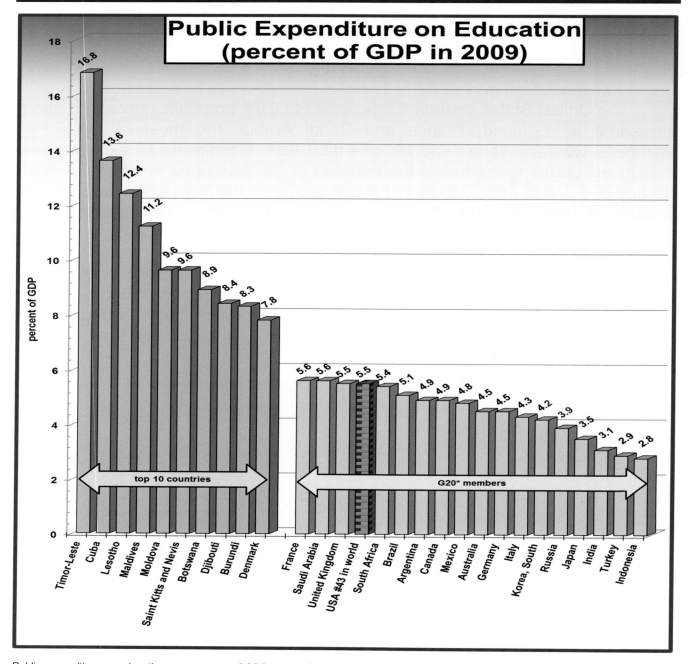

Public Expenditure on Education
(percent of GDP in 2009)

Public expenditure on education as a percent of GDP, where GDP (Gross Domestic Product) is the sum of all domestic purchases of final products and services + private domestic investment + government consumption + net trade (exports - imports). Government includes federal and state and local.

SOURCE: CIA, 2006–2009 databases accessed in October, 2011.

https://www.cia.gov/library/publications/the-world-factbook/rankorder/rankorderguide.html

*G20 Members (see Appendix I): Argentina, Australia, Brazil, Canada, China, France, Germany, India, Indonesia, Italy, Japan, South Korea, Mexico, Russian Federation, Saudi Arabia, South Africa, Turkey, United Kingdom, United States and the European Union**

**European Union (see Appendix II): Austria, Belgium, Bulgaria, Cyprus, Czech Rep., Denmark, Estonia, Finland, France, Germany, Greece, Hungary, Ireland, Italy, Latvia, Lithuania, Luxembourg, Malta, Netherlands, Poland, Portugal, Romania, Slovakia, Slovenia, Spain, Sweden, and the United Kingdom

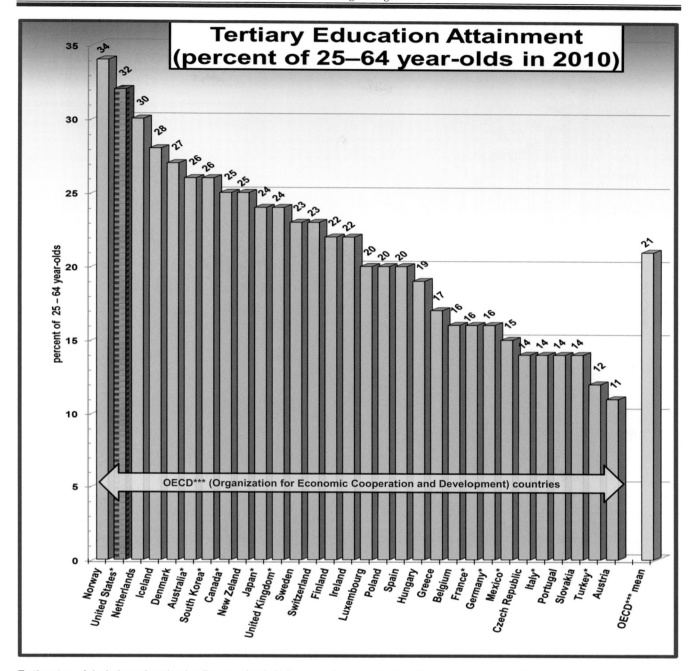

Tertiary-type A includes education leading to a bachelor's, master's, or equivalent degree, and advanced research programs. Includes all types of tertiary level degrees, including advanced research programs. Data are for the 25–64 year old population.

SOURCE: U.S. Census Bureau; 2009 database from the Organization for Economic Cooperation and Development (OECD), 2010, Education at a Glance 2010: OECD indicators, OECD Publishing (copyright). Internet release date: 9/30/2011

http://www.census.gov/compendia/statab/cats/international_statistics/vital_statistics_health_education.html

*G20 Members (see Appendix I): Argentina, Australia, Brazil, Canada, China, France, Germany, India, Indonesia, Italy, Japan, South Korea, Mexico, Russian Federation, Saudi Arabia, South Africa, Turkey, United Kingdom, United States and the European Union**

**European Union (see Appendix II): Austria, Belgium, Bulgaria, Cyprus, Czech Rep., Denmark, Estonia, Finland, France, Germany, Greece, Hungary, Ireland, Italy, Latvia, Lithuania, Luxembourg, Malta, Netherlands, Poland, Portugal, Romania, Slovakia, Slovenia, Spain, Sweden, and the United Kingdom

***OECD Countries (Organization for Economic Cooperation and Development) see Appendix III

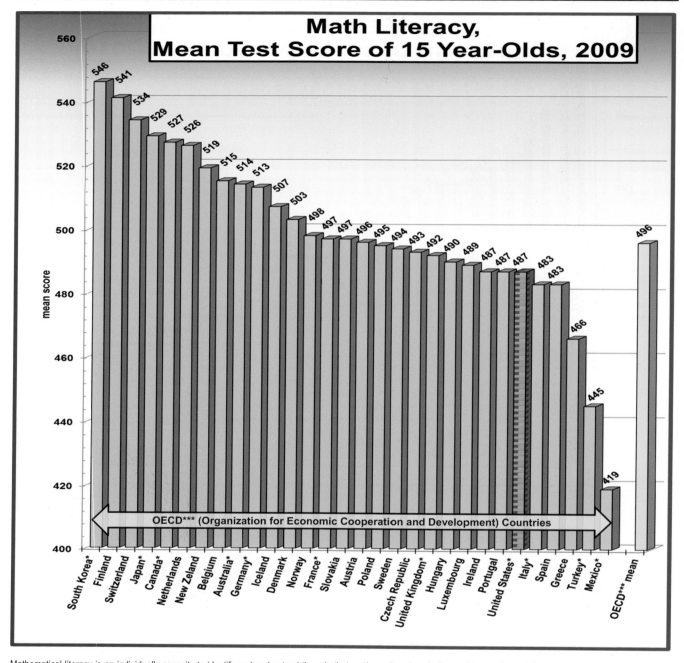

Math Literacy, Mean Test Score of 15 Year-Olds, 2009

Mean scores by country: South Korea* 546, Finland 541, Switzerland 534, Japan* 529, Canada* 527, Netherlands 526, New Zeland 519, Belgium 515, Australia* 514, Germany* 513, Iceland 507, Denmark 503, Norway 498, France* 497, Slovakia 497, Austria 496, Poland 495, Sweden 494, Czech Republic 493, United Kingdom* 492, Hungary 490, Luxembourg 489, Ireland 487, Portugal 487, United States* 487, Italy* 483, Spain 483, Greece 466, Turkey* 445, Mexico* 419, OECD*** mean 496.

OECD*** (Organization for Economic Cooperation and Development) Countries

Mathematical literacy is an individual's capacity to identify and understand the role that mathematics plays in the world, to make well-founded judgments, and to use and engage with mathematics in ways that meet the needs of that individual's life as a constructive, concerned and reflective citizen. To implement PISA (Program for International Student Assessment), each of the participating countries selects a nationally representative sample of fifteen-year-olds, regardless of grade level.

SOURCE: U.S. Census Bureau; 2009 database from the Organization for Economic Cooperation and Development (OECD), 2010, Education at a Glance 2010: OECD indicators, OECD Publishing (copyright). Internet release date: 9/30/2011

http://www.census.gov/compendia/statab/cats/international_statistics/vital_statistics_health_education.html

*G20 Members (see Appendix I): Argentina, Australia, Brazil, Canada, China, France, Germany, India, Indonesia, Italy, Japan, South Korea, Mexico, Russian Federation, Saudi Arabia, South Africa, Turkey, United Kingdom, United States and the European Union**

**European Union (see Appendix II): Austria, Belgium, Bulgaria, Cyprus, Czech Rep., Denmark, Estonia, Finland, France, Germany, Greece, Hungary, Ireland, Italy, Latvia, Lithuania, Luxembourg, Malta, Netherlands, Poland, Portugal, Romania, Slovakia, Slovenia, Spain, Sweden, and the United Kingdom

***OECD Countries (Organization for Economic Cooperation and Development) see Appendix III

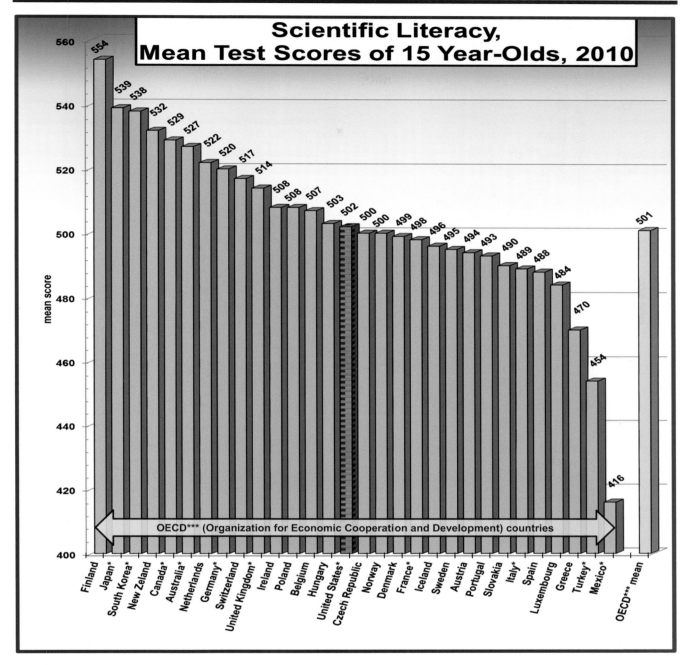

Scientific Literacy, Mean Test Scores of 15 Year-Olds, 2010

Finland 554, Japan* 539, South Korea* 538, New Zeland 532, Canada* 529, Australia* 527, Netherlands 522, Germany* 520, Switzerland 517, United Kingdom* 514, Ireland 508, Poland 508, Belgium 507, Hungary 503, United States* 502, Czech Republic 500, Norway 500, Denmark 499, France* 498, Iceland 496, Sweden 495, Austria 494, Portugal 493, Slovakia 490, Italy* 489, Spain 488, Luxembourg 484, Greece 470, Turkey* 454, Mexico* 416, OECD*** mean 501

OECD*** (Organization for Economic Cooperation and Development) countries

Scientific literacy is the capacity to use scientific knowledge, to identify questions; and to draw evidence-based conclusions in order to understand and help make decisions about the natural world and the changes made to it through human activity. To implement PISA (Program for International Student Assessment), each of the participating countries selects a nationally representative sample of fifteen-year-olds, regardless of grade level.

SOURCE: U.S. Census Bureau; 2009 database from the Organization for Economic Cooperation and Development (OECD); 2010, Education at a Glance 2010: OECD indicators, OECD Publishing (copyright). Internet release date: 9/30/2011

http://www.census.gov/compendia/statab/cats/international_statistics/vital_statistics_health_education.html

*G20 Members (see Appendix I): Argentina, Australia, Brazil, Canada, China, France, Germany, India, Indonesia, Italy, Japan, South Korea, Mexico, Russian Federation, Saudi Arabia, South Africa, Turkey, United Kingdom, United States and the European Union**

**European Union (see Appendix II): Austria, Belgium, Bulgaria, Cyprus, Czech Rep., Denmark, Estonia, Finland, France, Germany, Greece, Hungary, Ireland, Italy, Latvia, Lithuania, Luxembourg, Malta, Netherlands, Poland, Portugal, Romania, Slovakia, Slovenia, Spain, Sweden, and the United Kingdom

***OECD Countries (Organization for Economic Cooperation and Development) see Appendix III

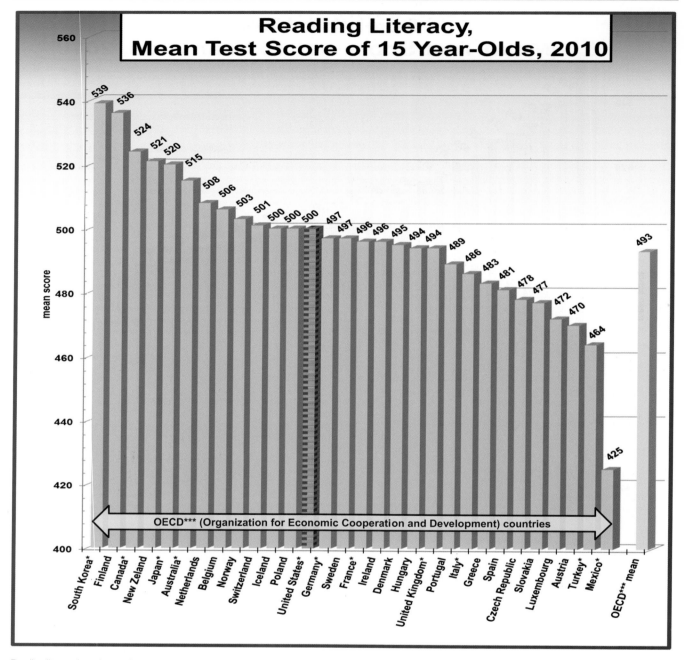

Reading Literacy, Mean Test Score of 15 Year-Olds, 2010

mean score

South Korea* 539
Finland 536
Canada* 524
New Zealand 521
Japan* 520
Australia* 515
Netherlands 508
Belgium 506
Norway 503
Switzerland 501
Iceland 500
Poland 500
United States* 500
Germany* 497
Sweden 497
France* 496
Ireland 496
Denmark 495
Hungary 494
United Kingdom* 494
Portugal 489
Italy* 486
Greece 483
Spain 481
Czech Republic 478
Slovakia 477
Luxembourg 472
Austria 470
Turkey* 464
Mexico* 425
OECD*** mean 493

OECD*** (Organization for Economic Cooperation and Development) countries

Reading literacy is understanding, using, and reflecting on written texts in order to achieve one's goals, to develop one's knowledge and potential, and to participate in society. To implement PISA (Program for International Student Assessment), each of the participating countries selects a nationally representative sample of fifteen-year-olds, regardless of grade level. In 2003, 5,456 students from public and private schools took the PISA assessment. Tests are typically administered to between 4,500 and 10,000 students in each country.

SOURCE: U.S. Census Bureau; 2009 database from the Organization for Economic Cooperation and Development (OECD), 2010, Education at a Glance 2010: OECD indicators, OECD Publishing (copyright). Internet release date: 9/30/2011

http://www.census.gov/compendia/statab/cats/international_statistics/vital_statistics_health_education.html

*G20 Members (see Appendix I): Argentina, Australia, Brazil, Canada, China, France, Germany, India, Indonesia, Italy, Japan, South Korea, Mexico, Russian Federation, Saudi Arabia, South Africa, Turkey, United Kingdom, United States and the European Union**

**European Union (see Appendix II): Austria, Belgium, Bulgaria, Cyprus, Czech Rep., Denmark, Estonia, Finland, France, Germany, Greece, Hungary, Ireland, Italy, Latvia, Lithuania, Luxembourg, Malta, Netherlands, Poland, Portugal, Romania, Slovakia, Slovenia, Spain, Sweden, and the United Kingdom

***OECD Countries (Organization for Economic Cooperation and Development) see Appendix III

Chapter 4: U.S. Education

Overview

In 2010, 14 percent of U.S. adults had not completed high school, while the high school drop-out rate was 7 percent, compared with 12 percent in 1980. The number of bachelor degrees awarded in the fields of science or engineering in the U.S. has doubled between 1969 and 2009.

In 2009, one-third of the doctoral degrees in science or engineering were awarded to foreigners, about the same percentage as in 1997; and one-quarter of those foreign recipients were from China. The total foreign enrollment in U.S. educational institutions has quadrupled between 1977 and 2010 but represents only 3.4 percent of total U.S. college enrollment.

Of 26 countries reporting tertiary education students "abroad" there are five countries where the majority of these students attended U.S. colleges; Japan led with 70 percent of their abroad students selecting to study in the United States.

Tertiary education includes all education leading to bachelor's, or master's degrees or advance research programs.

~

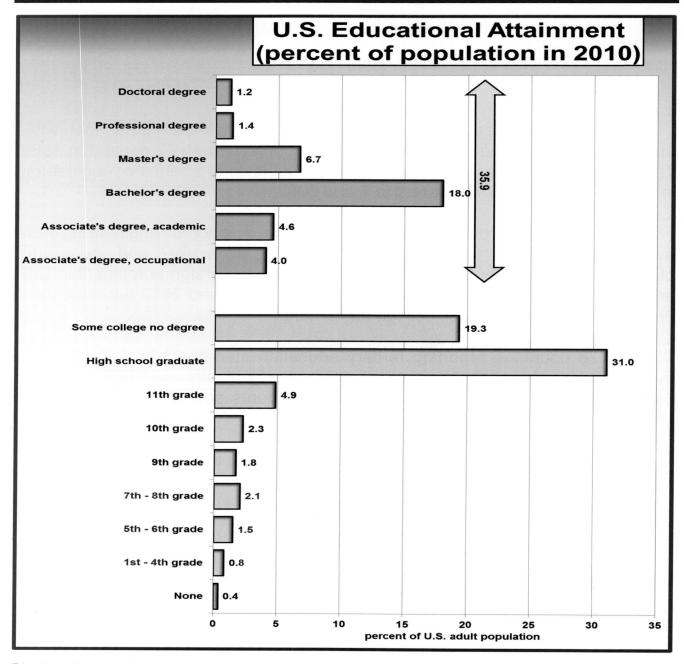

Educational Attainment of the population 18 years and over; numbers in percent; civilian non-institutionalized population.

SOURCE: U.S. Census Bureau, Current Population Reports, PPL-148, P-20, and earlier reports; and "School Enrollment."

http://www.census.gov/population/www/socdemo/school.html

Current Population Survey, 2010 Annual Social and Economic Supplement

http://www.census.gov/hhes/socdemo/education/data/cps/2010/tables.html

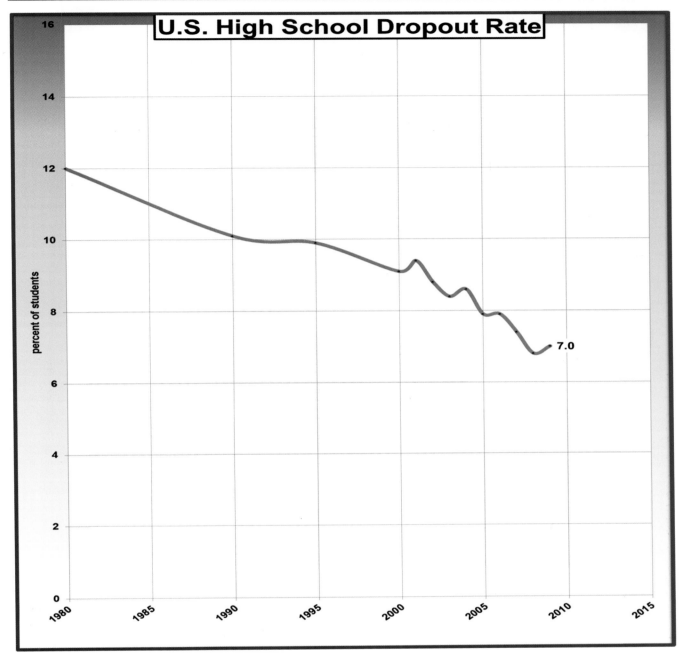

High school dropouts for persons 14 to 24 years old.

SOURCE: U.S. Census Bureau, Current Population Reports, PPL-148, P-20, and earlier reports; and "School Enrollment." Current Population Survey, 2010 Annual Social and Economic Supplement

http://www.census.gov/population/www/socdemo/school.html

http://www.census.gov/hhes/socdemo/education/data/cps/2010/tables.html

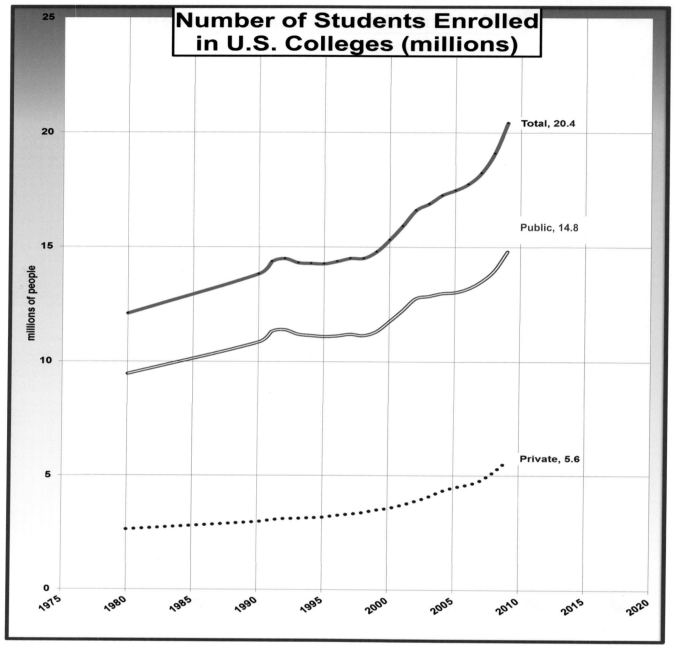

Number of Students Enrolled in U.S. Colleges (millions)

Total, 20.4

Public, 14.8

Private, 5.6

Enrollment is for students in U.S. colleges for fall of the previous year. Beginning 1996, data reflect a new classification of institutions; this classification includes some additional, primarily 2-year, colleges and excludes a few institutions that did not award degrees.

SOURCE: U.S. Census Bureau

http://www.census.gov/compendia/statab/cats/international_statistics/vital_statistics_health_education.html

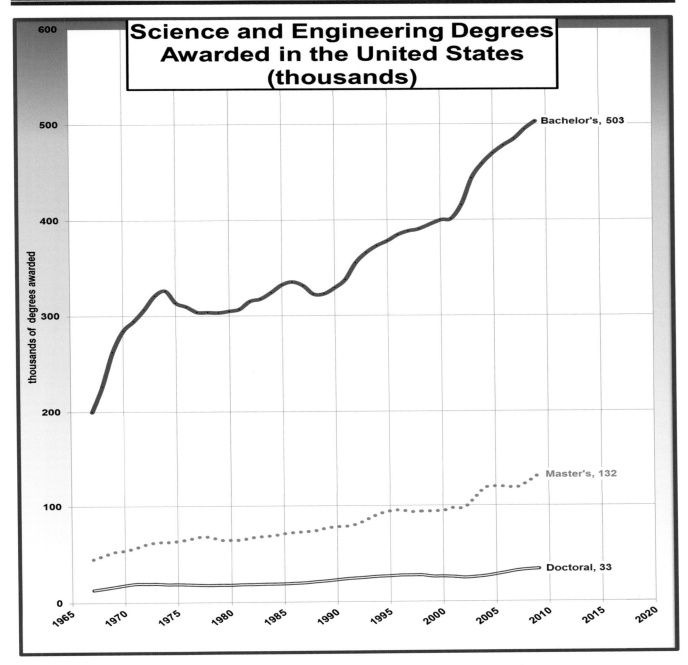

Science and Engineering Degrees Awarded in the United States (thousands)

For a description of science and engineering degree categories, see http://www.nsf.gov/statistics/nsf08321/.

SOURCE: U.S. Census Bureau

http://www.census.gov/compendia/statab/cats/international_statistics/vital_statistics_health_education.html

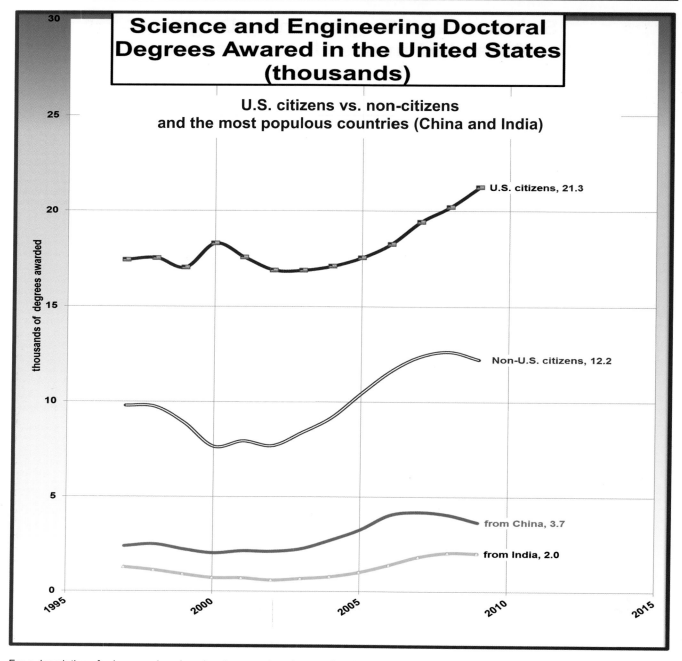

Science and Engineering Doctoral Degrees Awared in the United States (thousands)

U.S. citizens vs. non-citizens
and the most populous countries (China and India)

U.S. citizens, 21.3

Non-U.S. citizens, 12.2

from China, 3.7

from India, 2.0

For a description of science and engineering degree categories, see http://www.nsf.gov/statistics/nsf08321/.

SOURCE: U.S. Census Bureau

http://www.census.gov/compendia/statab/cats/international_statistics/vital_statistics_health_education.html

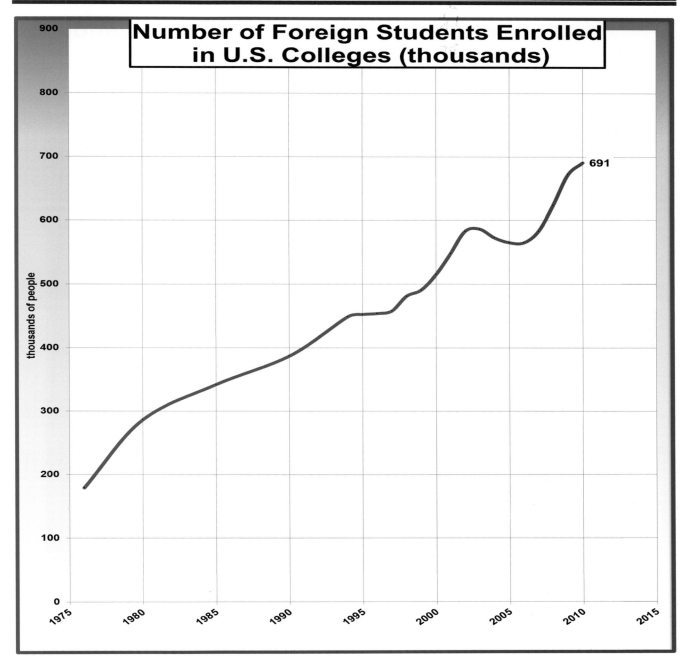

Number of Foreign Students Enrolled in U.S. Colleges (thousands)

691

Enrollment of students in U.S. colleges is for fall of the previous year. Foreign students are non-immigrants. Beginning 1996, data reflect a new classification of institutions; this classification includes some additional, primarily 2-year, colleges and excludes a few institutions that did not award degrees.

SOURCE: U.S. Census Bureau

http://www.census.gov/compendia/statab/cats/international_statistics/vital_statistics_health_education.html

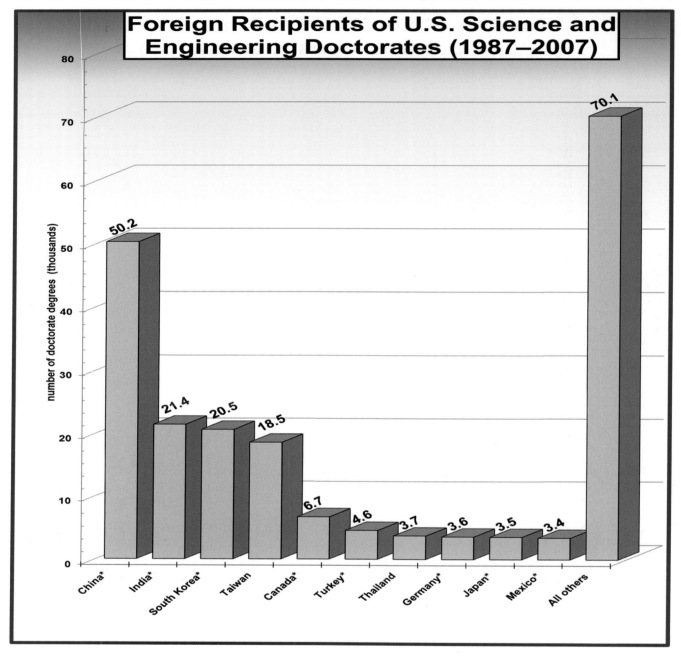

Foreign Recipients of U.S. Science and Engineering Doctorates (1987–2007)

number of doctorate degrees (thousands)

China* 50.2
India* 21.4
South Korea* 20.5
Taiwan 18.5
Canada* 6.7
Turkey* 4.6
Thailand 3.7
Germany* 3.6
Japan* 3.5
Mexico* 3.4
All others 70.1

Doctorate degrees awarded in science and engineering fields between 1987 and 2007. Foreign doctorate recipients include permanent and temporary residents.

SOURCE: National Science Foundation, Division of Science Resources Statistics, Survey of Earned Doctorates, special tabulations (2009).

http://www.nsf.gov/statistics/seind10/tables.htm

*G20 Members (see Appendix I): Argentina, Australia, Brazil, Canada, China, France, Germany, India, Indonesia, Italy, Japan, South Korea, Mexico, Russian Federation, Saudi Arabia, South Africa, Turkey, United Kingdom, United States and the European Union**

**European Union (see Appendix II): Austria, Belgium, Bulgaria, Cyprus, Czech Rep., Denmark, Estonia, Finland, France, Germany, Greece, Hungary, Ireland, Italy, Latvia, Lithuania, Luxembourg, Malta, Netherlands, Poland, Portugal, Romania, Slovakia, Slovenia, Spain, Sweden and the United Kingdom

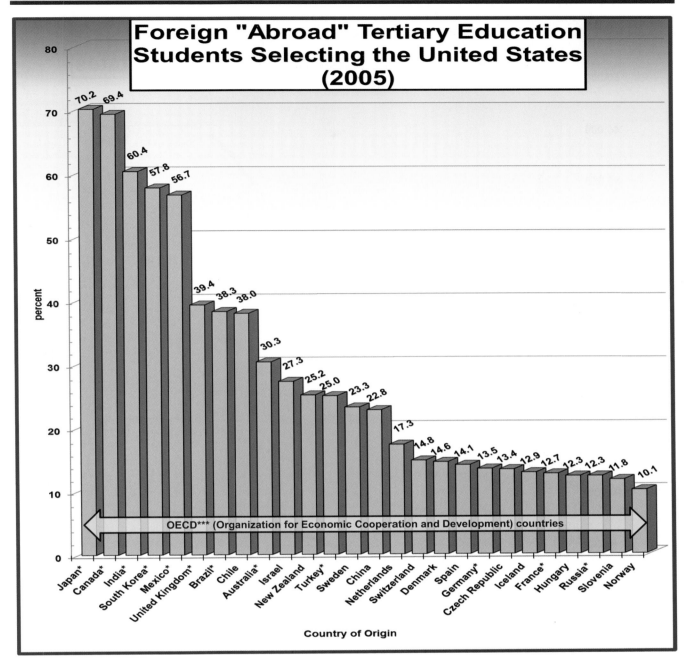

Foreign "Abroad" Tertiary Education Students Selecting the United States (2005)

percent — Country of Origin

Values by country:
- Japan* — 70.2
- Canada* — 69.4
- India* — 60.4
- South Korea* — 57.8
- Mexico* — 56.7
- United Kingdom* — 39.4
- Brazil* — 38.3
- Chile — 38.0
- Australia* — 30.3
- Israel — 27.3
- New Zealand — 25.2
- Turkey* — 25.0
- Sweden — 23.3
- China — 22.8
- Netherlands — 17.3
- Switzerland — 14.8
- Denmark — 14.6
- Spain — 14.1
- Germany* — 13.5
- Czech Republic — 13.4
- Iceland — 12.9
- France* — 12.7
- Hungary — 12.3
- Russia* — 12.3
- Slovenia — 11.8
- Norway — 10.1

OECD*** (Organization for Economic Cooperation and Development) countries

The proportion of students abroad is based only on the total number of students enrolled in countries reporting data to the OECD*** and UNESCO Institute for Statistics, 2005 database.

SOURCE: National Science Foundation, OECD***

http://www.nsf.gov/statistics/seind10/

*G20 Members (see Appendix I): Argentina, Australia, Brazil, Canada, China, France, Germany, India, Indonesia, Italy, Japan, South Korea, Mexico, Russian Federation, Saudi Arabia, South Africa, Turkey, United Kingdom, United States and the European Union**

**European Union (see Appendix II): Austria, Belgium, Bulgaria, Cyprus, Czech Rep., Denmark, Estonia, Finland, France, Germany, Greece, Hungary, Ireland, Italy, Latvia, Lithuania, Luxembourg, Malta, Netherlands, Poland, Portugal, Romania, Slovakia, Slovenia, Spain, Sweden and the United Kingdom

***OECD Countries (Organization for Economic Cooperation and Development) see Appendix III

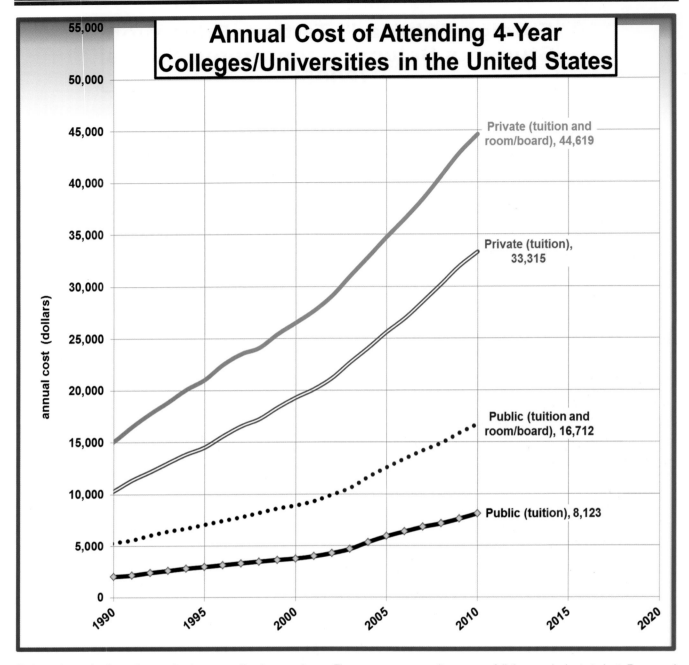

Estimated cost for the entire academic year ending in year shown. Figures are average charges per full-time equivalent student. Room and board are based on full-time students. For public institutions, data are for in-state students.

SOURCE: U.S. Census Bureau; U.S. National Center for Education Statistics, Digest of Education Statistics, annual. Database accessed September 2012

http://www.census.gov/compendia/statab/cats/education/higher_education_finances_fees_and_staff.html

Chapter 5: The U.S. Economy in Relation to the World

Overview

Gross Domestic Product (GDP) is the primary measure of a country's economic size, equal to private consumption + gross investment + government consumption (exclusive of transfer payments such as Social Security) + net trade [exports − imports]. U.S. GDP was $15.1 trillion in 2011, the largest in the world and 22 percent of the world's total. The U.S. GDP per capita at $48,400, ranked fourteenth in the world, about the same as Japan's or Canada's, and one-half of Luxembourg's.

In 2010, the largest component of U.S. GDP was personal consumption of services (47 percent), double the personal consumption of goods (23 percent), whereas in 1969 these components were both 30 percent. Government consumption, the combination of federal, state, and local consumption, contributed 21 percent, the same level as in 1951. Other government expenses, including transfer payments such as Medicare, Medicaid, and Social Security, are not included in GDP. The U.S. balance of trade deficit reduced GDP by 2.8 percent in 2010.

U.S. reserves, comprised of currencies and gold held by the Federal Reserve were valued at $.54 trillion in 2011. This was one-sixth the level of China's, whereas in 1998 both the United States and China held the same level. In 2010, U.S. reserves were at 3.3 percent of GDP compared with China's 49.2 percent.

U.S. federal debt was at 97 percent of GDP in 2011, the sixth highest in the world, two-thirds of Greece's percentage. The U.S. percentage doubled between 2007 and 2011 while Russia's halved in the same period from 18 percent to 9 percent.

~

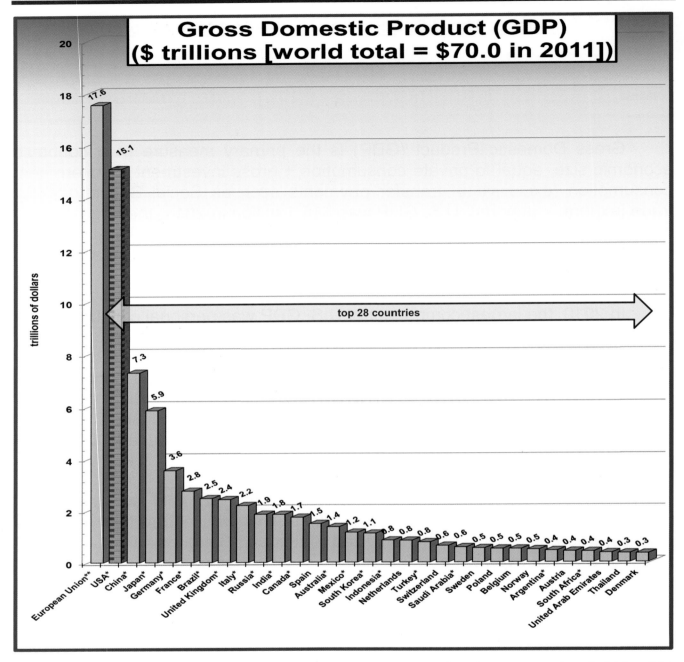

GDP = private consumption + gross investment + government consumption (exclusive of transfer payments such as Social Security) + [exports – imports]. GDP can be calculated at purchaser's prices as the sum of gross value added by all resident producers in the economy plus any product taxes and minus any subsidies not included in the value of the products. It is calculated without making deductions for depreciation of fabricated assets or for depletion and degradation of natural resources. Data are in current U.S. dollars. Dollar figures for GDP are converted from domestic currencies using single year official exchange rates. For a few countries where the official exchange rate does not reflect the rate effectively applied to actual foreign exchange transactions, an alternative conversion factor is used.

SOURCE: World Bank national accounts data, and OECD National Accounts data files.

http://data.worldbank.org/data-catalog/world-development-indicators?cid=GPD_WDI

*G20 Members (see Appendix I): Argentina, Australia, Brazil, Canada, China, France, Germany, India, Indonesia, Italy, Japan, South Korea, Mexico, Russian Federation, Saudi Arabia, South Africa, Turkey, United Kingdom, United States and the European Union**

**European Union (see Appendix II): Austria, Belgium, Bulgaria, Cyprus, Czech Rep., Denmark, Estonia, Finland, France, Germany, Greece, Hungary, Ireland, Italy, Latvia, Lithuania, Luxembourg, Malta, Netherlands, Poland, Portugal, Romania, Slovakia, Slovenia, Spain, Sweden and the United Kingdom

Gross Domestic Product (GDP) History ($ trillions)

The United States vs. leading countries and the most populous (China and India)

European Union**, 17.6

USA, 15.1

China, 7.3

Japan, 5.9

India, 1.8

GDP = private consumption + gross investment + government consumption (exclusive of transfer payments such as Social Security) + [exports − imports]. GDP can be calculated at purchaser's prices as the sum of gross value added by all resident producers in the economy plus any product taxes and minus any subsidies not included in the value of the products. It is calculated without making deductions for depreciation of fabricated assets or for depletion and degradation of natural resources. Data are in current U.S. dollars. Dollar figures for GDP are converted from domestic currencies using single year official exchange rates. For a few countries where the official exchange rate does not reflect the rate effectively applied to actual foreign exchange transactions, an alternative conversion factor is used.

SOURCE: World Bank national accounts data, and OECD*** National Accounts data files.

http://data.worldbank.org/data-catalog/world-development-indicators?cid=GPD_WDI

**European Union (see Appendix II): Austria, Belgium, Bulgaria, Cyprus, Czech Rep., Denmark, Estonia, Finland, France, Germany, Greece, Hungary, Ireland, Italy, Latvia, Lithuania, Luxembourg, Malta, Netherlands, Poland, Portugal, Romania, Slovakia, Slovenia, Spain, Sweden and the United Kingdom

***OECD Countries (Organization for Economic Cooperation and Development) see Appendix III

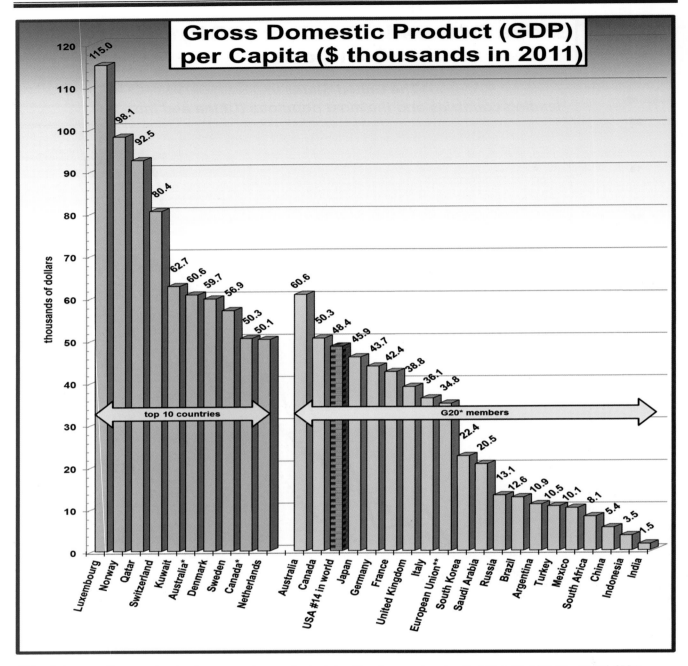

Gross Domestic Product (GDP) per Capita ($ thousands in 2011)

top 10 countries

G20* members

Luxembourg 115.0, Norway 98.1, Qatar 92.5, Switzerland 80.4, Kuwait 62.7, Australia* 60.6, Denmark 59.7, Sweden 56.9, Canada* 50.3, Netherlands 50.1

Australia 60.6, Canada 50.3, USA #14 in world 48.4, Japan 45.9, Germany 43.7, France 42.4, United Kingdom 38.8, Italy 36.1, European Union** 34.8, South Korea 22.4, Saudi Arabia 20.5, Russia 13.1, Brazil 12.6, Argentina 10.9, Turkey 10.5, Mexico 10.1, South Africa 8.1, China 5.4, Indonesia 3.5, India 1.5

thousands of dollars

GDP = private consumption + gross investment + government consumption (exclusive of transfer payments such as Social Security) + [exports − imports]. GDP is calculated at purchaser's prices as the sum of gross value added by all resident producers in the economy plus any product taxes and minus any subsidies not included in the value of the products. It is calculated without making deductions for depreciation of fabricated assets or for depletion and degradation of natural resources. Data are in current U.S. dollars converted from domestic currencies using single year official exchange rates. GDP per capita is gross domestic product divided by midyear population.

SOURCE: World Bank national accounts data, and OECD*** National Accounts data files. 2011 database accessed September, 2012,

http://data.worldbank.org/data-catalog/world-development-indicators?cid=GPD_WDI.

*G20 Members (see Appendix I): Argentina, Australia, Brazil, Canada, China, France, Germany, India, Indonesia, Italy, Japan, South Korea, Mexico, Russian Federation, Saudi Arabia, South Africa, Turkey, United Kingdom, United States and the European Union**

**European Union (see Appendix II): Austria, Belgium, Bulgaria, Cyprus, Czech Rep., Denmark, Estonia, Finland, France, Germany, Greece, Hungary, Ireland, Italy, Latvia, Lithuania, Luxembourg, Malta, Netherlands, Poland, Portugal, Romania, Slovakia, Slovenia, Spain, Sweden and the United Kingdom

***OECD Countries (Organization for Economic Cooperation and Development) see Appendix III

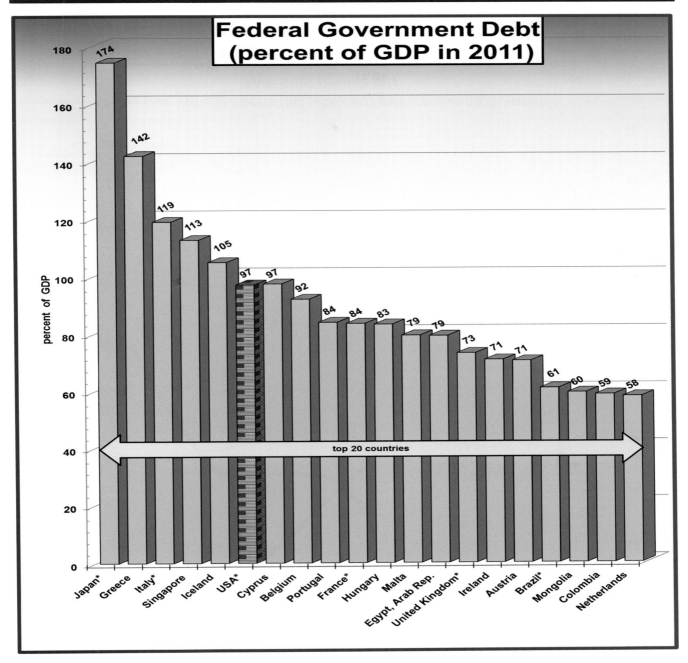

Debt is the entire stock of direct government fixed-term contractual obligations to others outstanding on a particular date. It includes domestic and foreign liabilities such as currency and money deposits, securities other than shares, and loans. It is the gross amount of government liabilities reduced by the amount of equity and financial derivatives held by the government. Because debt is a stock rather than a flow, it is measured as of a given date, usually the last day of the fiscal year. GDP = private consumption + gross investment + government consumption (exclusive of transfer payments such as Social Security) + [exports − imports].

SOURCE: World Bank. International Monetary Fund, Government Finance Statistics Yearbook and data files, and World Bank and OECD GDP estimates. 2009 database accessed January, 2012, except the U.S. is for year 2011 per U.S. Federal Reserve.

http://data.worldbank.org/data-catalog/world-development-indicators?cid=GPD_WDI

*G20 Members (see Appendix I): Argentina, Australia, Brazil, Canada, China, France, Germany, India, Indonesia, Italy, Japan, South Korea, Mexico, Russian Federation, Saudi Arabia, South Africa, Turkey, United Kingdom, United States and the European Union**

**European Union (see Appendix II): Austria, Belgium, Bulgaria, Cyprus, Czech Rep., Denmark, Estonia, Finland, France, Germany, Greece, Hungary, Ireland, Italy, Latvia, Lithuania, Luxembourg, Malta, Netherlands, Poland, Portugal, Romania, Slovakia, Slovenia, Spain, Sweden and the United Kingdom

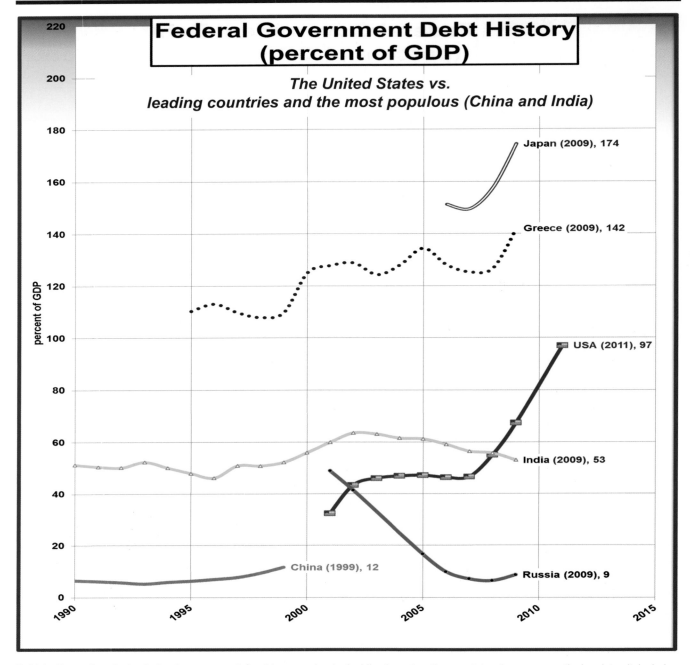

Federal Government Debt History (percent of GDP)

The United States vs. leading countries and the most populous (China and India)

Japan (2009), 174

Greece (2009), 142

USA (2011), 97

India (2009), 53

China (1999), 12

Russia (2009), 9

percent of GDP

Debt is the entire stock of direct government fixed-term contractual obligations to others outstanding on a particular date. It includes domestic and foreign liabilities such as currency and money deposits, securities other than shares, and loans. It is the gross amount of government liabilities reduced by the amount of equity and financial derivatives held by the government. Because debt is a stock rather than a flow, it is measured as of a given date, usually the last day of the fiscal year. GDP = private consumption + gross investment + government consumption (exclusive of transfer payments such as Social Security) + [exports − imports].

SOURCE: World Bank. International Monetary Fund, Government Finance Statistics Yearbook and data files, and World Bank and OECD GDP estimates; 2009 database accessed January 2012, except the U.S. is for year 2011 per the U.S. Federal Reserve.

http://data.worldbank.org/data-catalog/world-development-indicators?cid=GPD_WDI

**European Union (see Appendix II): Austria, Belgium, Bulgaria, Cyprus, Czech Rep., Denmark, Estonia, Finland, France, Germany, Greece, Hungary, Ireland, Italy, Latvia, Lithuania, Luxembourg, Malta, Netherlands, Poland, Portugal, Romania, Slovakia, Slovenia, Spain, Sweden and the United Kingdom

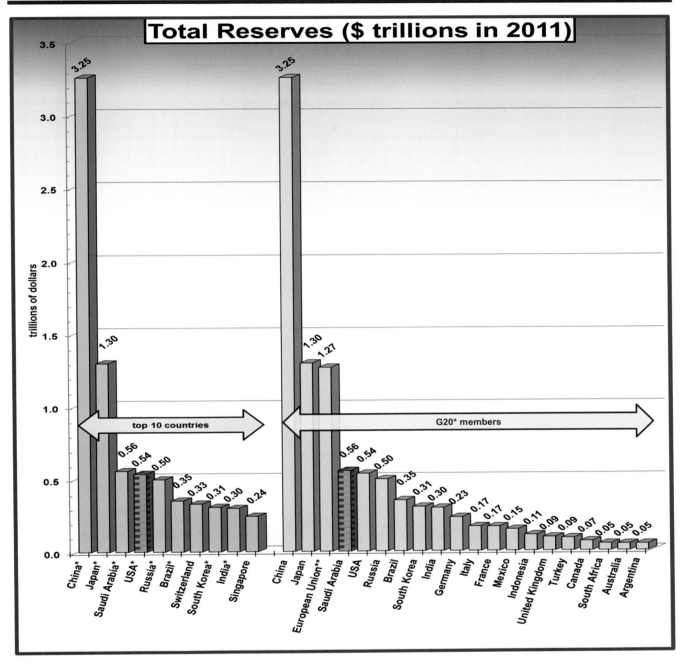

Total Reserves ($ trillions in 2011)

Total reserves comprise holdings of monetary gold, special drawing rights, reserves of IMF (International Monetary Fund) members held by the IMF, and holdings of foreign exchange under the control of monetary authorities. The gold component of these reserves is valued at year-end (December 31) London prices. Data are in current U.S. dollars.

SOURCE: World Bank. International Monetary Fund, International Financial Statistics and data files; 2011 database accessed in September 2012

http://data.worldbank.org/data-catalog/world-development-indicators?cid=GPD_WDI

*G20 Members (see Appendix I): Argentina, Australia, Brazil, Canada, China, France, Germany, India, Indonesia, Italy, Japan, South Korea, Mexico, Russian Federation, Saudi Arabia, South Africa, Turkey, United Kingdom, United States and the European Union**

**European Union (see Appendix II): Austria, Belgium, Bulgaria, Cyprus, Czech Rep., Denmark, Estonia, Finland, France, Germany, Greece, Hungary, Ireland, Italy, Latvia, Lithuania, Luxembourg, Malta, Netherlands, Poland, Portugal, Romania, Slovakia, Slovenia, Spain, Sweden and the United Kingdom

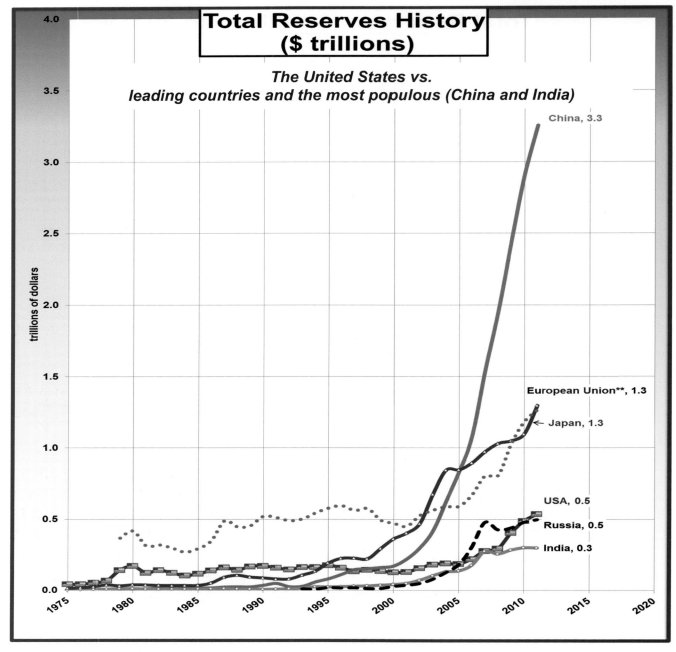

Total Reserves History ($ trillions)

The United States vs. leading countries and the most populous (China and India)

China, 3.3

European Union**, 1.3

Japan, 1.3

USA, 0.5

Russia, 0.5

India, 0.3

trillions of dollars

Total reserves comprise holdings of monetary gold, special drawing rights, reserves of IMF members held by the IMF, and holdings of foreign exchange under the control of monetary authorities. The gold component of these reserves is valued at year-end (December 31) London prices. Data are in current U.S. dollars.

SOURCE: World Bank. International Monetary Fund, International Financial Statistics and data files. Primarily 2010 database accessed in January 2012

http://data.worldbank.org/data-catalog/world-development-indicators?cid=GPD_WDI

**European Union (see Appendix II): Austria, Belgium, Bulgaria, Cyprus, Czech Rep., Denmark, Estonia, Finland, France, Germany, Greece, Hungary, Ireland, Italy, Latvia, Lithuania, Luxembourg, Malta, Netherlands, Poland, Portugal, Romania, Slovakia, Slovenia, Spain, Sweden and the United Kingdom

Chapter 6: U.S. Economy

Overview

Federal debt is the total outstanding amount of money owed by the U.S. federal government. It is the net, cumulative sum of all budget deficits/surpluses. In 2012, the U.S. debt grew to a record $15.9 trillion. The portion held by foreigners, primarily as U.S. Treasury notes and bonds, increased to $5.29 trillion, four times as much as in 2000, and one-fourth of foreign debt was held by China, the largest creditor. The Federal Reserve or intra-government agencies held 42 percent of federal debt, including obligations to U.S. trust funds such as Social Security and Medicare.

Between 2000 and 2010, annual federal expenditures for social programs increased from $.77 trillion to $1.71 trillion, whereas interest payments on the debt have remained almost unchanged at $.28 trillion during that period.

In 2011, sales volume of new single family homes declined to one-fourth their 2006 level, while average home prices declined by one-third. In 2011, fixed home mortgage interest rates declined to approximately 4.0 percent.

In 1970, 32 percent of the U.S. population was below the poverty level, which declined to 11 percent in 2000. By 2009 the level increased to 14.3 percent. Between 1970 and 2009 the number of food stamp recipients increased from 5 to 45 million people at a cost of $75.3 billion. During this period, mean household income for the bottom three-fifths of the population increased by 19 percent to $30,600, while mean income for the top one-fifth rose 56 percent to $173,700. Mean income for the top 400 individual income tax filers in 2008 was $270.5 million and they paid federal income taxes at an average tax rate of 18.1 percent. In 2010, the national mean household income was $49,450.

In 2009, the top 2.8 percent tax filers paid 50 percent of all personal income tax collected, while the bottom 50 percent of filers contributed 2 percent.

~

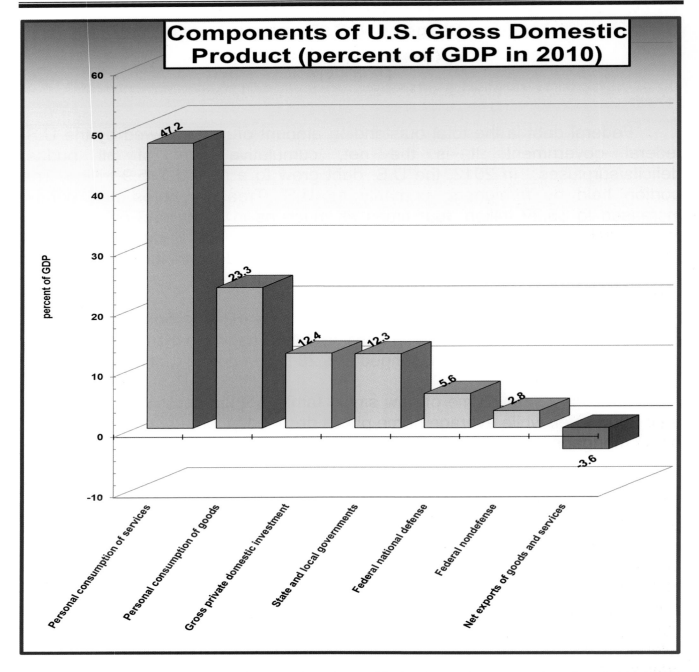

Components of U.S. Gross Domestic Product (percent of GDP in 2010)

GDP (Gross Domestic Product) is the sum of all domestic purchases of final products and services + private domestic investment + government consumption + net trade (exports - imports). Government includes federal + state + local. [In 2010, the negative U.S. trade imbalance reduced GDP by 3.6 percent.]

SOURCE: Bureau of Economic Analysis, 2010

http://www.bea.gov/national/nipaweb/SelectTable.asp?Selected=N

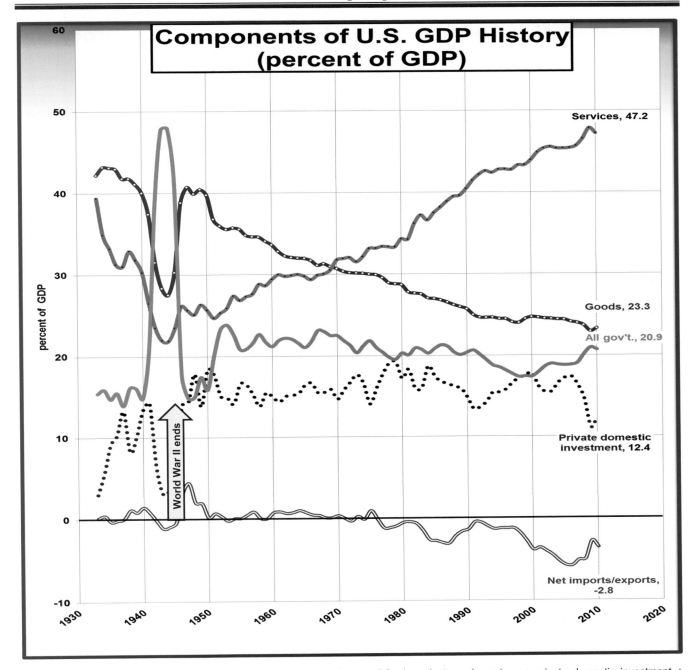

Components of U.S. GDP History (percent of GDP)

- Services, 47.2
- Goods, 23.3
- All gov't., 20.9
- Private domestic investment, 12.4
- Net imports/exports, -2.8
- World War II ends

percent of GDP

GDP (Gross Domestic Product) is the sum of all domestic purchases of final products and services + private domestic investment + government consumption + net trade (exports - imports). Government includes federal + state + local.

SOURCE: Bureau of Economic Analysis

http://www.bea.gov/national/nipaweb/SelectTable.asp?Selected=N

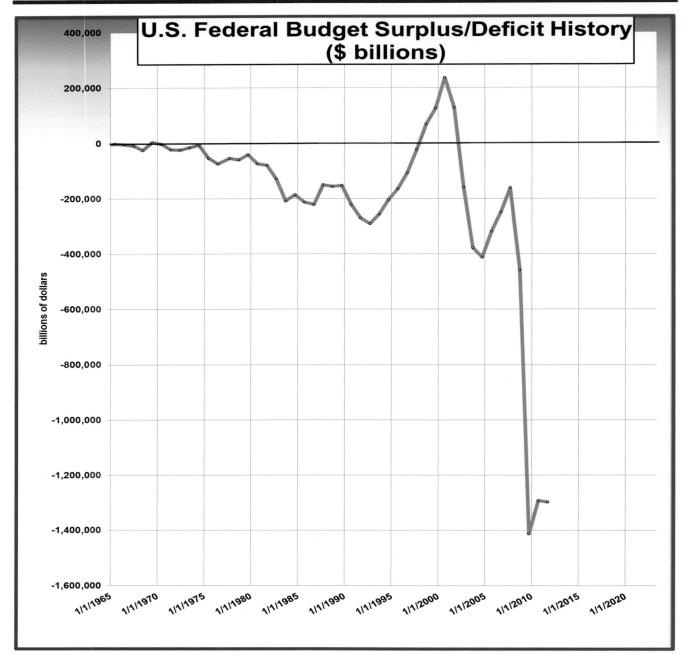

Annual U.S. federal budget net surplus/deficit

SOURCE: Federal Reserve Bank of St. Louis; U.S. Department of Commerce: Census Bureau

http://research.stlouisfed.org/fred2/data/FYFSD.txt

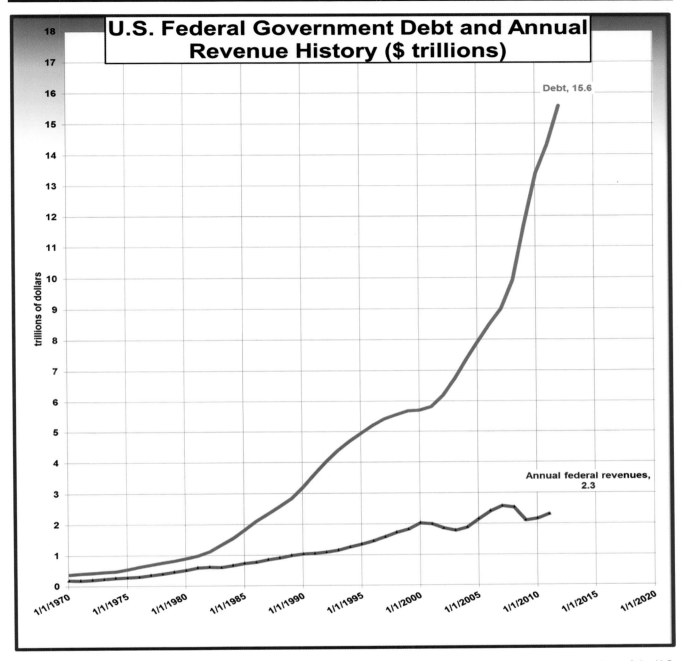

U.S. Federal Government Debt and Annual Revenue History ($ trillions)

Debt, 15.6

Annual federal revenues, 2.3

trillions of dollars

1/1/1970 1/1/1975 1/1/1980 1/1/1985 1/1/1990 1/1/1995 1/1/2000 1/1/2005 1/1/2010 1/1/2015 1/1/2020

Total Federal receipts (revenues) consist of taxes and other federal income. Cumulative debt are the total current obligations of the U.S. government.

SOURCE: Federal Reserve Bank of St. Louis; U.S. Department of Commerce: Bureau of Economic Analysis

http://research.stlouisfed.org/

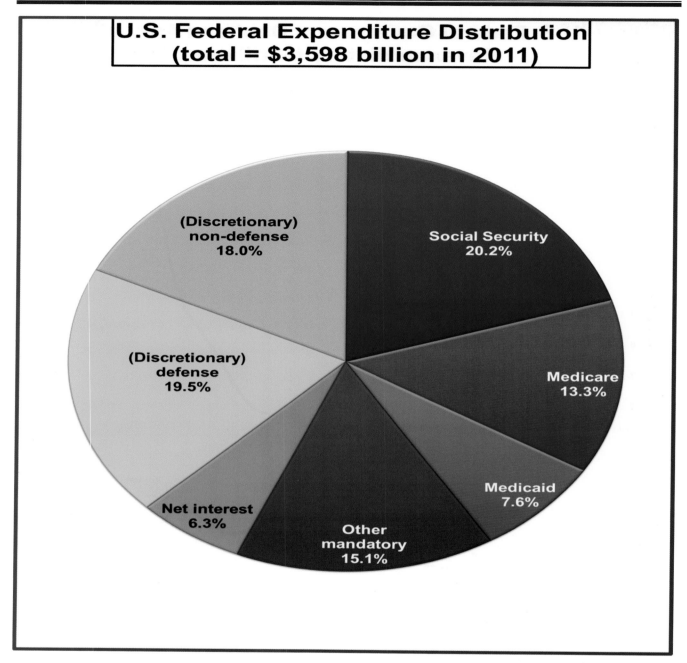

U.S. Federal Expenditure Distribution (total = $3,598 billion in 2011)

- Social Security 20.2%
- Medicare 13.3%
- Medicaid 7.6%
- Other mandatory 15.1%
- Net interest 6.3%
- (Discretionary) defense 19.5%
- (Discretionary) non-defense 18.0%

Total federal expenditures for 2011.

SOURCE: Congressional Budget Office

http://www.cbo.gov/ftpdocs/125xx/doc12577/budgetinfographic.htm

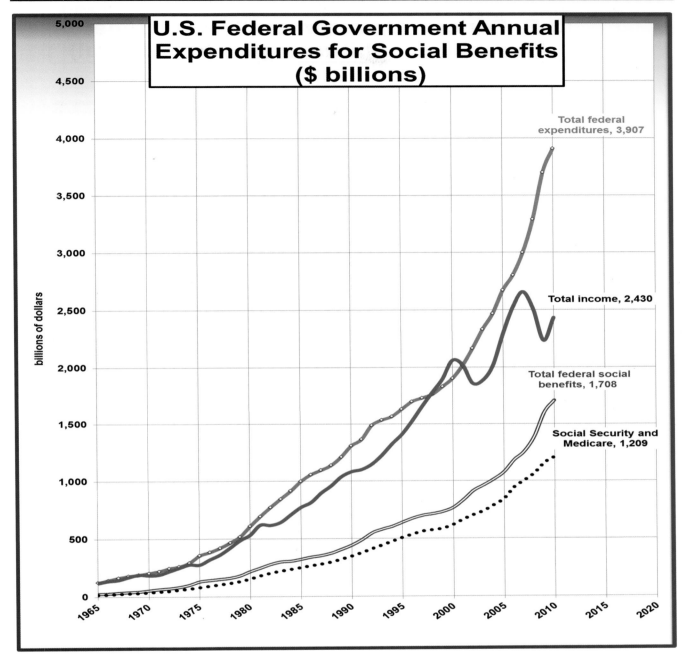

Government social benefit expenditures. Social benefits include Medicare, Social Security, Medicaid, veteran's benefits, food stamps, and unemployment.

SOURCE: Bureau of Economic Analysis

http://www.bea.gov/national/nipaweb/SelectTable.asp?Selected=N

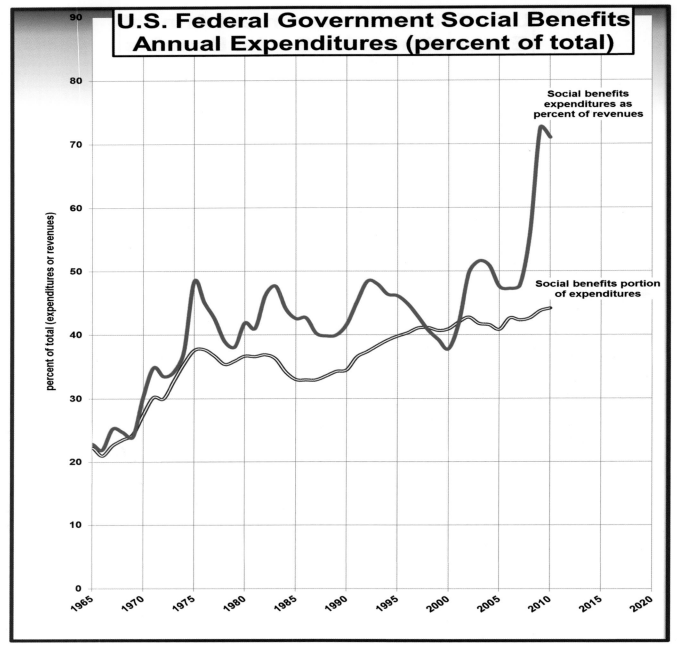

U.S. Federal Government Social Benefits Annual Expenditures (percent of total)

Federal government social benefit expenditures includes Medicare, Medicaid, Social Security, veteran's benefits, unemployment, and food stamps.

SOURCE: Bureau of Economic Analysis

http://www.bea.gov/national/nipaweb/SelectTable.asp?Selected=N

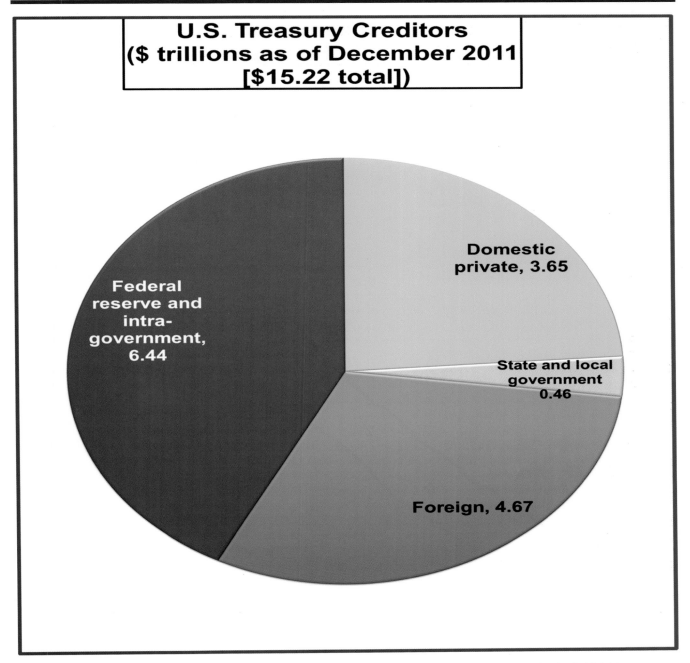

U.S. Treasury Creditors
($ trillions as of December 2011
[$15.22 total])

Domestic private, 3.65

State and local government 0.46

Federal reserve and intra-government, 6.44

Foreign, 4.67

U.S. Treasury creditors, as of December 2011, totaled $15.22 trillion, of which $4.67 trillion (30.7 percent) was foreign held debt.

SOURCE: U.S. Treasury Dept.

http://www.treasury.gov/resource-center/data-chart-center/tic/Documents/mfh.txt

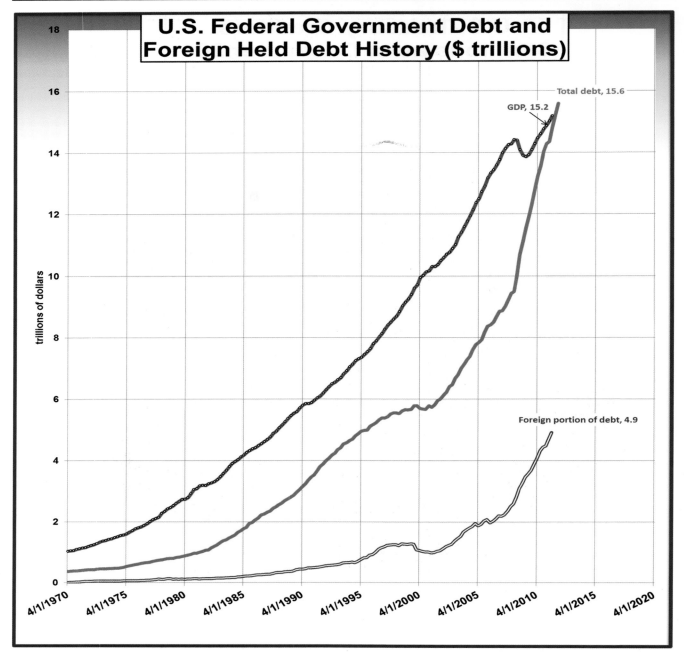

U.S. Federal Government Debt and Foreign Held Debt History ($ trillions)

Total debt, 15.6

GDP, 15.2

Foreign portion of debt, 4.9

trillions of dollars

4/1/1970 4/1/1975 4/1/1980 4/1/1985 4/1/1990 4/1/1995 4/1/2000 4/1/2005 4/1/2010 4/1/2015 4/1/2020

Federal debt held by foreign and international investors; total federal receipts are taxes and other federal income. GDP (Gross Domestic Product) is the sum of all domestic purchases of final products and services + private domestic investment + government consumption + net trade (exports - imports).

SOURCE: Federal Reserve Bank of St. Louis; U.S. Department of Commerce: Bureau of Economic Analysis

http://research.stlouisfed.org/

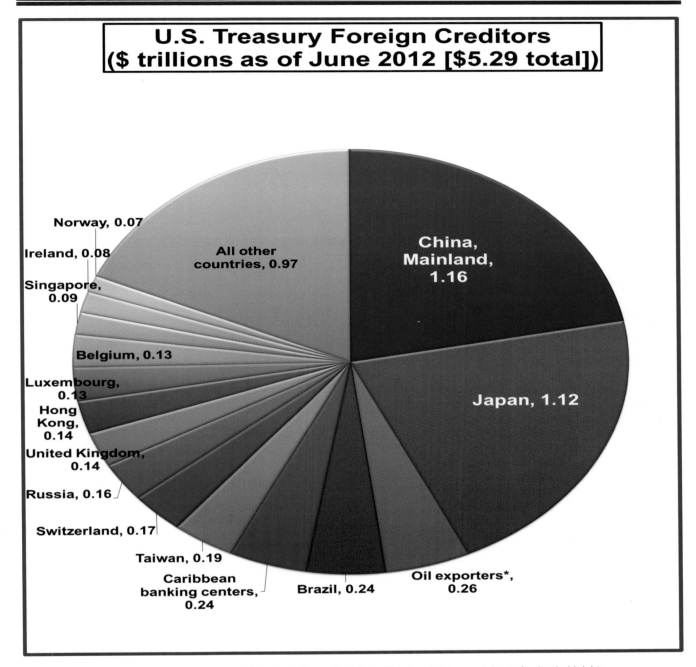

U.S. Treasury Foreign Creditors ($ trillions as of June 2012 [$5.29 total])

China, Mainland, 1.16

Japan, 1.12

Oil exporters*, 0.26

Brazil, 0.24

Caribbean banking centers, 0.24

Taiwan, 0.19

Switzerland, 0.17

Russia, 0.16

United Kingdom, 0.14

Hong Kong, 0.14

Luxembourg, 0.13

Belgium, 0.13

Singapore, 0.09

Ireland, 0.08

Norway, 0.07

All other countries, 0.97

U.S. Treasury creditors, as of June, 2012, totaled $15.58 trillion, of which $5.29 trillion (33.9 percent) was foreign held debt.

*Oil exporters include Ecuador, Venezuela, Indonesia, Bahrain, Iran, Iraq, Kuwait, Oman, Qatar, Saudi Arabia, the United Arab Emirates, Algeria, Gabon, Libya, and Nigeria

SOURCE: U.S. Treasury Dept.

http://www.treasury.gov/resource-center/data-chart-center/tic/Documents/mfh.txt

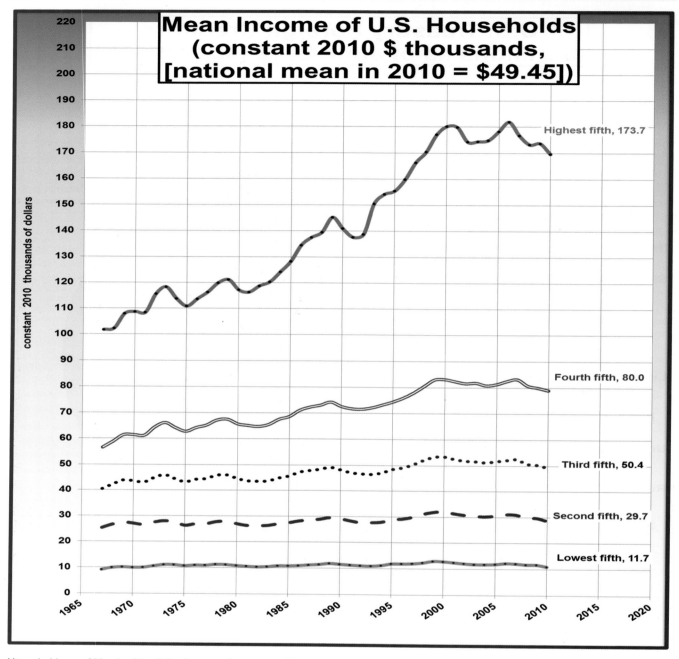

Mean Income of U.S. Households (constant 2010 $ thousands, [national mean in 2010 = $49.45])

Highest fifth, 173.7

Fourth fifth, 80.0

Third fifth, 50.4

Second fifth, 29.7

Lowest fifth, 11.7

constant 2010 thousands of dollars

Households as of March of the following year, in constant 2010 dollars; the shares method ranks households from lowest to highest on the basis on income and then divides them into groups of equal population size, typically quintiles. The aggregate income of each group is then divided by the overall aggregate income to derive shares; based on Current Population Survey, Annual Social and Economic Supplement (ASEC); income at selected positions in constant (2010) dollars.

SOURCE: U.S. Census Bureau, accessed in December 2011.

http://www.census.gov/hhes/www/p60_238sa.pdf

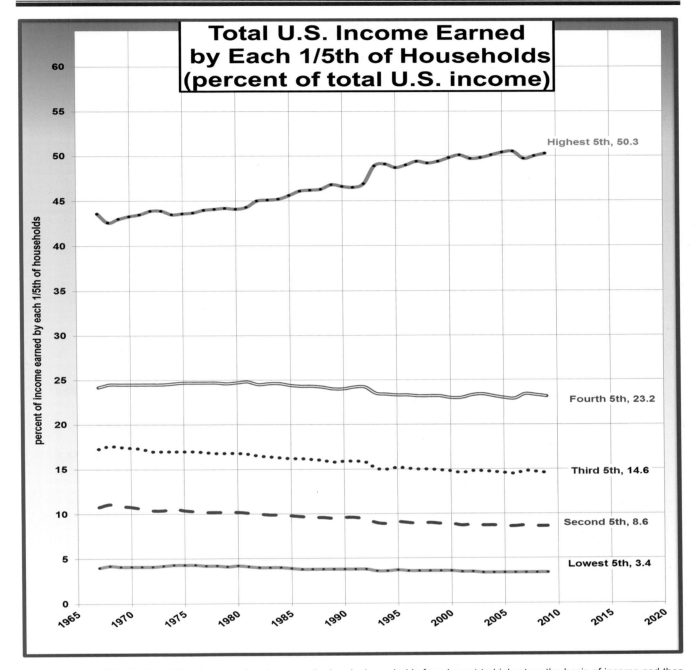

Total U.S. Income Earned by Each 1/5th of Households (percent of total U.S. income)

Highest 5th, 50.3

Fourth 5th, 23.2

Third 5th, 14.6

Second 5th, 8.6

Lowest 5th, 3.4

Households as of March of the following year; the shares method ranks households from lowest to highest on the basis of income and then divides them into groups of equal population size, typically quintiles. The aggregate income of each group is then divided by the overall aggregate income to derive shares; based on Current Population Survey, Annual Social and Economic Supplement (ASEC). Income at selected positions in constant (2010) dollars.

SOURCE: U.S. Census Bureau, accessed in December 2011.

http://www.census.gov/hhes/www/p60_238sa.pdf

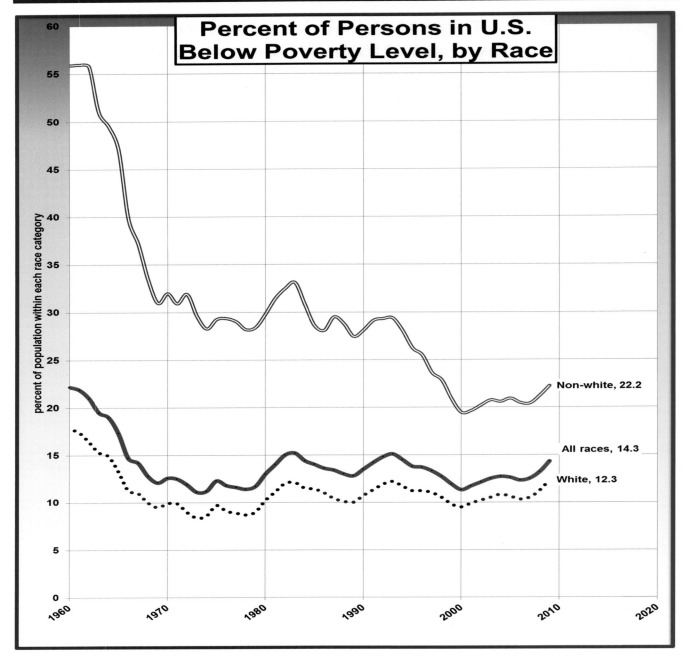

Percent of Persons in U.S. Below Poverty Level, by Race

Non-white, 22.2

All races, 14.3

White, 12.3

percent of population within each race category

Persons as of March of the following year; based on Current Population Survey, Annual Social and Economic Supplement (ASEC); see text, this section and Section 1, Appendix III.

For data collection changes over time, see http://www.census.gov/hhes/www/income/data/historical/history.html. The Census Bureau uses a set of money income thresholds that vary by family size and composition to determine who is in poverty. If a family's total income is less than the family's threshold, then that family and every individual in it is considered in poverty. The official poverty thresholds do not vary geographically, but they are updated for inflation using Consumer Price Index (CPI-U). The official poverty definition uses money income before taxes and does not include capital gains or noncash benefits (such as public housing, Medicaid, and food stamps).

SOURCE: U.S. Census Bureau, accessed in December 2011.

http://www.census.gov/compendia/statab/cats/international_statistics/vital_statistics_health_education.html

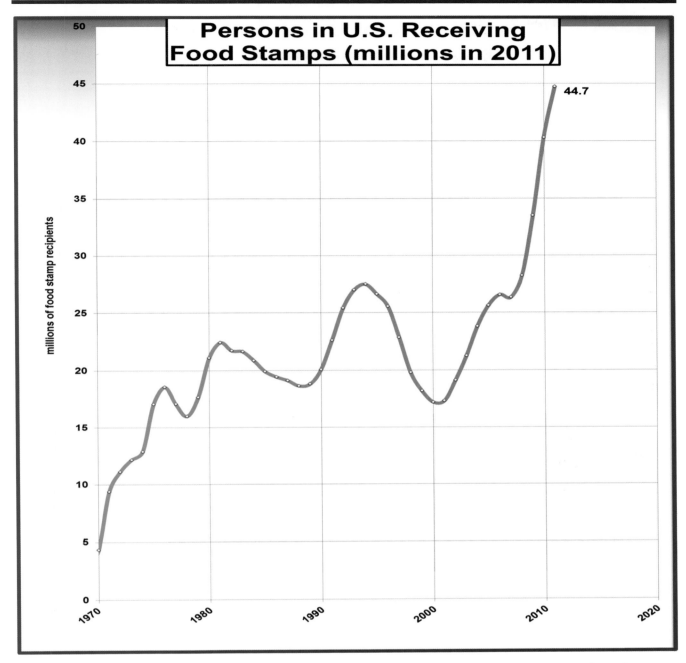

Persons in U.S. Receiving Food Stamps (millions in 2011)

44.7

Supplemental Nutrition Assistance Program Participation; in 2008 the U.S. Department of Agriculture renamed the Food Stamp Program as SNAP (Supplemental Nutrition Assistance Program).

SOURCE: U.S. Department of Agriculture

http://www.fns.usda.gov/pd/29SNAPcurrPP.htm

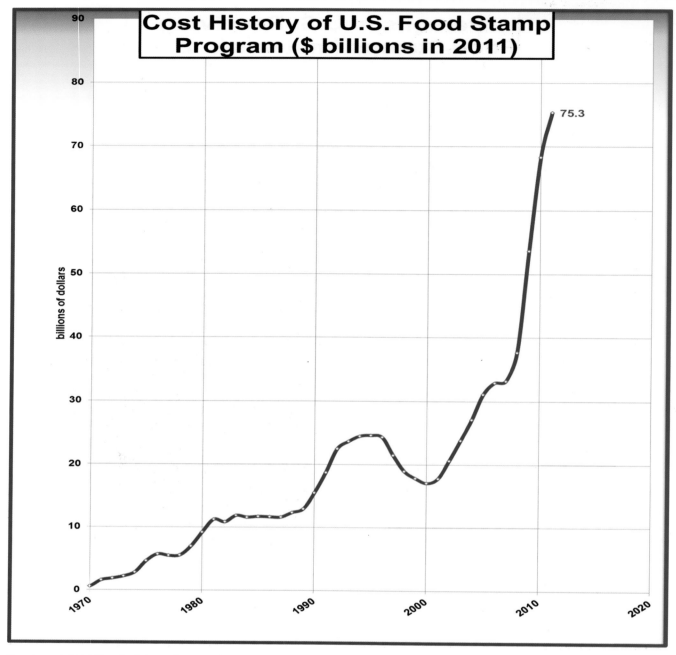

Cost History of U.S. Food Stamp Program ($ billions in 2011)

Supplemental Nutrition Assistance Program Costs; in 2008 the U.S. Department of Agriculture renamed the Food Stamp Program as SNAP (Supplemental Nutrition Assistance Program).

SOURCE: U.S. Department of Agriculture

http://www.fns.usda.gov/pd/29SNAPcurrPP.htm

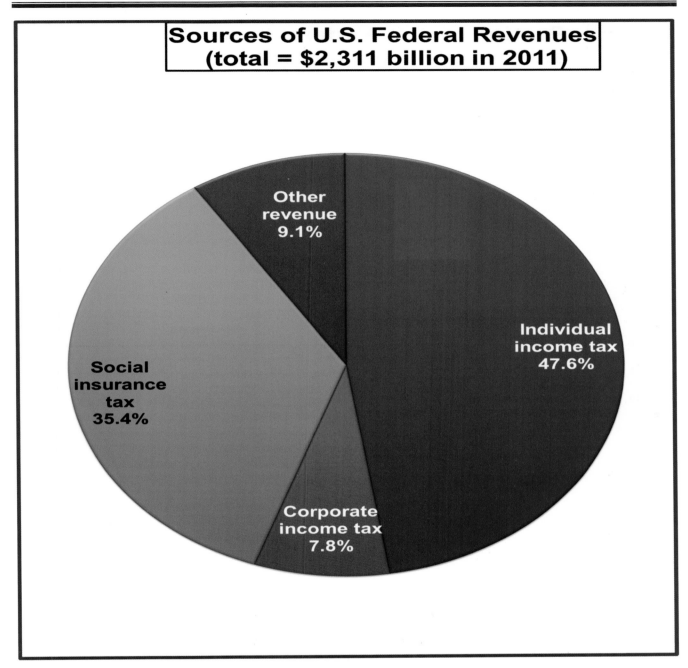

Sources of U.S. Federal Revenues (total = $2,311 billion in 2011)

- Other revenue 9.1%
- Individual income tax 47.6%
- Corporate income tax 7.8%
- Social insurance tax 35.4%

Total federal receipts (revenue) was $2,311 billion in 2011.

SOURCE: Congressional Budget Office

http://www.cbo.gov/ftpdocs/125xx/doc12577/budgetinfographic.htm

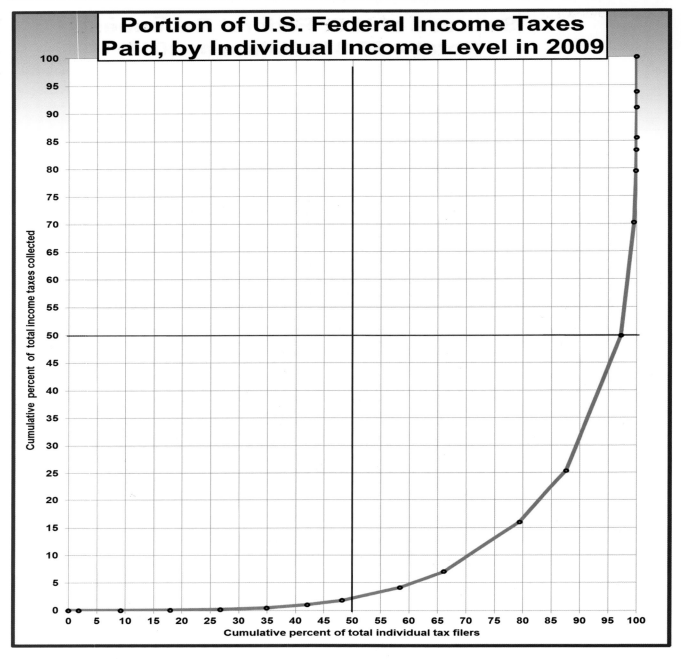

Personal income taxes for U.S. population in 2009

SOURCE: Internal Revenue Service

http://www.irs.gov/pub/irs-soi/08intop400.pdf

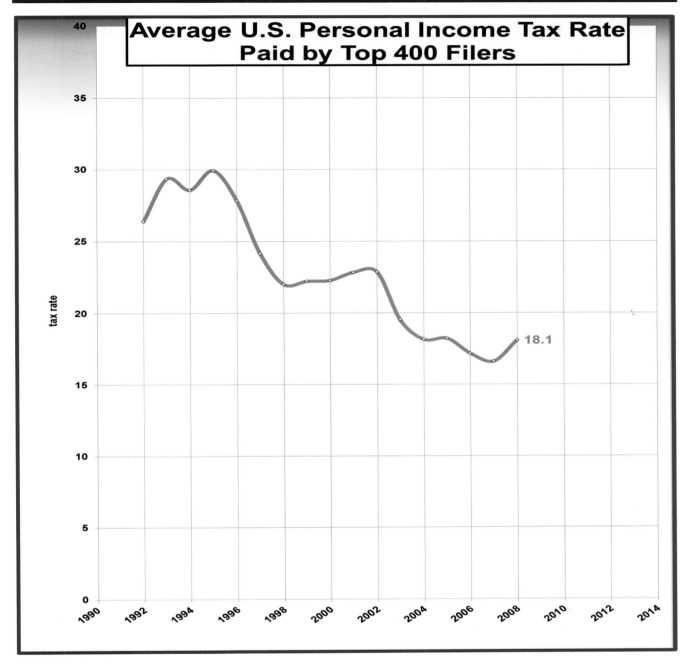

Average U.S. Personal Income Tax Rate Paid by Top 400 Filers

Effective personal income tax rate for the 400 individual income tax returns reporting the highest adjusted gross incomes each year, 1992–2008

SOURCE: Internal Revenue Service

http://www.irs.gov/pub/irs-soi/08intop400.pdf

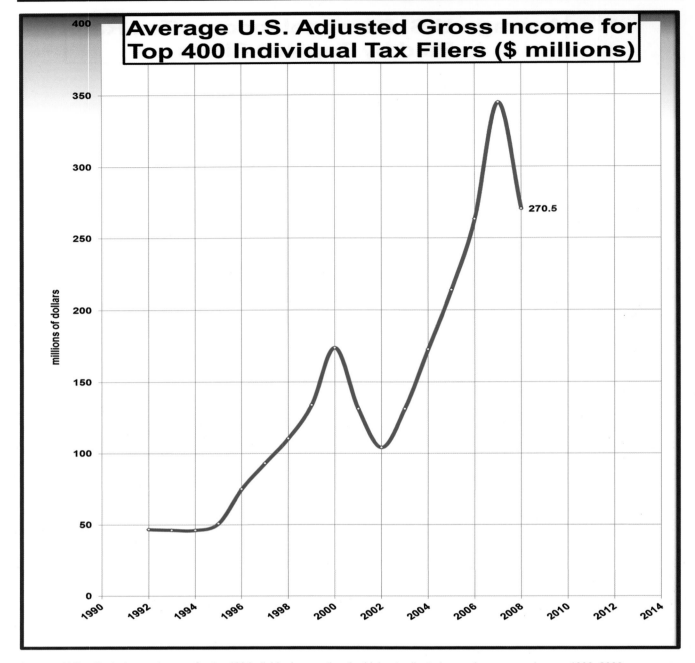

Average U.S. Adjusted Gross Income for Top 400 Individual Tax Filers ($ millions)

270.5

millions of dollars

1990 1992 1994 1996 1998 2000 2002 2004 2006 2008 2010 2012 2014

Average U.S. adjusted gross income for the 400 individuals reporting the highest adjusted gross incomes each year, 1992–2008

SOURCE: Internal Revenue Service

http://www.irs.gov/pub/irs-soi/08intop400.pdf

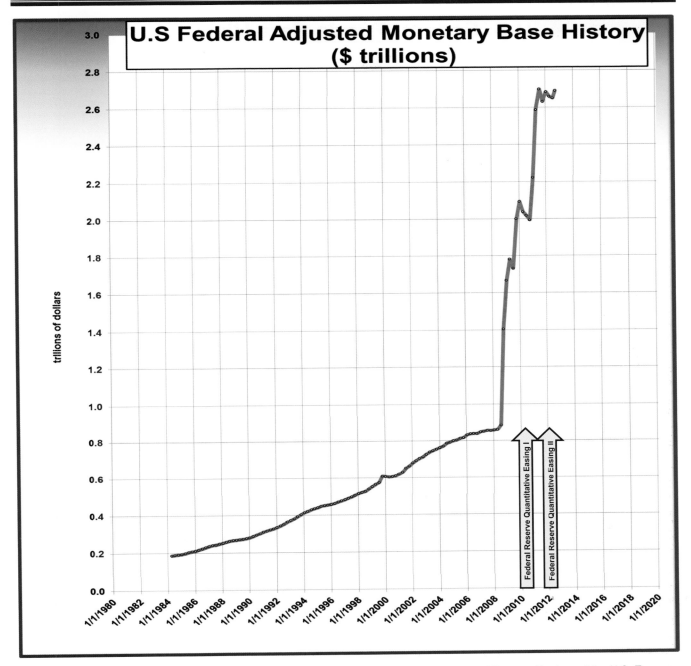

U.S Federal Adjusted Monetary Base History ($ trillions)

The Adjusted Monetary Base is the sum of currency (including coin) in circulation outside Federal Reserve Banks and the U.S. Treasury, plus deposits held by depository institutions at Federal Reserve Banks.

SOURCE: Federal Reserve Bank of St. Louis

http://research.stlouisfed.org/publications/review/03/09/Anderson.pdf.

http://research.stlouisfed.org/fred2/data/FYFSD.txt

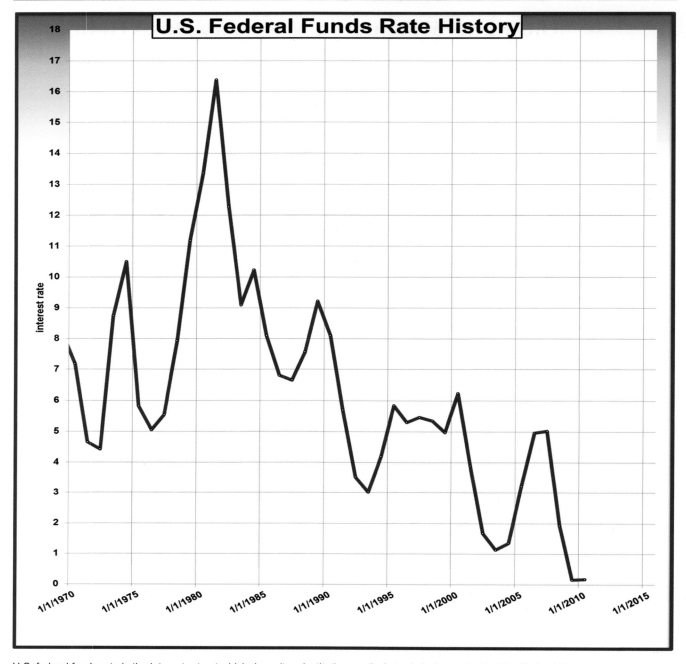

U.S. federal funds rate is the interest rate at which depository institutions actively trade balances held at the Federal Reserve.

SOURCE: Federal Reserve Bank of St. Louis

http://research.stlouisfed.org/

U.S. 30-Year Mortgage Rate History

30 year conventional, fixed mortage rates

SOURCE: Federal Reserve Bank of St. Louis

http://research.stlouisfed.org/

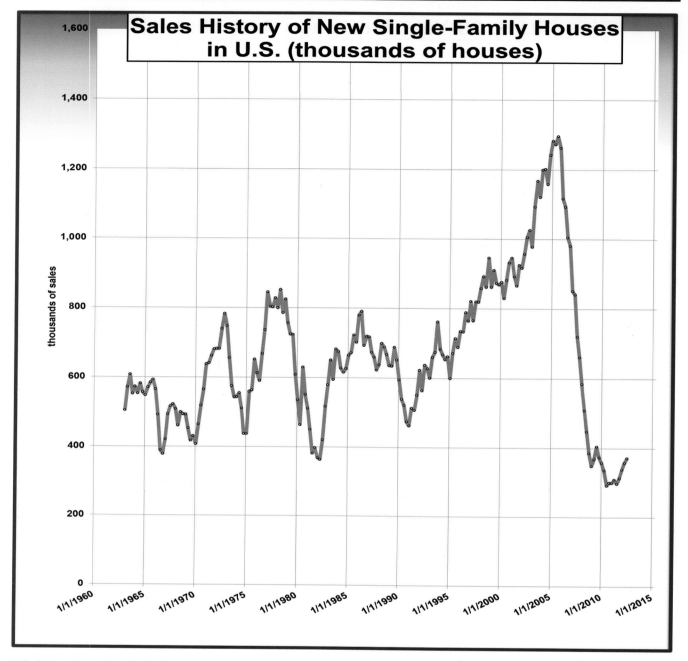

Sales History of New Single-Family Houses in U.S. (thousands of houses)

U.S. Sales of new single-family houses

SOURCE: Federal Reserve Bank of St. Louis; U.S. Department of Commerce: Census Bureau

http://research.stlouisfed.org/

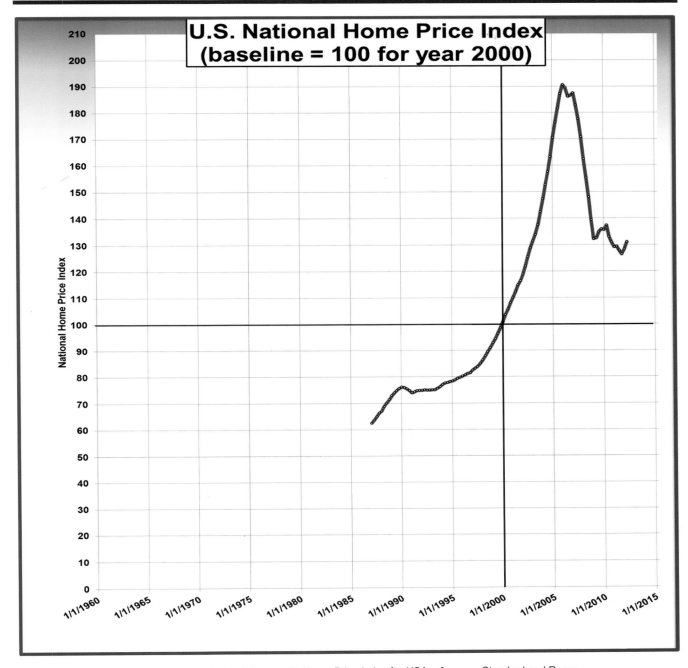

U.S. National Home Price Index (baseline = 100 for year 2000)

U.S. sales of new single-family houses; National Composite Home Price Index for USA reference: Standard and Poors

SOURCE: Federal Reserve Bankiof St. Louis; U.S. Department of Commerce: Census Bureau

http://research.stlouisfed.org/

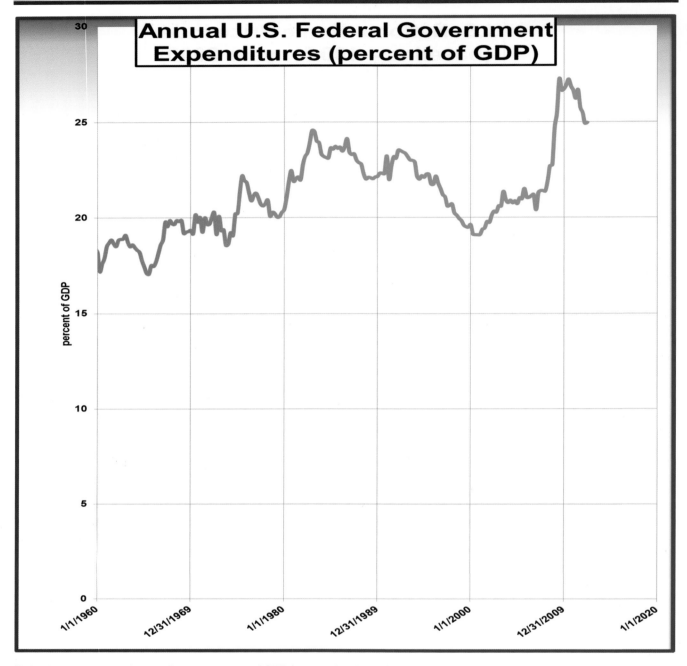

Annual U.S. Federal Government Expenditures (percent of GDP)

Federal government total expenditures as percent of GDP (seasonally adjusted).

SOURCE: Bureau of Economic Analysis

http://www.bea.gov/iTable/iTable.cfm?ReqID=9&step=1

GDP (Gross Domestic Product) is the sum of all domestic purchases of final products and services + private domestic investment + government consumption + net trade (exports - imports). Government includes federal, state and local.

Chapter 7: The U.S. Role in International Trade

Overview

International trade, the sum of imports + exports, was 29 percent of total U.S. GDP in 2010, two times the 1973 percentage, and ranked nineteenth among the G20* members. This compared with 78.6 percent of GDP for the European Union** and 55.2 percent for China.

In 2010, the United States was the world's largest exporter at $1.84 trillion and the largest importer at $2.36 trillion, which resulted in the world's largest trade deficit of $517 billion. This deficit was 4.7 times larger than India's, the second largest trade deficit in the world, compared with China's surplus of $232 billion. The largest single U.S. import product was crude oil at $252 billion while civilian aircraft and parts were the largest single export product category at $72 billion. Shares of U.S. stock traded were also the largest in the world, at $30.8 trillion, versus China's $7.7 trillion.

In 2009, the U.S. airlines transported 30 percent of the world's airline passengers, a decline from 53 percent in 1970, while China's share has grown from zero to 10 percent. U.S. also transported 30 percent of the world's air freight in 2009, a decline from 45 percent in 1973 while China's share has grown from zero to 6 percent.

In 2008, U.S. investors owned or controlled $3.2 trillion in foreign businesses, two times the 2002 level, and exceeded foreign investment in the U.S. by .91 trillion.

~

*G20 Members (see Appendix I): Argentina, Australia, Brazil, Canada, China, France, Germany, India, Indonesia, Italy, Japan, South Korea, Mexico, Russian Federation, Saudi Arabia, South Africa, Turkey, United Kingdom, United States and the European Union**

**European Union (see Appendix II): Austria, Belgium, Bulgaria, Cyprus, Czech Rep., Denmark, Estonia, Finland, France, Germany, Greece, Hungary, Ireland, Italy, Latvia, Lithuania, Luxembourg, Malta, Netherlands, Poland, Portugal, Romania, Slovakia, Slovenia, Spain, Sweden and the United Kingdom

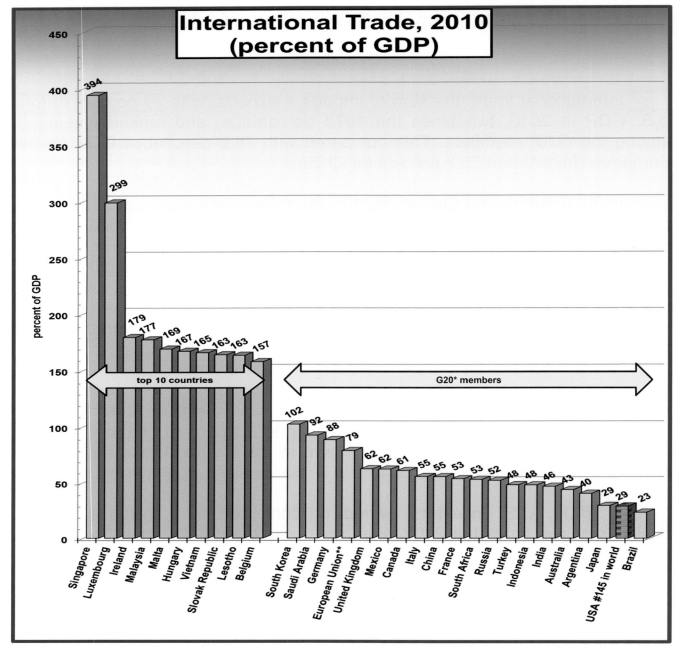

Trade is the sum of exports and imports of goods and services measured as a share of gross domestic product. The foreign-trade ratio for a country can exceed 100 percent of GDP because GDP is the sum of four components: consumption, investment, government spending plus net exports. The last component, net exports requires subtracting imports from exports. In contrast, a country's total trade is the result of adding exports to imports. GDP = private consumption + gross investment + government consumption (exclusive of transfer payments such as Social Security) + [exports − imports].

SOURCE: World Bank national accounts data, and OECD National Accounts data files. 2010 database accessed in October 2011.

http://data.worldbank.org/data-catalog/world-development-indicators?cid=GPD_WDI

*G20 Members (see Appendix I): Argentina, Australia, Brazil, Canada, China, France, Germany, India, Indonesia, Italy, Japan, South Korea, Mexico, Russian Federation, Saudi Arabia, South Africa, Turkey, United Kingdom, United States and the European Union**

**European Union (see Appendix II): Austria, Belgium, Bulgaria, Cyprus, Czech Rep., Denmark, Estonia, Finland, France, Germany, Greece, Hungary, Ireland, Italy, Latvia, Lithuania, Luxembourg, Malta, Netherlands, Poland, Portugal, Romania, Slovakia, Slovenia, Spain, Sweden and the United Kingdom

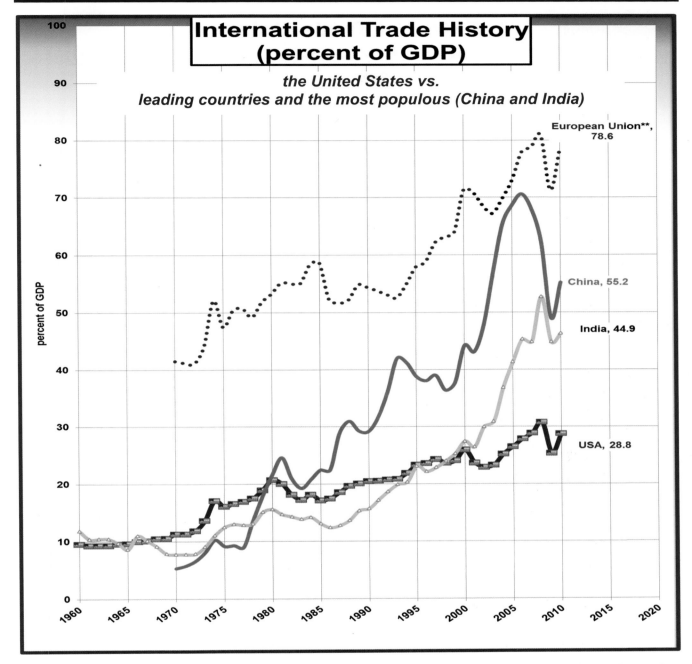

International Trade History (percent of GDP)

the United States vs.
leading countries and the most populous (China and India)

European Union**, 78.6

China, 55.2

India, 44.9

USA, 28.8

percent of GDP

Trade is the sum of exports and imports of goods and services measured as a share of gross domestic product. The foreign-trade ratio for a country can exceed 100 percent of GDP because GDP is the sum of four components: consumption, investment, government spending plus net exports. The last component, net exports requires subtracting imports from exports. In contrast, a country's total trade is the result of adding exports to imports. GDP = private consumption + gross investment + government consumption (exclusive of transfer payments such as Social Security) + [exports − imports].

SOURCE: World Bank national accounts data, and OECD National Accounts data files. 2010 database accessed in October 2011.

http://data.worldbank.org/data-catalog/world-development-indicators?cid=GPD_WDI

**European Union (see Appendix II): Austria, Belgium, Bulgaria, Cyprus, Czech Rep., Denmark, Estonia, Finland, France, Germany, Greece, Hungary, Ireland, Italy, Latvia, Lithuania, Luxembourg, Malta, Netherlands, Poland, Portugal, Romania, Slovakia, Slovenia, Spain, Sweden and the United Kingdom

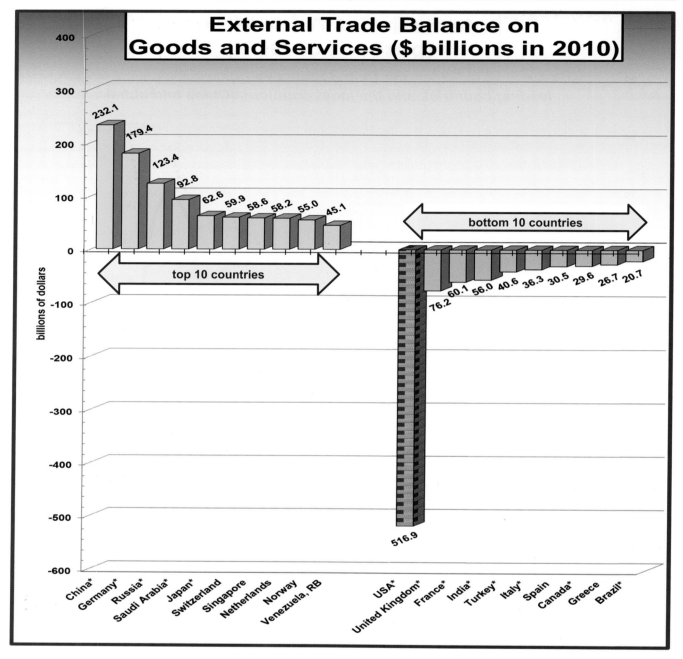

External Trade Balance on Goods and Services ($ billions in 2010)

billions of dollars

top 10 countries: China* 232.1, Germany* 179.4, Russia* 123.4, Saudi Arabia* 92.8, Japan* 62.6, Switzerland 59.9, Singapore 58.6, Netherlands 58.2, Norway 55.0, Venezuela, RB 45.1

bottom 10 countries: USA* 516.9, United Kingdom* 76.2, France* 60.1, India* 56.0, Turkey* 40.6, Italy* 36.3, Spain 30.5, Canada* 29.6, Greece 26.7, Brazil* 20.7

External trade balance on goods and services (formerly resource balance) equals exports of goods and services minus imports of goods and services (previously nonfactor services).

SOURCE: World Bank national accounts data, and OECD*** National Accounts data files; 2010 database accessed in April 2012.

http://data.worldbank.org/data-catalog/world-development-indicators?cid=GPD_WDI

*G20 Members (see Appendix I): Argentina, Australia, Brazil, Canada, China, France, Germany, India, Indonesia, Italy, Japan, South Korea, Mexico, Russian Federation, Saudi Arabia, South Africa, Turkey, United Kingdom, United States and the European Union**

**European Union (see Appendix II): Austria, Belgium, Bulgaria, Cyprus, Czech Rep., Denmark, Estonia, Finland, France, Germany, Greece, Hungary, Ireland, Italy, Latvia, Lithuania, Luxembourg, Malta, Netherlands, Poland, Portugal, Romania, Slovakia, Slovenia, Spain, Sweden and the United Kingdom

***OECD (see Appendix III) Organization for Economic Cooperation and Development

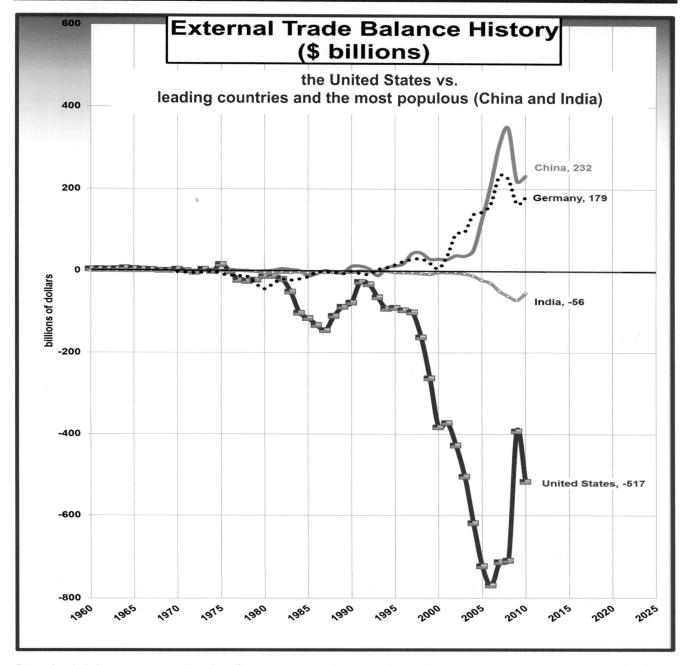

External Trade Balance History ($ billions)

the United States vs.
leading countries and the most populous (China and India)

China, 232

Germany, 179

India, -56

United States, -517

External trade balance on goods and services (formerly resource balance) equals exports of goods and services minus imports of goods and services (previously nonfactor services).

SOURCE: World Bank national accounts data, and OECD*** National Accounts data files; 2010 database accessed in April, 2012.

http://data.worldbank.org/data-catalog/world-development-indicators?cid=GPD_WDI

***OECD (see Appendix III) Organization for Economic Cooperation and Development

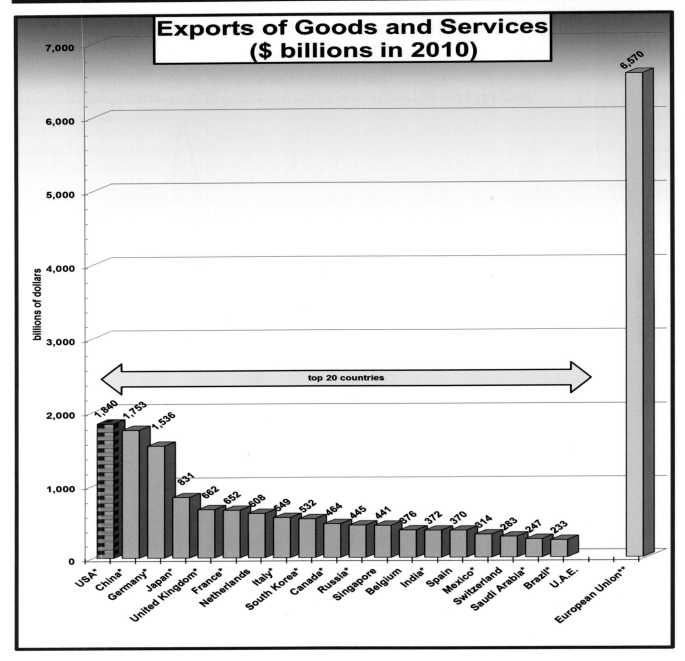

Exports of Goods and Services ($ billions in 2010)

billions of dollars

top 20 countries

USA*	1,840
China*	1,753
Germany*	1,536
Japan*	831
United Kingdom*	662
France*	652
Netherlands	608
Italy*	549
South Korea*	532
Canada*	464
Russia*	445
Singapore	441
Belgium	376
India*	372
Spain	370
Mexico*	314
Switzerland	283
Saudi Arabia*	247
Brazil*	233
U.A.E.	
European Union**	6,570

Exports of goods and services represent the value of all goods and other market services provided to the rest of the world. They include the value of merchandise, freight, insurance, transport, travel, royalties, license fees, and other services, such as communication, construction, financial, information, business, personal, and government services. They exclude compensation of employees and investment income (formerly called factor services) and transfer payments. Data are in current U.S. dollars.

SOURCE: World Bank national accounts data, and OECD National Accounts data files. 2010 database accessed in April 2012

http://data.worldbank.org/data-catalog/world-development-indicators?cid=GPD_WDI

*G20 Members (see Appendix I): Argentina, Australia, Brazil, Canada, China, France, Germany, India, Indonesia, Italy, Japan, South Korea, Mexico, Russian Federation, Saudi Arabia, South Africa, Turkey, United Kingdom, United States and the European Union**

**European Union (see Appendix II): Austria, Belgium, Bulgaria, Cyprus, Czech Rep., Denmark, Estonia, Finland, France, Germany, Greece, Hungary, Ireland, Italy, Latvia, Lithuania, Luxembourg, Malta, Netherlands, Poland, Portugal, Romania, Slovakia, Slovenia, Spain, Sweden and the United Kingdom

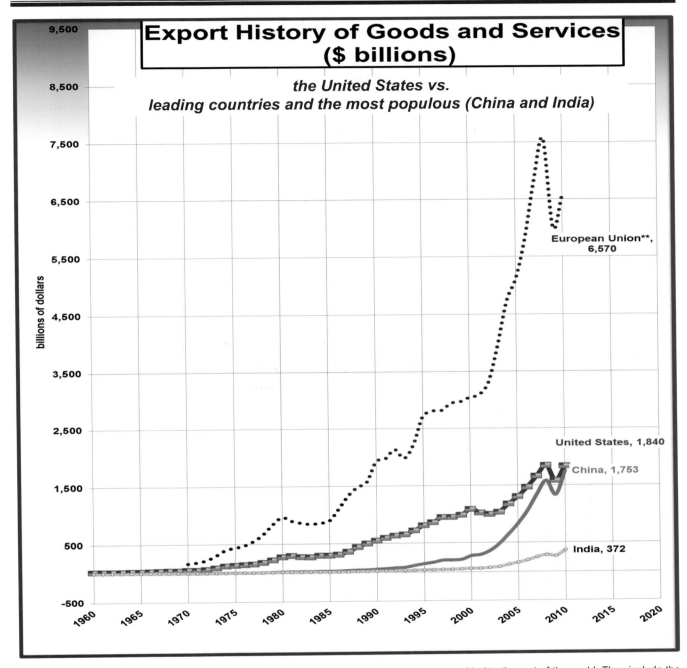

Export History of Goods and Services ($ billions)

the United States vs.
leading countries and the most populous (China and India)

European Union**, 6,570

United States, 1,840

China, 1,753

India, 372

billions of dollars

Exports of goods and services represent the value of all goods and other market services provided to the rest of the world. They include the value of merchandise, freight, insurance, transport, travel, royalties, license fees, and other services, such as communication, construction, financial, information, business, personal, and government services. They exclude compensation of employees and investment income (formerly called factor services) and transfer payments. Data are in current U.S. dollars.

SOURCE: World Bank national accounts data, and OECD National Accounts data files; 2010 database accessed in January 2012

http://data.worldbank.org/data-catalog/world-development-indicators?cid=GPD_WDI

**European Union (see Appendix II): Austria, Belgium, Bulgaria, Cyprus, Czech Rep., Denmark, Estonia, Finland, France, Germany, Greece, Hungary, Ireland, Italy, Latvia, Lithuania, Luxembourg, Malta, Netherlands, Poland, Portugal, Romania, Slovakia, Slovenia, Spain, Sweden and the United Kingdom

***OECD (see Appendix III) Organization for Economic Cooperation and Development

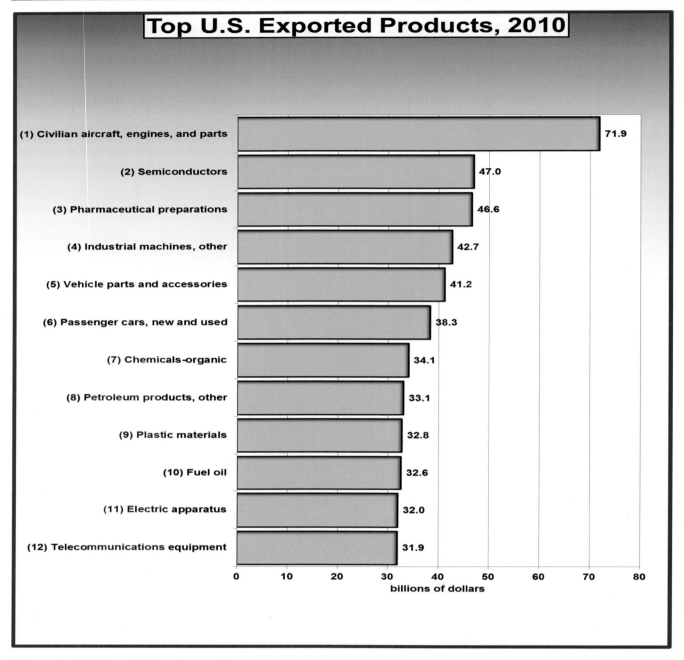

Top U.S. Exported Products, 2010

Product	billions of dollars
(1) Civilian aircraft, engines, and parts	71.9
(2) Semiconductors	47.0
(3) Pharmaceutical preparations	46.6
(4) Industrial machines, other	42.7
(5) Vehicle parts and accessories	41.2
(6) Passenger cars, new and used	38.3
(7) Chemicals-organic	34.1
(8) Petroleum products, other	33.1
(9) Plastic materials	32.8
(10) Fuel oil	32.6
(11) Electric apparatus	32.0
(12) Telecommunications equipment	31.9

U.S. exports, 2010, classified by end-use code

SOURCE: Census Bureau Foreign Trade, Data Dissemination Branch of the Foreign Trade Division

http://www.census.gov/foreign-trade/statistics/product/enduse/exports/c0000.html#questions

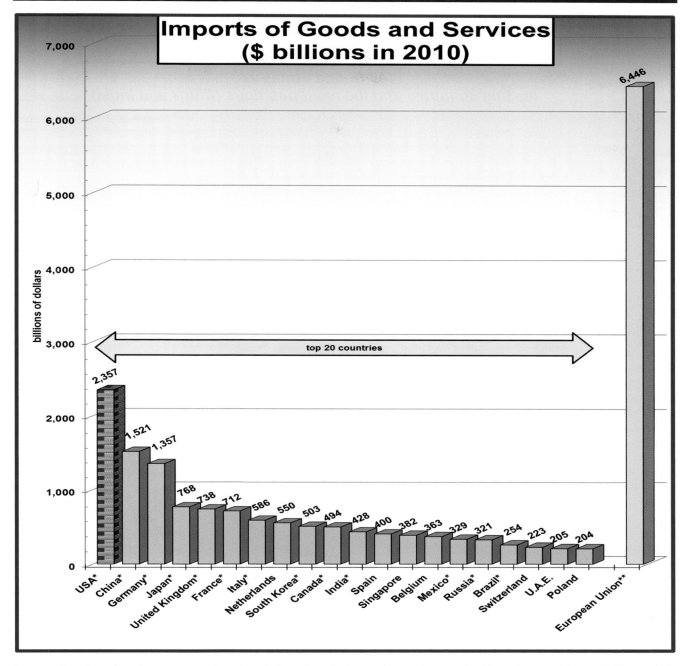

Imports of Goods and Services ($ billions in 2010)

top 20 countries

USA* 2,357
China* 1,521
Germany* 1,357
Japan* 768
United Kingdom* 738
France* 712
Italy* 586
Netherlands 550
South Korea* 503
Canada* 494
India* 428
Spain 400
Singapore 382
Belgium 363
Mexico* 329
Russia* 321
Brazil* 254
Switzerland 223
U.A.E. 205
Poland 204
European Union** 6,446

Imports of goods and services represent the value of all goods and other market services received from the rest of the world. They include the value of merchandise, freight, insurance, transport, travel, royalties, license fees, and other services, such as communication, construction, financial, information, business, personal, and government services. They exclude compensation of employees and investment income (formerly called factor services) and transfer payments. Data are in current U.S. dollars.

SOURCE: World Bank national accounts data, and OECD National Accounts data files; 2010 database accessed in April 2012

http://data.worldbank.org/data-catalog/world-development-indicators?cid=GPD_WDI

**European Union (see Appendix II): Austria, Belgium, Bulgaria, Cyprus, Czech Rep., Denmark, Estonia, Finland, France, Germany, Greece, Hungary, Ireland, Italy, Latvia, Lithuania, Luxembourg, Malta, Netherlands, Poland, Portugal, Romania, Slovakia, Slovenia, Spain, Sweden and the United Kingdom

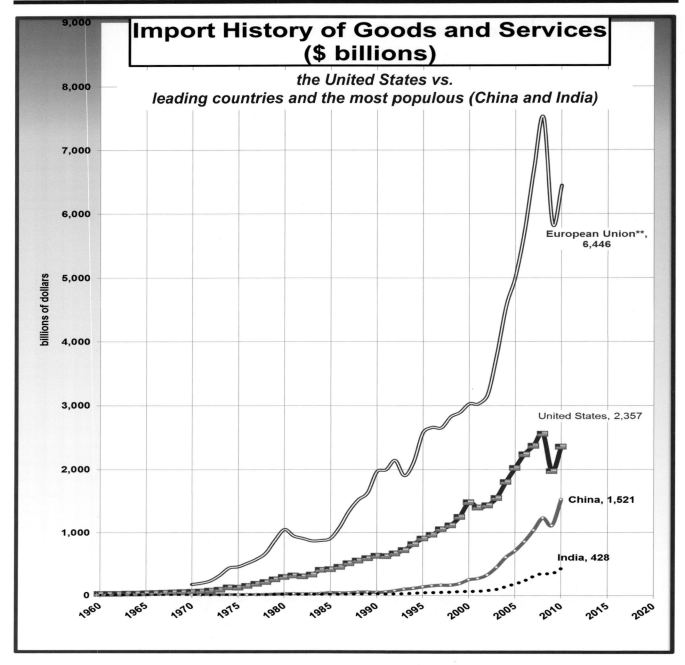

Import History of Goods and Services ($ billions)

the United States vs.
leading countries and the most populous (China and India)

billions of dollars

European Union**, 6,446

United States, 2,357

China, 1,521

India, 428

Imports of goods and services represent the value of all goods and other market services received from the rest of the world. They include the value of merchandise, freight, insurance, transport, travel, royalties, license fees, and other services, such as communication, construction, financial, information, business, personal, and government services. They exclude compensation of employees and investment income (formerly called factor services) and transfer payments. Data are in current U.S. dollars.

SOURCE: World Bank national accounts data, and OECD National Accounts data files; 2010 database accessed in April 2012

http://data.worldbank.org/data-catalog/world-development-indicators?cid=GPD_WDI

**European Union (see Appendix II): Austria, Belgium, Bulgaria, Cyprus, Czech Rep., Denmark, Estonia, Finland, France, Germany, Greece, Hungary, Ireland, Italy, Latvia, Lithuania, Luxembourg, Malta, Netherlands, Poland, Portugal, Romania, Slovakia, Slovenia, Spain, Sweden and the United Kingdom

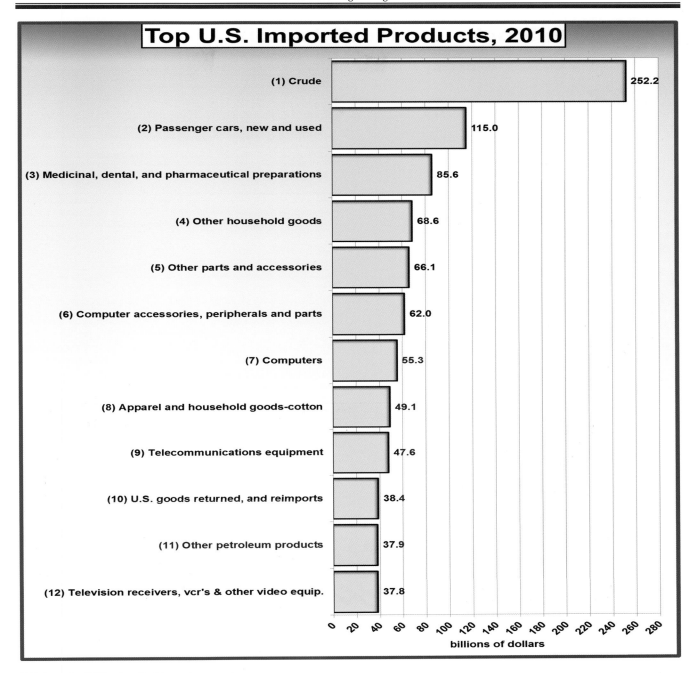

Top U.S. Imported Products, 2010

Product	billions of dollars
(1) Crude	252.2
(2) Passenger cars, new and used	115.0
(3) Medicinal, dental, and pharmaceutical preparations	85.6
(4) Other household goods	68.6
(5) Other parts and accessories	66.1
(6) Computer accessories, peripherals and parts	62.0
(7) Computers	55.3
(8) Apparel and household goods-cotton	49.1
(9) Telecommunications equipment	47.6
(10) U.S. goods returned, and reimports	38.4
(11) Other petroleum products	37.9
(12) Television receivers, vcr's & other video equip.	37.8

U.S. imports, 2010, classified by end-use code.

SOURCE: U.S. Census Bureau Foreign Trade, Data Dissemination Branch of the Foreign Trade Division

http://www.census.gov/foreign-trade/statistics/product/enduse/exports/c0000.html#questions

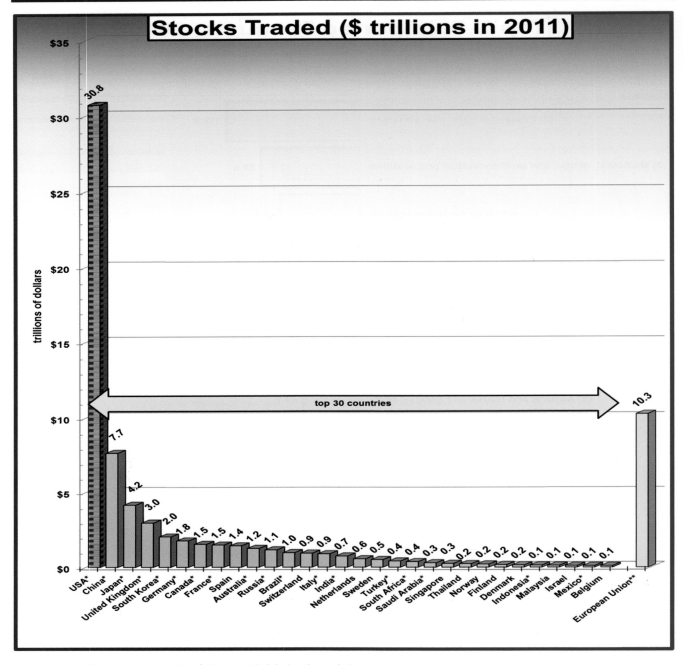

Stocks Traded ($ trillions in 2011)

top 30 countries

USA* 30.8
China* 7.7
Japan* 4.2
United Kingdom* 3.0
South Korea* 2.0
Germany* 1.8
Canada* 1.5
France* 1.5
Spain 1.4
Australia* 1.2
Russia* 1.1
Brazil* 1.0
Switzerland 0.9
Italy* 0.9
India* 0.7
Netherlands 0.6
Sweden 0.5
Turkey* 0.4
South Africa* 0.4
Saudi Arabia* 0.3
Singapore 0.3
Thailand 0.2
Norway 0.2
Finland 0.2
Denmark 0.2
Indonesia* 0.1
Malaysia 0.1
Israel 0.1
Mexico* 0.1
Belgium 0.1
European Union** 10.3

Stocks traded refers to the total value of shares traded during the period.

SOURCE: The World Bank, 2011 database accessed September 2012. Standard & Poor's, Global Stock Markets Factbook and supplemental S&P data.

http://data.worldbank.org/data-catalog/world-development-indicators?cid=GPD_WDI

*G20 Members (see Appendix I): Argentina, Australia, Brazil, Canada, China, France, Germany, India, Indonesia, Italy, Japan, South Korea, Mexico, Russian Federation, Saudi Arabia, South Africa, Turkey, United Kingdom, United States and the European Union**

**European Union (see Appendix II): Austria, Belgium, Bulgaria, Cyprus, Czech Rep., Denmark, Estonia, Finland, France, Germany, Greece, Hungary, Ireland, Italy, Latvia, Lithuania, Luxembourg, Malta, Netherlands, Poland, Portugal, Romania, Slovakia, Slovenia, Spain, Sweden and the United Kingdom

U.S. Dollar Exchange Rate Index of Major Currencies (March 1973 = 100)

The U.S. dollar exchange rate index (designated TWEXMPA) is a weighted average of the foreign exchange value of the U.S. dollar against a subset of the broad index currencies that circulate widely outside the country of issue. March 1973 is set equal to100.0. The index includes the Euro Area, Canada, Japan, United Kingdom, Switzerland, Australia, and Sweden. For more information about trade-weighted indexes see http://www.federalreserve.gov/pubs/bulletin/2005/winter05_index.pdf.

SOURCE: U.S. Federal Reserve Bank of St. Louis

http://research.stlouisfed.org/fred2/series/TWEXMPA/downloaddata?cid=105

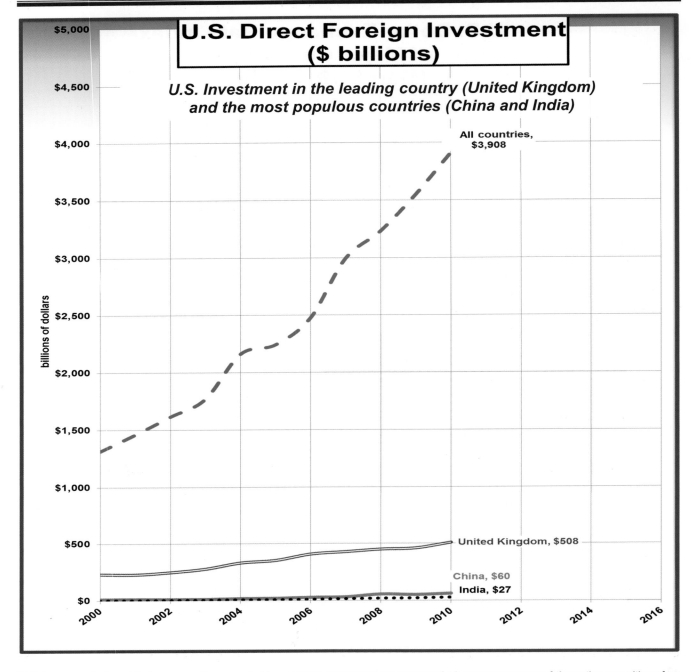

U.S. Direct Foreign Investment ($ billions)

U.S. Investment in the leading country (United Kingdom) and the most populous countries (China and India)

All countries, $3,908

United Kingdom, $508

China, $60

India, $27

billions of dollars

U.S. investment abroad is the ownership or control by one U.S. person or corporation of 10 percent or more of the voting securities of an incorporated foreign business enterprise or an equivalent interest in an unincorporated foreign business enterprise. Negative position can occur when a U.S. parent company's liabilities to the foreign affiliate are greater than its equity in and loans to the foreign affiliate.

SOURCE: U.S. Census Bureau, accessed in December, 2011. U.S. Bureau of Economic Analysis, Survey of Current Business, July 2011.

http://www.census.gov/compendia/statab/cats/international_statistics/vital_statistics_health_education.html

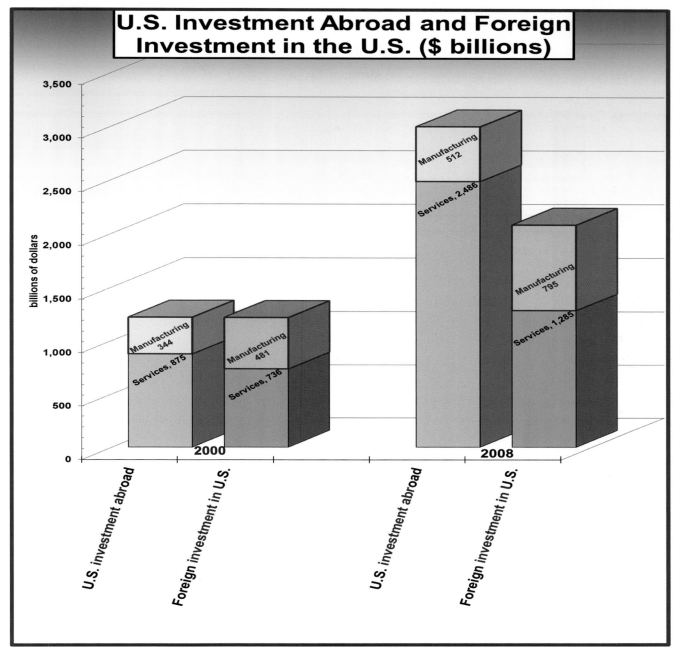

Stock of U.S. direct investment abroad and foreign direct investment in the United States, by selected industry/service: 2000 and 2008

SOURCE: National Science Foundation, Bureau of Economic Analysis, International Economic Accounts, U.S. Direct Investment Abroad, Balance of Payments and Direct Investment Position Data and Foreign Direct Investment in the United States: Balance of Payments and Direct Investment Position Data, http://www.bea.gov/international/di1fdibal.htm, accessed 15 September 2009.

http://www.nsf.gov/statistics/seind10/tables

http://www.bea.gov/international/di1usdbal.htm

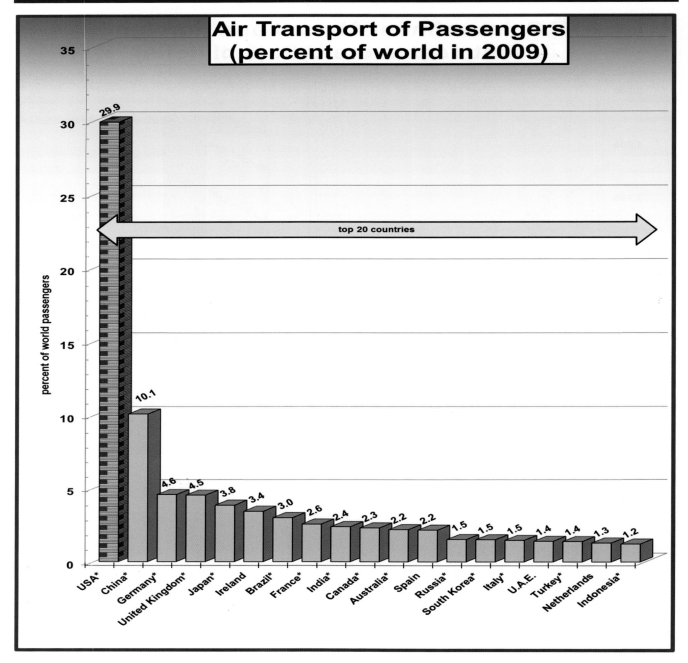

Air Transport of Passengers (percent of world in 2009)

percent of world passengers

top 20 countries

USA* 29.9
China* 10.1
Germany* 4.6
United Kingdom* 4.5
Japan* 3.8
Ireland 3.4
Brazil* 3.0
France* 2.6
India* 2.4
Canada* 2.3
Australia* 2.2
Spain 2.2
Russia* 1.5
South Korea* 1.5
Italy* 1.5
U.A.E. 1.4
Turkey* 1.4
Netherlands 1.3
Indonesia* 1.2

Air passengers carried include both domestic and international aircraft passengers of air carriers registered in the country.

SOURCE: International Civil Aviation Organization, Civil Aviation Statistics of the World and ICAO staff estimates. 2009 database accessed April 2012

http://data.worldbank.org/data-catalog/world-development-indicators?cid=GPD_WDI

*G20 Members (see Appendix I): Argentina, Australia, Brazil, Canada, China, France, Germany, India, Indonesia, Italy, Japan, South Korea, Mexico, Russian Federation, Saudi Arabia, South Africa, Turkey, United Kingdom, United States and the European Union**

**European Union (see Appendix II): Austria, Belgium, Bulgaria, Cyprus, Czech Rep., Denmark, Estonia, Finland, France, Germany, Greece, Hungary, Ireland, Italy, Latvia, Lithuania, Luxembourg, Malta, Netherlands, Poland, Portugal, Romania, Slovakia, Slovenia, Spain, Sweden and the United Kingdom

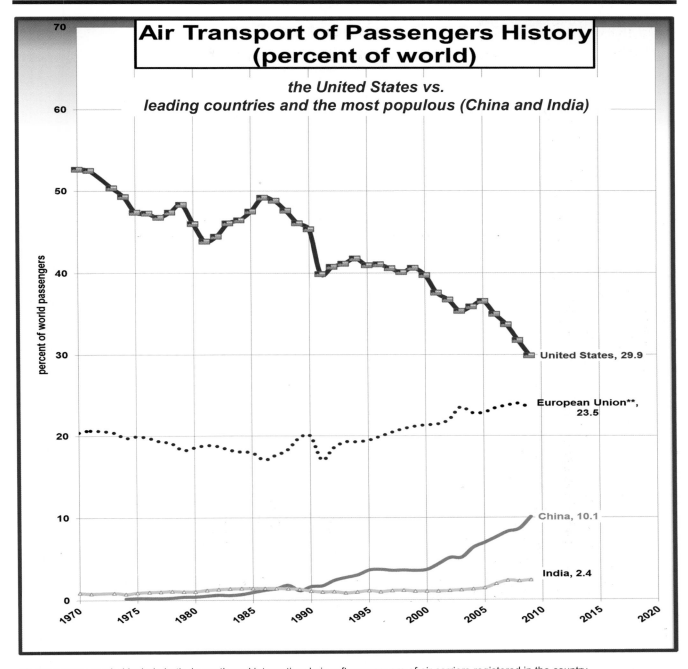

Air Transport of Passengers History (percent of world)

the United States vs.
leading countries and the most populous (China and India)

United States, 29.9

European Union**, 23.5

China, 10.1

India, 2.4

Air passengers carried include both domestic and international aircraft passengers of air carriers registered in the country.

SOURCE: World Bank. International Civil Aviation Organization, Civil Aviation Statistics of the World and ICAO staff estimates; 2009 database accessed April 2012

http://data.worldbank.org/data-catalog/world-development-indicators?cid=GPD_WDI.

**European Union (see Appendix II): Austria, Belgium, Bulgaria, Cyprus, Czech Rep., Denmark, Estonia, Finland, France, Germany, Greece, Hungary, Ireland, Italy, Latvia, Lithuania, Luxembourg, Malta, Netherlands, Poland, Portugal, Romania, Slovakia, Slovenia, Spain, Sweden and the United Kingdom

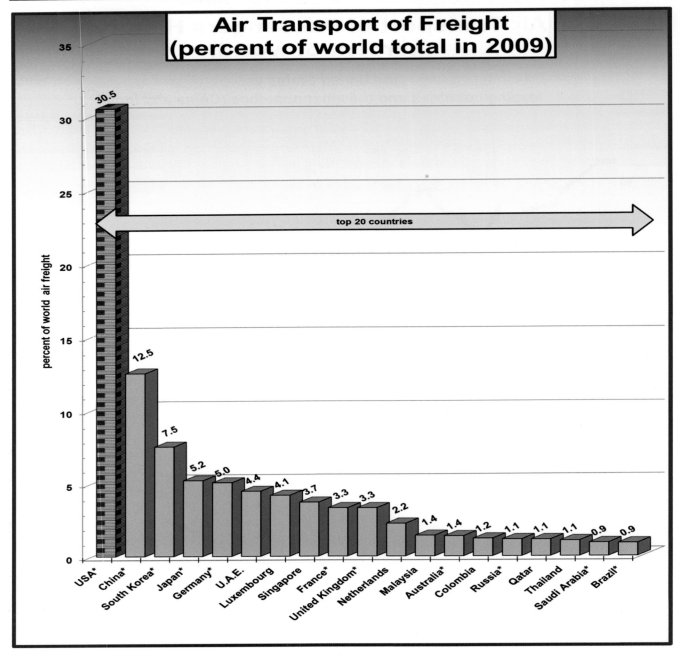

**Air Transport of Freight
(percent of world total in 2009)**

top 20 countries

percent of world air freight

USA*	China*	South Korea*	Japan*	Germany*	U.A.E.	Luxembourg	Singapore	France*	United Kingdom*	Netherlands	Malaysia	Australia*	Colombia	Russia*	Qatar	Thailand	Saudi Arabia*	Brazil*
30.5	12.5	7.5	5.2	5.0	4.4	4.1	3.7	3.3	3.3	2.2	1.4	1.4	1.2	1.1	1.1	1.1	0.9	0.9

Air freight is the volume of freight, express, and diplomatic bags carried on each flight stage (operation of an aircraft from takeoff to its next landing), measured in metric tons times kilometers traveled.

SOURCE: World Bank. International Civil Aviation Organization, Civil Aviation Statistics of the World and ICAO staff estimates; 2009 database accessed April 2012

http://data.worldbank.org/data-catalog/world-development-indicators?cid=GPD_WDI.

*G20 Members (see Appendix I): Argentina, Australia, Brazil, Canada, China, France, Germany, India, Indonesia, Italy, Japan, South Korea, Mexico, Russian Federation, Saudi Arabia, South Africa, Turkey, United Kingdom, United States and the European Union**

**European Union (see Appendix II): Austria, Belgium, Bulgaria, Cyprus, Czech Rep., Denmark, Estonia, Finland, France, Germany, Greece, Hungary, Ireland, Italy, Latvia, Lithuania, Luxembourg, Malta, Netherlands, Poland, Portugal, Romania, Slovakia, Slovenia, Spain, Sweden and the United Kingdom

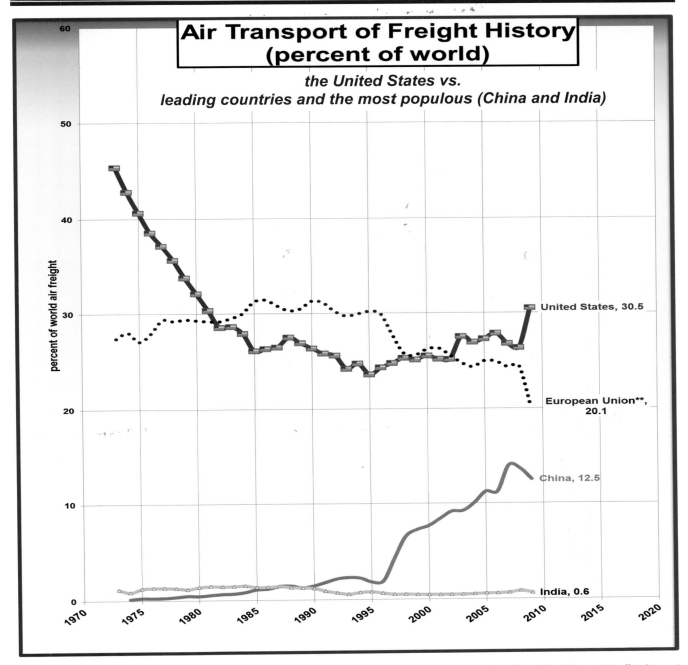

Air Transport of Freight History (percent of world)

the United States vs.
leading countries and the most populous (China and India)

United States, 30.5

European Union**, 20.1

China, 12.5

India, 0.6

percent of world air freight

Air freight is the volume of freight, express, and diplomatic bags carried on each flight stage (operation of an aircraft from takeoff to its next landing), measured in metric tons times kilometers traveled.

SOURCE: World Bank. International Civil Aviation Organization, Civil Aviation Statistics of the World and ICAO staff estimates; 2009 database accessed April 2012

http://data.worldbank.org/data-catalog/world-development-indicators?cid=GPD_WDI

**European Union (see Appendix II): Austria, Belgium, Bulgaria, Cyprus, Czech Rep., Denmark, Estonia, Finland, France, Germany, Greece, Hungary, Ireland, Italy, Latvia, Lithuania, Luxembourg, Malta, Netherlands, Poland, Portugal, Romania, Slovakia, Slovenia, Spain, Sweden and the United Kingdom

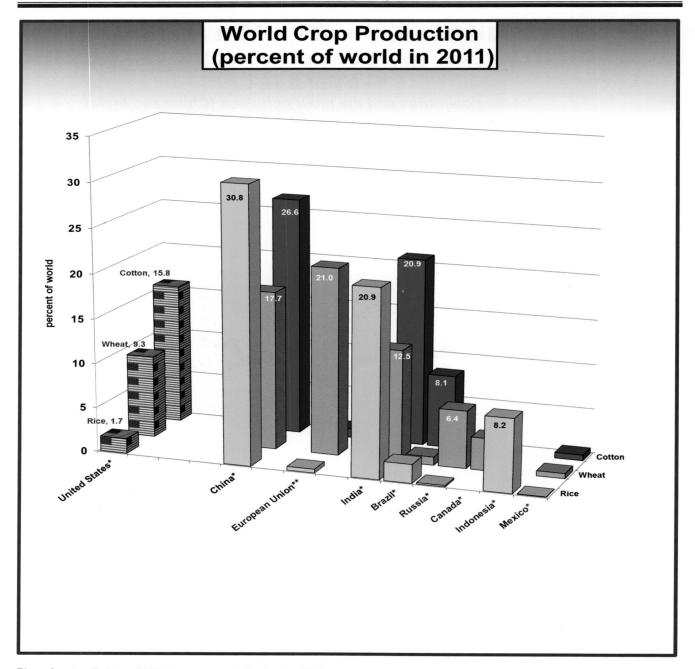

World Crop Production (percent of world in 2011)

Rice refers to milled rice; 2011 data accessed in September 2012.

SOURCE: U.S. Census Bureau, Agriculture, Foreign Agricultural Service, World Agricultural Production, annual.

http://www.census.gov/compendia/statab/cats/international_statistics/agricultural_production_and_trade.html

*G20 Members (see Appendix I): Argentina, Australia, Brazil, Canada, China, France, Germany, India, Indonesia, Italy, Japan, South Korea, Mexico, Russian Federation, Saudi Arabia, South Africa, Turkey, United Kingdom, United States and the European Union**

**European Union (see Appendix II): Austria, Belgium, Bulgaria, Cyprus, Czech Rep., Denmark, Estonia, Finland, France, Germany, Greece, Hungary, Ireland, Italy, Latvia, Lithuania, Luxembourg, Malta, Netherlands, Poland, Portugal, Romania, Slovakia, Slovenia, Spain, Sweden and the United Kingdom

Chapter 8: U.S. Employment in Relation to the World

Overview

In 2002, 21 percent of the U.S. workforce was employed in industry, the same percentage as in China, and by 2009 the U.S. percentage declined to 20 percent; while China's increased to 27 percent.

"Industry" consists of manufacturing, construction, mining, quarrying (including oil production), and public utilities (electricity, gas, and water).

In 2009, 79 percent of all U.S. workers were employed in services, approximately the same percentage as the United Kingdom, the highest among G20* members. "Services" include wholesale and retail trade, hotels, restaurants, transport, government, financial, professional, and personal services such as education, health care, and real estate services.

In 2010, U.S. manufacturing value added was the highest in the world, and approximately the same as China's. Since 1993 U.S. manufacturing value added increased 50 percent while China's increased 1,000 percent.

U.S. productivity tied for second place in the world in 2010, approximately the same as Belgium, Netherlands, Ireland, and France, but behind Norway which was 25 percent higher. During the 1970–2010 period, U.S. productivity increased each year.

~

*G20 Members (see Appendix I): Argentina, Australia, Brazil, Canada, China, France, Germany, India, Indonesia, Italy, Japan, South Korea, Mexico, Russian Federation, Saudi Arabia, South Africa, Turkey, United Kingdom, United States and the European Union**

**European Union (see Appendix II): Austria, Belgium, Bulgaria, Cyprus, Czech Rep., Denmark, Estonia, Finland, France, Germany, Greece, Hungary, Ireland, Italy, Latvia, Lithuania, Luxembourg, Malta, Netherlands, Poland, Portugal, Romania, Slovakia, Slovenia, Spain, Sweden and the United Kingdom

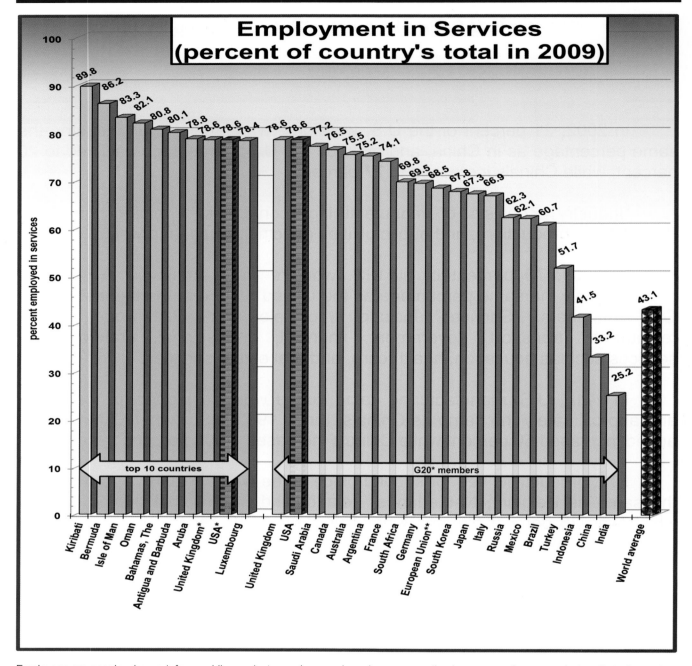

**Employment in Services
(percent of country's total in 2009)**

Employees are people who work for a public or private employer and receive remuneration in wages, salary, commission, tips, piece rates, or pay in kind. Services correspond to divisions 6-9 (ISIC revision 2) or tabulation categories G-P (ISIC revision 3), and include wholesale and retail trade and restaurants and hotels; transport, storage, and communications; financing, insurance, real estate, and business services; and community, social, and personal services.

SOURCE: World Bank. International Labour Organization, Key Indicators of the Labour Market database. Primarily 2008/2009 databases accessed in April 2012

http://data.worldbank.org/data-catalog/world-development-indicators?cid=GPD_WDI

*G20 Members (see Appendix I): Argentina, Australia, Brazil, Canada, China, France, Germany, India, Indonesia, Italy, Japan, South Korea, Mexico, Russian Federation, Saudi Arabia, South Africa, Turkey, United Kingdom, United States and the European Union**

**European Union (see Appendix II): Austria, Belgium, Bulgaria, Cyprus, Czech Rep., Denmark, Estonia, Finland, France, Germany, Greece, Hungary, Ireland, Italy, Latvia, Lithuania, Luxembourg, Malta, Netherlands, Poland, Portugal, Romania, Slovakia, Slovenia, Spain, Sweden and the United Kingdom

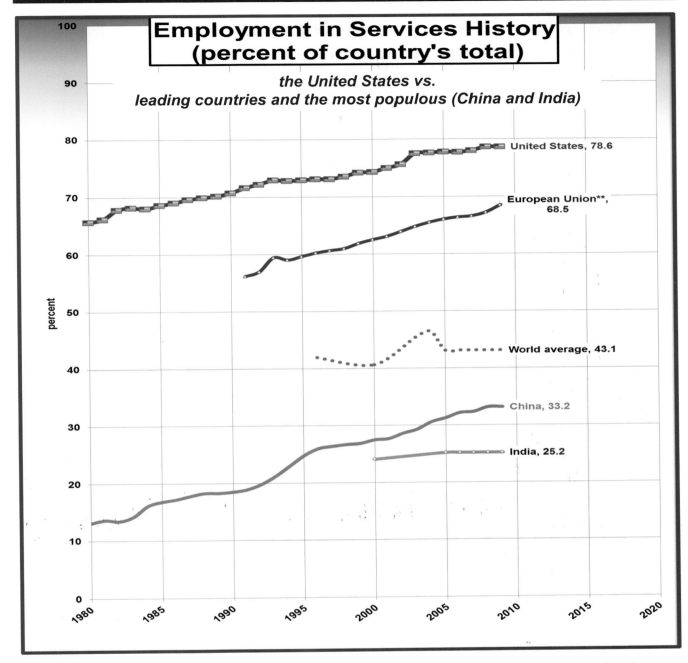

Employment in Services History (percent of country's total)

the United States vs. leading countries and the most populous (China and India)

United States, 78.6

European Union**, 68.5

World average, 43.1

China, 33.2

India, 25.2

Employees are people who work for a public or private employer and receive remuneration in wages, salary, commission, tips, piece rates, or pay in kind. Services correspond to divisions 6-9 (ISIC revision 2) or tabulation categories G-P (ISIC revision 3), and include wholesale and retail trade and restaurants and hotels; transport, storage, and communications; financing, insurance, real estate, and business services; and community, social, and personal services.

SOURCE: World Bank. International Labour Organization, Key Indicators of the Labour Market database. Primarily 2008/2009 databases accessed in April 2012

http://data.worldbank.org/data-catalog/world-development-indicators?cid=GPD_WDI

**European Union (see Appendix II): Austria, Belgium, Bulgaria, Cyprus, Czech Rep., Denmark, Estonia, Finland, France, Germany, Greece, Hungary, Ireland, Italy, Latvia, Lithuania, Luxembourg, Malta, Netherlands, Poland, Portugal, Romania, Slovakia, Slovenia, Spain, Sweden and the United Kingdom

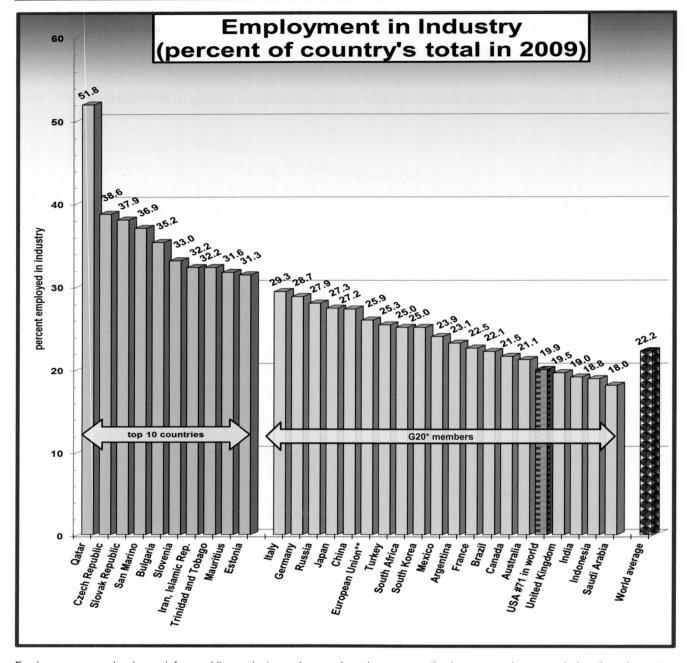

Employment in Industry
(percent of country's total in 2009)

percent employed in industry

top 10 countries

G20* members

Qatar 51.8
Czech Republic 38.6
Slovak Republic 37.9
San Marino 36.9
Bulgaria 35.2
Slovenia 33.0
Iran, Islamic Rep. 32.2
Trinidad and Tobago 32.2
Mauritius 31.6
Estonia 31.3

Italy 29.3
Germany 28.7
Russia 27.9
Japan 27.3
China 27.2
European Union** 25.9
Turkey 25.3
South Africa 25.0
South Korea 25.0
Mexico 23.9
Argentina 23.1
France 22.5
Brazil 22.1
Canada 21.5
Australia 21.1
USA #71 in world 19.9
United Kingdom 19.5
India 19.0
Indonesia 18.8
Saudi Arabia 18.0

World average 22.2

Employees are people who work for a public or private employer and receive remuneration in wages, salary, commission, tips, piece rates, or pay in kind. Industry corresponds to divisions 2-5 (ISIC revision 2) or tabulation categories C-F (ISIC revision 3); and includes mining and quarrying (including oil production), manufacturing, construction, and public utilities (electricity, gas, and water).

SOURCE: World Bank. International Labour Organization, Key Indicators of the Labour Market database. Primarily 2008/2009 databases accessed in April 2012

http://data.worldbank.org/data-catalog/world-development-indicators?cid=GPD_WDI

*G20 Members (see Appendix I): Argentina, Australia, Brazil, Canada, China, France, Germany, India, Indonesia, Italy, Japan, South Korea, Mexico, Russian Federation, Saudi Arabia, South Africa, Turkey, United Kingdom, United States and the European Union**

**European Union (see Appendix II): Austria, Belgium, Bulgaria, Cyprus, Czech Rep., Denmark, Estonia, Finland, France, Germany, Greece, Hungary, Ireland, Italy, Latvia, Lithuania, Luxembourg, Malta, Netherlands, Poland, Portugal, Romania, Slovakia, Slovenia, Spain, Sweden and the United Kingdom

Employment in Industry History (percent of country's total)

the United States vs.
the most populous (China and India)

China, 27.2

United States, 19.9

India, 19.0

percent

Employees are people who work for a public or private employer and receive remuneration in wages, salary, commission, tips, piece rates, or pay in kind. Industry corresponds to divisions 2-5 (ISIC revision 2) or tabulation categories C-F (ISIC revision 3), and includes mining and quarrying (including oil production), manufacturing, construction, and public utilities (electricity, gas, and water).

SOURCE: World Bank. International Labour Organization, Key Indicators of the Labour Market database. Primarily 2008/2009 databases accessed in April 2012

http://data.worldbank.org/data-catalog/world-development-indicators?cid=GPD_WDI

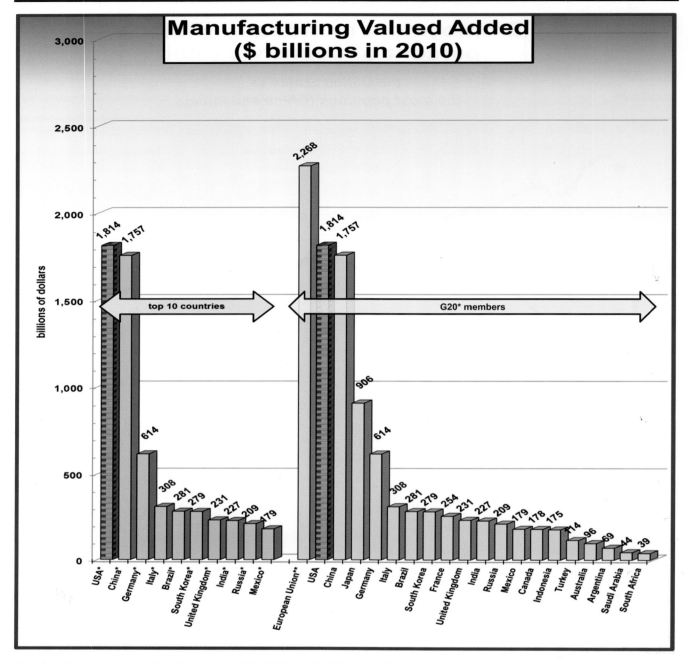

Manufacturing Valued Added
($ billions in 2010)

Manufacturing refers to industries belonging to ISIC divisions 15-37. Value added is the net output of a sector after adding all outputs and subtracting intermediate inputs. It is calculated without making deductions for depreciation of fabricated assets or depletion and degradation of natural resources. The origin of value added is determined by the International Standard Industrial Classification (ISIC), revision 3. Data are in current U.S. dollars.

SOURCE: World Bank national accounts data, and OECD National Accounts data files. Primarily 2010 database accessed in April 2012

http://data.worldbank.org/data-catalog/world-development-indicators?cid=GPD_WDI

*G20 Members (see Appendix I): Argentina, Australia, Brazil, Canada, China, France, Germany, India, Indonesia, Italy, Japan, South Korea, Mexico, Russian Federation, Saudi Arabia, South Africa, Turkey, United Kingdom, United States and the European Union**

**European Union (see Appendix II): Austria, Belgium, Bulgaria, Cyprus, Czech Rep., Denmark, Estonia, Finland, France, Germany, Greece, Hungary, Ireland, Italy, Latvia, Lithuania, Luxembourg, Malta, Netherlands, Poland, Portugal, Romania, Slovakia, Slovenia, Spain, Sweden and the United Kingdom

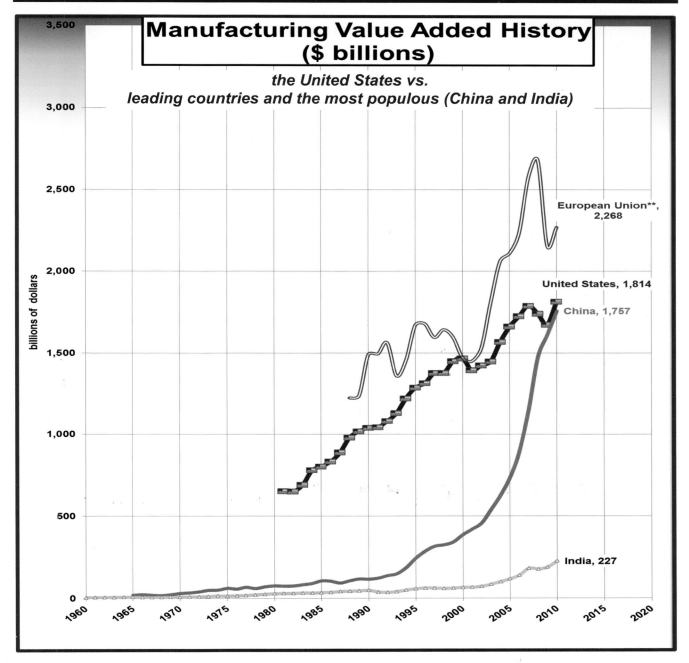

Manufacturing Value Added History ($ billions)

the United States vs.
leading countries and the most populous (China and India)

European Union**, 2,268

United States, 1,814

China, 1,757

India, 227

Manufacturing refers to industries belonging to ISIC divisions 15-37. Value added is the net output of a sector after adding all outputs and subtracting intermediate inputs. It is calculated without making deductions for depreciation of fabricated assets or depletion and degradation of natural resources. The origin of value added is determined by the International Standard Industrial Classification (ISIC), revision 3. Data are in current U.S. dollars.

SOURCE: World Bank national accounts data, and OECD National Accounts data files. Primarily 2010 database accessed in January 2012

http://data.worldbank.org/data-catalog/world-development-indicators?cid=GPD_WDI

**European Union (see Appendix II): Austria, Belgium, Bulgaria, Cyprus, Czech Rep., Denmark, Estonia, Finland, France, Germany, Greece, Hungary, Ireland, Italy, Latvia, Lithuania, Luxembourg, Malta, Netherlands, Poland, Portugal, Romania, Slovakia, Slovenia, Spain, Sweden and the United Kingdom

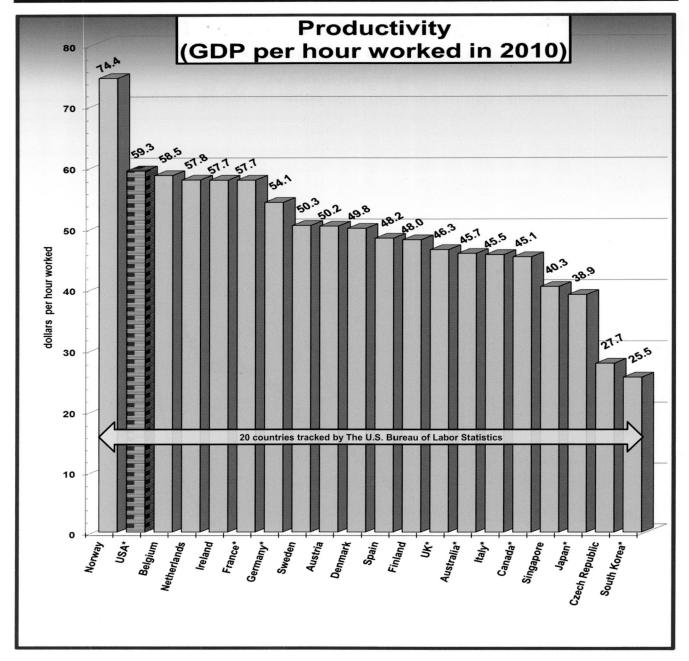

Productivity (GDP per hour worked in 2010)

Norway 74.4, USA* 59.3, Belgium 58.5, Netherlands 57.8, Ireland 57.7, France* 57.7, Germany* 54.1, Sweden 50.3, Austria 50.2, Denmark 49.8, Spain 48.2, Finland 48.0, UK* 46.3, Australia* 45.7, Italy* 45.5, Canada* 45.1, Singapore 40.3, Japan* 38.9, Czech Republic 27.7, South Korea* 25.5

dollars per hour worked

20 countries tracked by The U.S. Bureau of Labor Statistics

GDP (Gross Domestic Product) is the sum of all domestic purchases of final products and services + private domestic investment + government consumption + net trade (exports - imports). Government includes federal + state + local. GDP per hour worked converted to U.S. dollars using 2010 Purchasing Power Parities^^.

SOURCE: U.S. Bureau of Labor Statistics, 2010 database.

http://www.bls.gov/ilc/

*G20 Members (see Appendix I): Argentina, Australia, Brazil, Canada, China, France, Germany, India, Indonesia, Italy, Japan, South Korea, Mexico, Russian Federation, Saudi Arabia, South Africa, Turkey, United Kingdom, United States and the European Union**

**European Union (see Appendix II): Austria, Belgium, Bulgaria, Cyprus, Czech Rep., Denmark, Estonia, Finland, France, Germany, Greece, Hungary, Ireland, Italy, Latvia, Lithuania, Luxembourg, Malta, Netherlands, Poland, Portugal, Romania, Slovakia, Slovenia, Spain, Sweden and the United Kingdom

^^(Purchasing Power Parities are a measure of how expensive goods and services are in a country relative to the United States.)

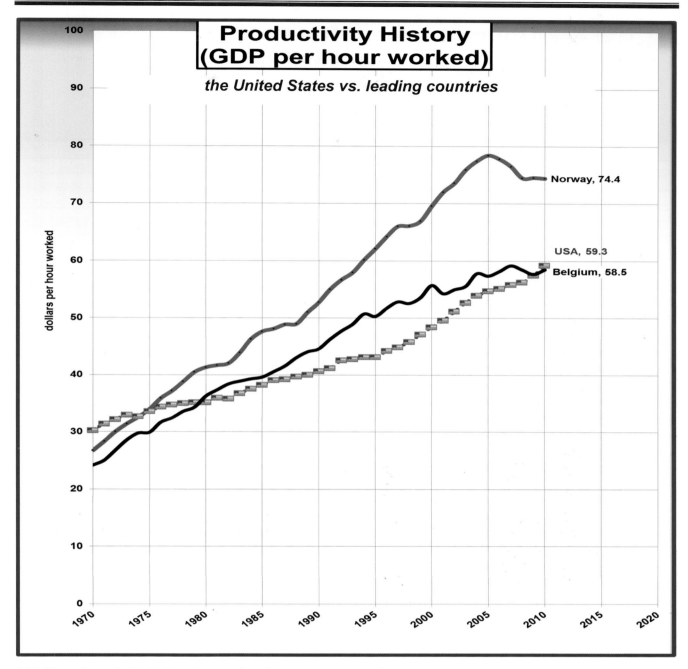

**Productivity History
(GDP per hour worked)**
the United States vs. leading countries

Norway, 74.4

USA, 59.3

Belgium, 58.5

dollars per hour worked

(y-axis: 0, 10, 20, 30, 40, 50, 60, 70, 80, 90, 100)

(x-axis: 1970, 1975, 1980, 1985, 1990, 1995, 2000, 2005, 2010, 2015, 2020)

GDP (Gross Domestic Product) is the sum of all domestic purchases of final products and services + private domestic investment + government consumption + net trade (exports - imports). Government includes federal + state + local. GDP per hour worked converted to U.S. dollars using 2010 Purchasing Power Parities^^.

SOURCE: U.S. Bureau of Labor Statistics, 2010 database.

http://www.bls.gov/ilc/

^^(Purchasing Power Parities are a measure of how expensive goods and services are in a country relative to the United States.)

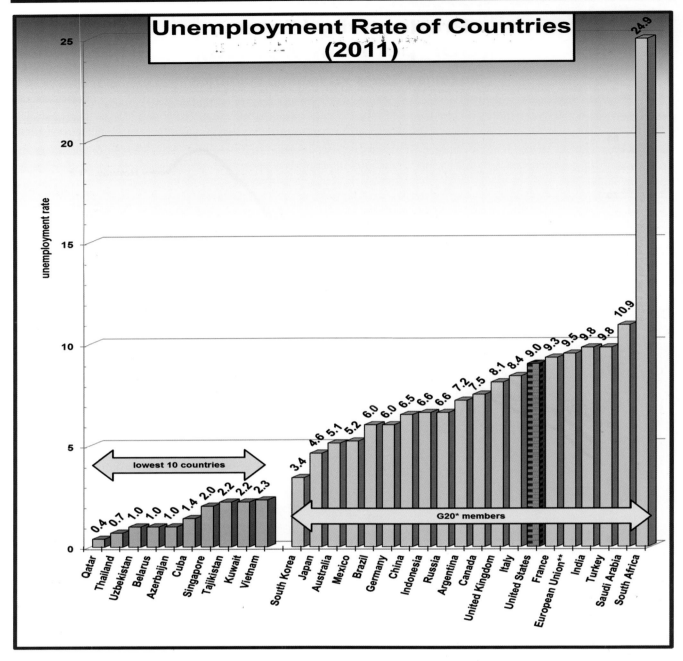

Unemployment Rate of Countries (2011)

unemployment rate

lowest 10 countries

G20* members

Qatar 0.4, Thailand 0.7, Uzbekistan 1.0, Belarus 1.0, Azerbaijan 1.0, Cuba 1.4, Singapore 2.0, Tajikistan 2.2, Kuwait 2.2, Vietnam 2.3

South Korea 3.4, Japan 4.6, Australia 5.1, Mexico 5.2, Brazil 6.0, Germany 6.0, China 6.5, Indonesia 6.6, Russia 6.6, Argentina 7.2, Canada 7.5, United Kingdom 8.1, Italy 8.4, United States 9.0, France 9.3, European Union** 9.5, India 9.8, Turkey 9.8, Saudi Arabia 10.9, South Africa 24.9

Percent of the labor force without jobs.

SOURCE: CIA, 2011 database accessed in September 2012.

https://www.cia.gov/library/publications/the-world-factbook/rankorder/2129rank.html

*G20 Members (see Appendix I): Argentina, Australia, Brazil, Canada, China, France, Germany, India, Indonesia, Italy, Japan, South Korea, Mexico, Russian Federation, Saudi Arabia, South Africa, Turkey, United Kingdom, United States and the European Union**

**European Union (see Appendix II): Austria, Belgium, Bulgaria, Cyprus, Czech Rep., Denmark, Estonia, Finland, France, Germany, Greece, Hungary, Ireland, Italy, Latvia, Lithuania, Luxembourg, Malta, Netherlands, Poland, Portugal, Romania, Slovakia, Slovenia, Spain, Sweden and the United Kingdom

Chapter 9: U.S. Employment

Overview

In 2009, 24 percent of U.S. workers were employed in education/health services versus 10 percent in manufacturing. Fifty-one percent of all U.S. private industry workers were employed by companies with more than 500 employees, while 11 percent were employed by companies with less than 10. However, 78.3 percent of all businesses have no employees. In 2012, there were twice as many civilian government employees as workers in the manufacturing sector.

In 2011, there were 132 million U.S. workers, 16.7 percent of which were public employees and two-thirds of those were local, i.e., non-federal and non-state, government employees. Of all federal employees, 98 percent or 2.84 million, were civilian personal employed by the executive branch. Between 2000–2010; the average annual compensation for federal employees, including salary and benefits, increased 60 percent to $123,000—double the average private compensation.

~

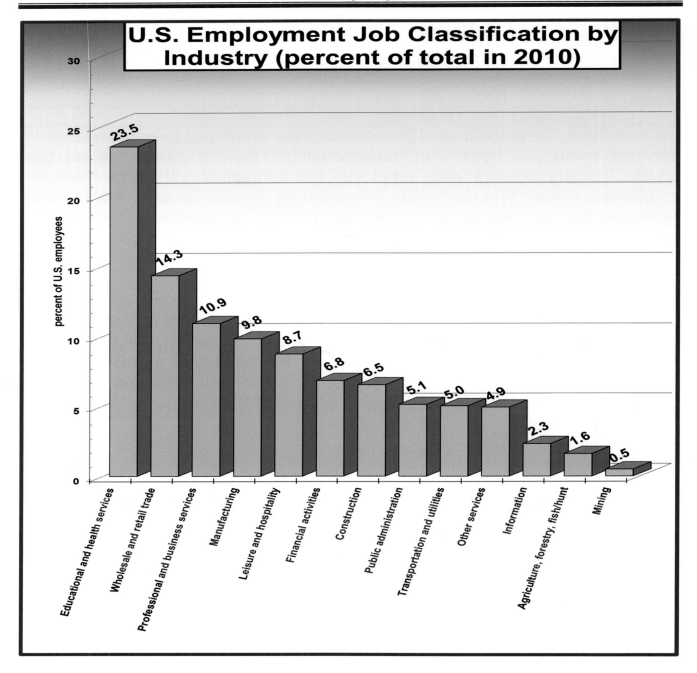

U.S. Employment Job Classification by Industry (percent of total in 2010)

Industry sector of employed civilian workers 16 years old and over in 2010; total number = 137 million.

SOURCE: U.S. Census Bureau Current Population Survey, annual social and economic supplement, 2010

http://quickfacts.census.gov/qfd/states/00000.html

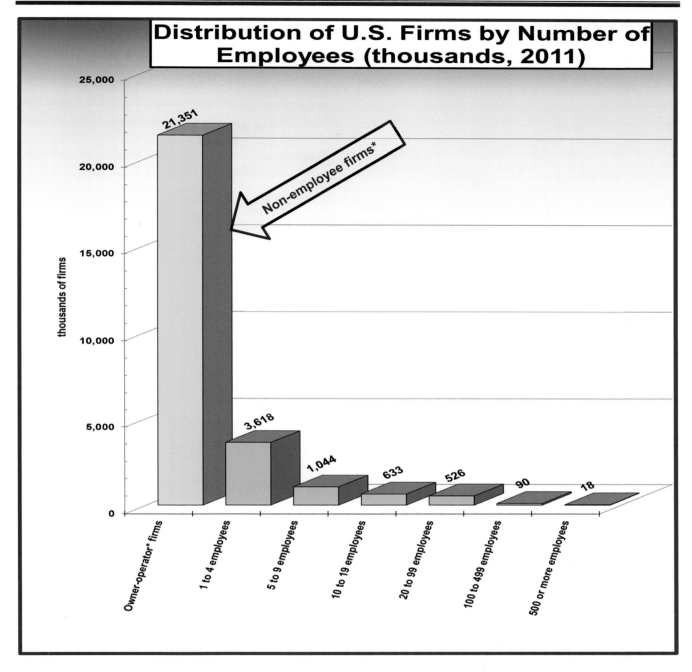

Distribution of U.S. Firms by Number of Employees (thousands, 2011)

In 2007, there were 27.3 million firms in the U.S. including 21.4 million owner operated businesses without employees.

*78.3 percent of all U.S. business firms are non-employee firms and are owner operated. Most are self-employed persons operating unincorporated businesses, and may or may not be the owner's principal source of income. Because non-employers account for only about 3.4 percent of business receipts, they are not included in most business statistics, for example, most reports from the Economic Census.

SOURCE: U.S. Census Bureau.

http://www.census.gov/econ/smallbus.html

U.S. Employment Distribution by Firm Size (thousands of employees in 2011)

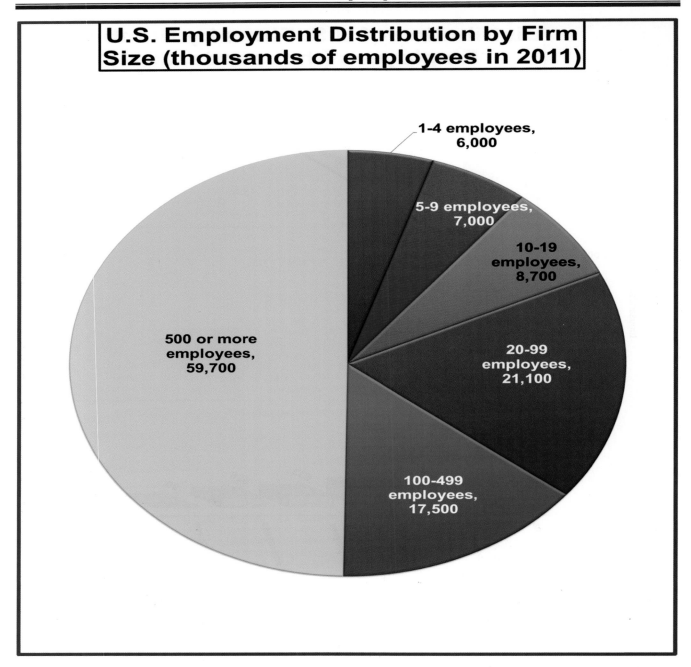

1-4 employees, 6,000

5-9 employees, 7,000

10-19 employees, 8,700

20-99 employees, 21,100

100-499 employees, 17,500

500 or more employees, 59,700

Millions of workers employed based on the total employment size of the firm in 2011; total number of employees are 119,894,009 and excludes firms that are owner operated with no emplyees. An establishment is a single physical location at which business is conducted or where services or industrial operations are performed. An enterprise is a business organization consisting of one or more domestic establishments under common ownership or control. [Total employed = 119.9 million workers in firms with 1 or more employees]

SOURCE: Source: U.S. Census Bureau, Statistics of U.S. Businesses, accessed March 2011.

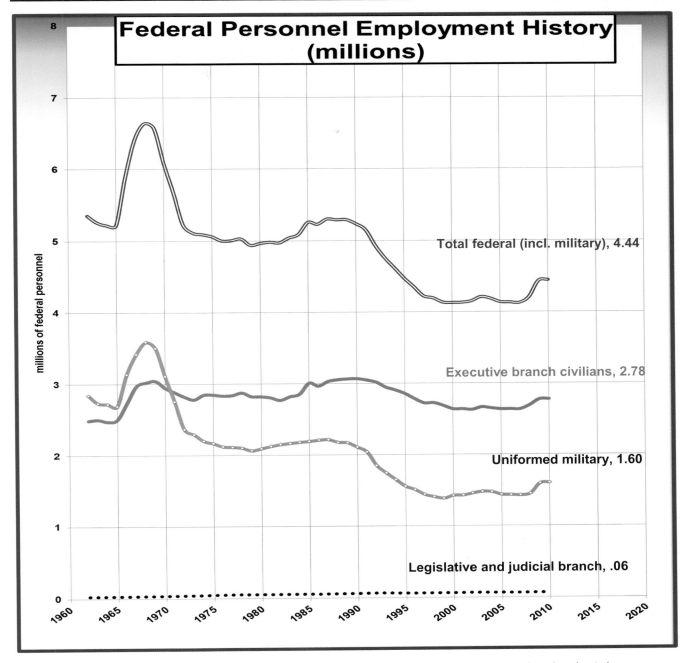

Federal Personnel Employment History (millions)

Total federal (incl. military), 4.44

Executive branch civilians, 2.78

Uniformed military, 1.60

Legislative and judicial branch, .06

millions of federal personnel

Executive branch includes the Postal Service, and, beginning in 1970, includes various disadvantaged youth and worker-trainee programs. Uniformed Military Personnel data comes from the Department of Defense.

SOURCE: Office of Policy Management

http://www.opm.gov/feddata/HistoricalTables/TotalGovernmentSince1962.asp

Data comes from 113 monthly submissions and covers total end-of-year civilian employment of full-time permanent, temporary, part-time, and intermittent employees.

http://www.opm.gov/feddata/HistoricalTables/TotalGovernmentSince1962.asp

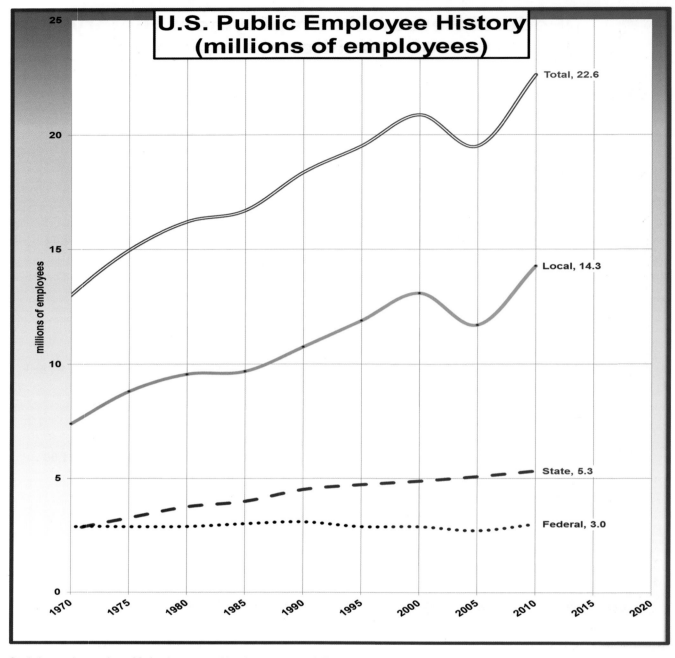

U.S. Public Employee History (millions of employees)

millions of employees

Total, 22.6

Local, 14.3

State, 5.3

Federal, 3.0

25
20
15
10
5
0

1970 1975 1980 1985 1990 1995 2000 2005 2010 2015 2020

Statistics on the number of federal, state, and local government civilian employees include full-time and part-time.

SOURCE: U.S. Census Bureau, accessed in February 2012, and U.S. Bureau of Economic Analysis, Survey of Current Business, April 2011, see also http://www.bea.gov/scb/index.htm

http://www.census.gov//govs/apes/index.html

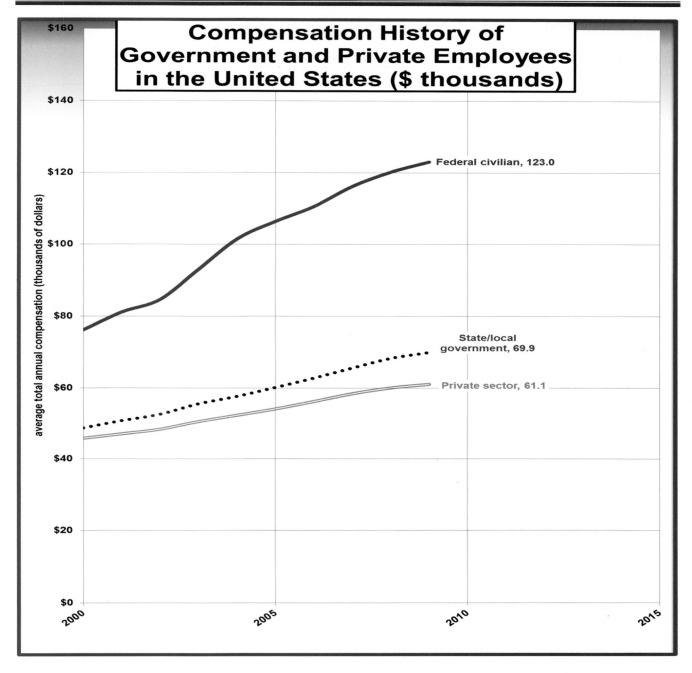

Compensation History of Government and Private Employees in the United States ($ thousands)

Federal civilian, 123.0

State/local government, 69.9

Private sector, 61.1

average total annual compensation (thousands of dollars)

Statistics on the number of federal, state, and local government civilian employees and includes full-time and part-time. Annual total compensation and wages and salary accruals per full-time equivalent employee. Wage and salary accruals include executives' compensation, bonuses, tips, and payments-in-kind; total compensation includes in addition to wages and salaries, employer contributions for social insurance, employer contributions to private and welfare funds, director's fees, jury and witness fees, etc.

SOURCE: U.S. Census Bureau, accessed in February 2012, and U.S. Bureau of Economic Analysis, Survey of Current Business, April 2011, see also <http://www.bea.gov/scb/index.htm>.

http://www.census.gov//govs/apes/index.html

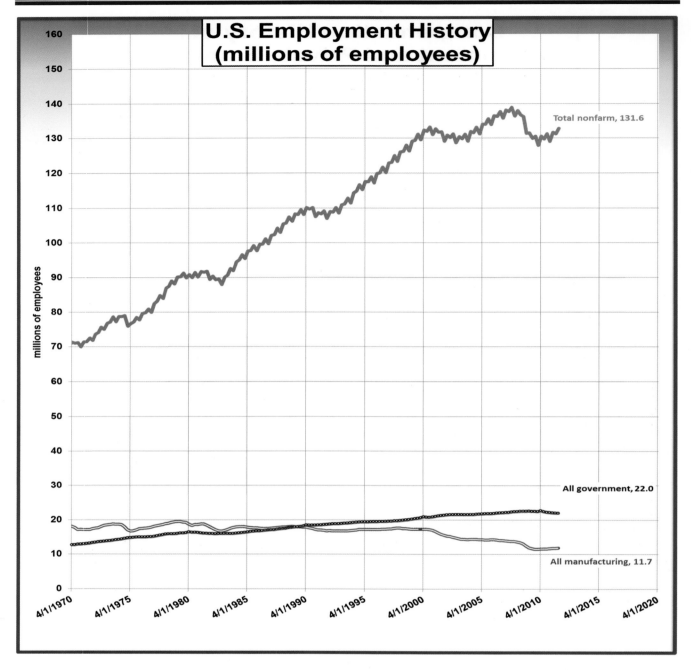

U.S. employment in government jobs includes federal (civilian), state and local government.

SOURCE: Federal Reserve Bank of St. Louis; U.S. Department of Labor: Bureau of Labor Statistics

http://research.stlouisfed.org/

Chapter 10: U.S. Energy in Relation to the World

Overview

In 2010, the U.S. and China were tied in first place for total energy consumption. Russia and India each consumed about one-fourth the U.S. level. Between 1972–2010, U.S. consumption declined by one-third, while China's increased by 270 percent. Based on per capita consumption the U.S. was tenth in the world, about the same as Canada's level.

The United States was the number one importer of oil in the world at 10.3 million barrels per day in 2011, approximately equal to the 9.7 million barrels per day produced in the U.S. One-fourth of U.S. oil imports originated from Canada and 55 percent from OPEC* nations and the Persian Gulf region.

U.S. proved oil reserves ranked thirteenth in the world, about the same as China's, and are equal to only 7 percent of Saudi Arabia's.

U.S. natural gas proved reserves ranked fifth in the world, only 16 percent of Russia's. The United States had the second largest amount of "technically recoverable" shale gas in the world, equivalent to two-thirds of China's. In 2010, U.S. "proved" reserves of coal were the largest in the world.

The U.S. emitted 17 percent of the world's CO_2 in 2008, down from 31 percent in 1960, while China emitted 22 percent of the world's 2008 total. The U.S. ranked tenth in the world for CO_2 per capita, about the same level as Australia or Saudi Arabia, and 3.7 times China's per capita level.

~

*Organization of Petroleum Exporting Countries (see Appendix IV)
United Kingdom

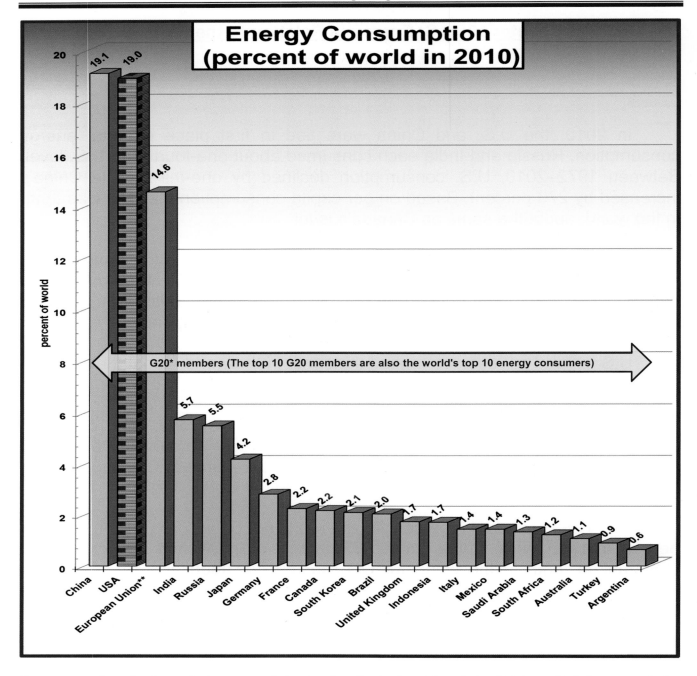

Energy consumption refers to use of primary energy before transformation to other end-use fuels, which is equal to indigenous production plus imports and stock changes, minus exports and fuels supplied to ships and aircraft engaged in international transport.

SOURCE: World Bank. International Energy Agency (IEA Statistics © OECD/IEA, http://www.iea.org/stats/index.asp). 2009/2010 databases.

http://data.worldbank.org/data-catalog/world-development-indicators?cid=GPD_WDI

*G20 Members (see Appendix I): Argentina, Australia, Brazil, Canada, China, France, Germany, India, Indonesia, Italy, Japan, South Korea, Mexico, Russian Federation, Saudi Arabia, South Africa, Turkey, United Kingdom, United States and the European Union**

**European Union (see Appendix II): Austria, Belgium, Bulgaria, Cyprus, Czech Rep., Denmark, Estonia, Finland, France, Germany, Greece, Hungary, Ireland, Italy, Latvia, Lithuania, Luxembourg, Malta, Netherlands, Poland, Portugal, Romania, Slovakia, Slovenia, Spain, Sweden and the United Kingdom

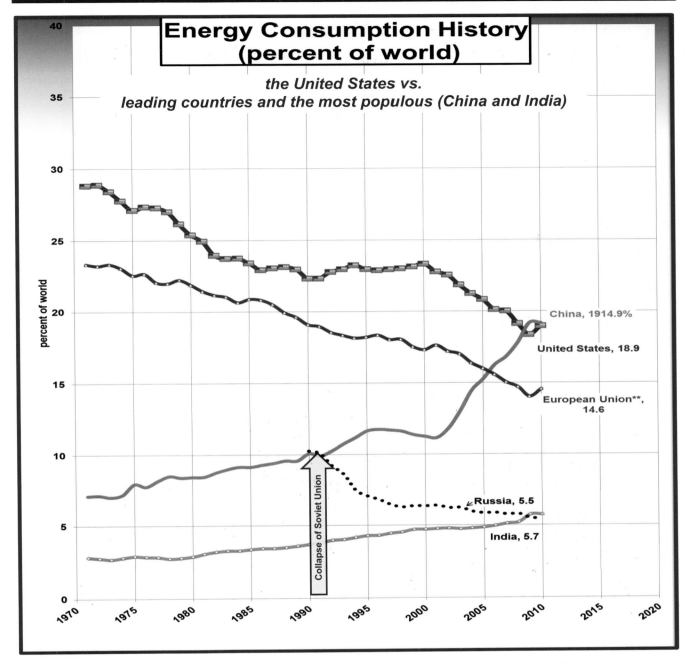

Energy Consumption History (percent of world)

the United States vs.
leading countries and the most populous (China and India)

China, 1914.9%

United States, 18.9

European Union**, 14.6

Collapse of Soviet Union

Russia, 5.5

India, 5.7

Energy use refers to use of primary energy before transformation to other end-use fuels, which is equal to indigenous production plus imports and stock changes, minus exports and fuels supplied to ships and aircraft engaged in international transport.

SOURCE: World Bank. International Energy Agency (IEA Statistics © OECD/IEA, http://www.iea.org/stats/index.asp); 2009/2010 databases

http://data.worldbank.org/data-catalog/world-development-indicators?cid=GPD_WDI

**European Union (see Appendix II): Austria, Belgium, Bulgaria, Cyprus, Czech Rep., Denmark, Estonia, Finland, France, Germany, Greece, Hungary, Ireland, Italy, Latvia, Lithuania, Luxembourg, Malta, Netherlands, Poland, Portugal, Romania, Slovakia, Slovenia, Spain, Sweden and the United Kingdom

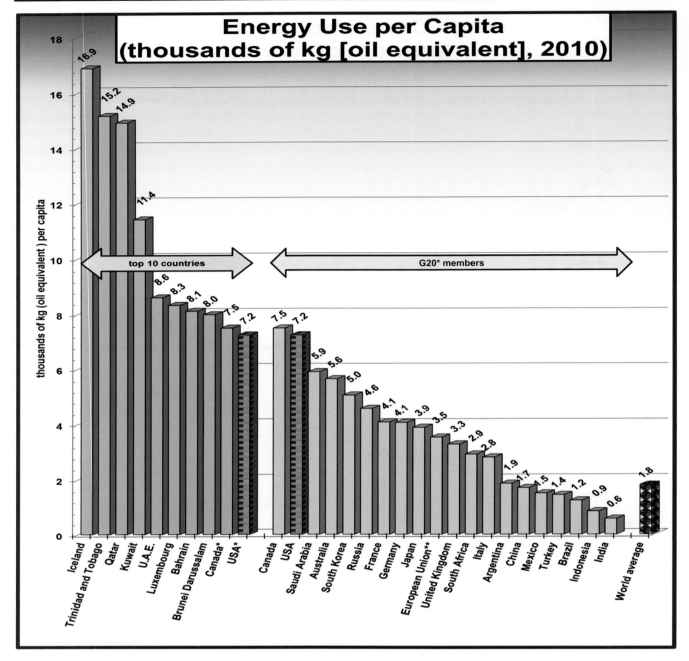

Energy use refers to use of primary energy before transformation to other end-use fuels, which is equal to indigenous production plus imports and stock changes, minus exports and fuels supplied to ships and aircraft engaged in international transport.

SOURCE: World Bank. International Energy Agency (IEA Statistics © OECD/IEA, http://www.iea.org/stats/index.asp); 2009/2010 databases accessed in April 2012

http://data.worldbank.org/data-catalog/world-development-indicators?cid=GPD_WDI

*G20 Members (see Appendix I): Argentina, Australia, Brazil, Canada, China, France, Germany, India, Indonesia, Italy, Japan, South Korea, Mexico, Russian Federation, Saudi Arabia, South Africa, Turkey, United Kingdom, United States and the European Union**

**European Union (see Appendix II): Austria, Belgium, Bulgaria, Cyprus, Czech Rep., Denmark, Estonia, Finland, France, Germany, Greece, Hungary, Ireland, Italy, Latvia, Lithuania, Luxembourg, Malta, Netherlands, Poland, Portugal, Romania, Slovakia, Slovenia, Spain, Sweden and the United Kingdom

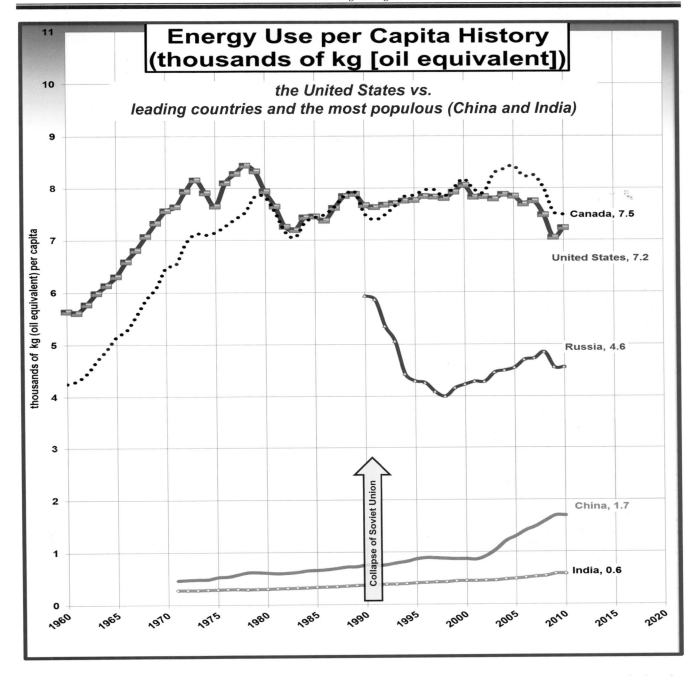

Energy Use per Capita History (thousands of kg [oil equivalent])

the United States vs.
leading countries and the most populous (China and India)

Canada, 7.5

United States, 7.2

Russia, 4.6

China, 1.7

India, 0.6

Collapse of Soviet Union

Energy use refers to use of primary energy before transformation to other end-use fuels, which is equal to indigenous production plus imports and stock changes, minus exports and fuels supplied to ships and aircraft engaged in international transport.

SOURCE: World Bank. International Energy Agency (IEA Statistics © OECD/IEA, http://www.iea.org/stats/index.asp); 2009/2010 databases accessed in January 2012

http://data.worldbank.org/data-catalog/world-development-indicators?cid=GPD_WDI

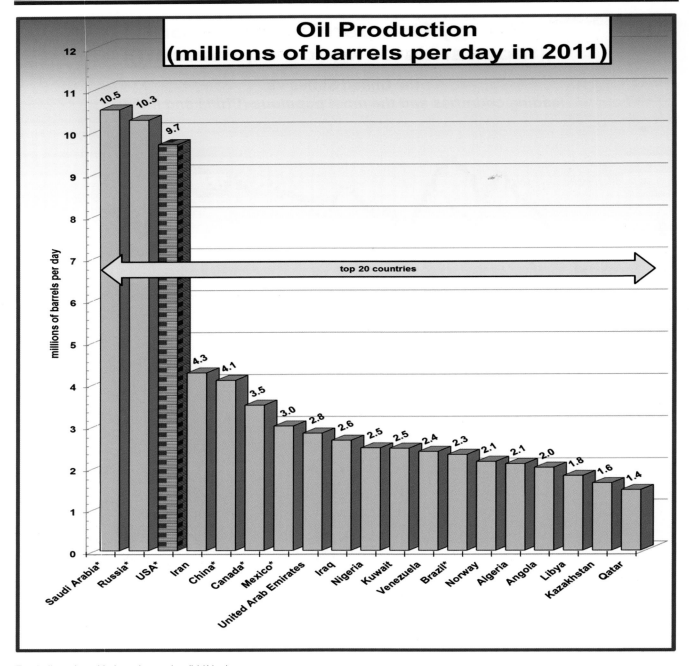

Oil Production
(millions of barrels per day in 2011)

millions of barrels per day

top 20 countries

10.5 10.3 9.7 4.3 4.1 3.5 3.0 2.8 2.6 2.5 2.5 2.4 2.3 2.1 2.1 2.0 1.8 1.6 1.4

Saudi Arabia* Russia* USA* Iran China* Canada* Mexico* United Arab Emirates Iraq Nigeria Kuwait Venezuela Brazil* Norway Algeria Angola Libya Kazakhstan Qatar

Total oil produced in barrels per day (bbl/day).

SOURCE: CIA, 2011 database accessed in September 2012

https://www.cia.gov/library/publications/the-world-factbook/rankorder/rankorderguide.html

*G20 Members (see Appendix I): Argentina, Australia, Brazil, Canada, China, France, Germany, India, Indonesia, Italy, Japan, South Korea, Mexico, Russian Federation, Saudi Arabia, South Africa, Turkey, United Kingdom, United States and the European Union**

**European Union (see Appendix II): Austria, Belgium, Bulgaria, Cyprus, Czech Rep., Denmark, Estonia, Finland, France, Germany, Greece, Hungary, Ireland, Italy, Latvia, Lithuania, Luxembourg, Malta, Netherlands, Poland, Portugal, Romania, Slovakia, Slovenia, Spain, Sweden and the United Kingdom

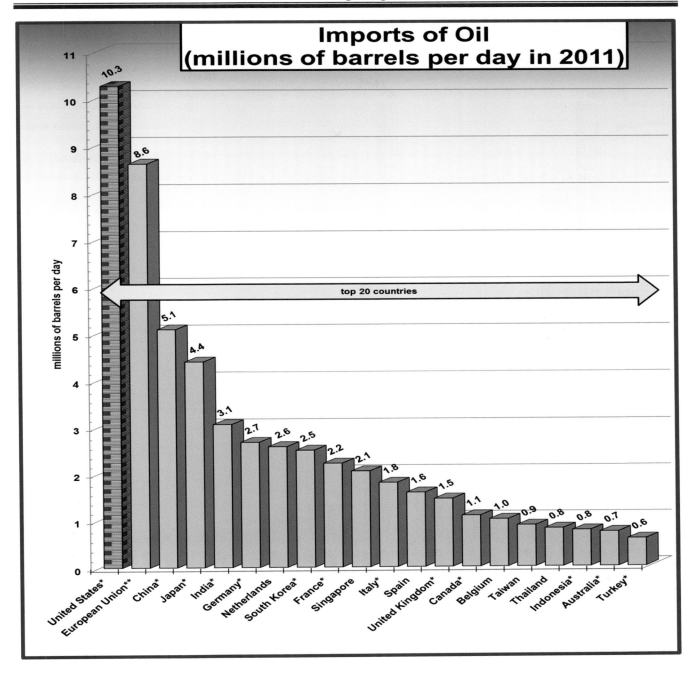

**Imports of Oil
(millions of barrels per day in 2011)**

millions of barrels per day

top 20 countries

United States* 10.3
European Union** 8.6
China* 5.1
Japan* 4.4
India* 3.1
Germany* 2.7
Netherlands 2.6
South Korea* 2.5
France* 2.2
Singapore 2.1
Italy* 1.8
Spain 1.6
United Kingdom* 1.5
Canada* 1.1
Belgium 1.0
Taiwan 0.9
Thailand 0.8
Indonesia* 0.8
Australia* 0.7
Turkey* 0.6

Total oil imported in barrels per day (bbl/day), including both crude oil and oil products.

SOURCE: CIA, 2011 database accessed in September 2012

https://www.cia.gov/library/publications/the-world-factbook/rankorder/rankorderguide.html

*G20 Members (see Appendix I): Argentina, Australia, Brazil, Canada, China, France, Germany, India, Indonesia, Italy, Japan, South Korea, Mexico, Russian Federation, Saudi Arabia, South Africa, Turkey, United Kingdom, United States and the European Union**

**European Union (see Appendix II): Austria, Belgium, Bulgaria, Cyprus, Czech Rep., Denmark, Estonia, Finland, France, Germany, Greece, Hungary, Ireland, Italy, Latvia, Lithuania, Luxembourg, Malta, Netherlands, Poland, Portugal, Romania, Slovakia, Slovenia, Spain, Sweden and the United Kingdom

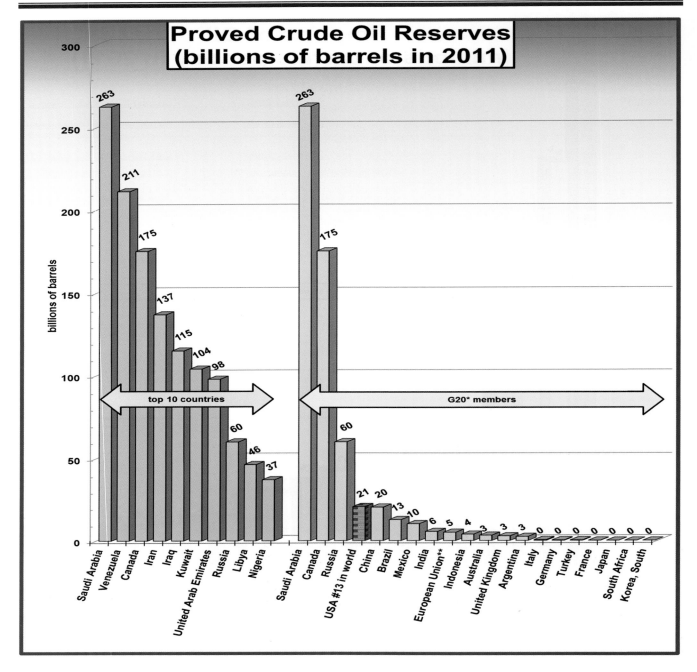

Proved Crude Oil Reserves (billions of barrels in 2011)

Stock of proved reserves of crude oil in barrels (bbl) where proved reserves are those quantities of petroleum that, by analysis of geological and engineering data, can be estimated with a high degree of confidence to be commercially recoverable from a given date forward, from known reservoirs and under current economic conditions.

SOURCE: CIA, 2011 database accessed in October 2011.

https://www.cia.gov/library/publications/the-world-factbook/rankorder/rankorderguide.html

*G20 Members (see Appendix I): Argentina, Australia, Brazil, Canada, China, France, Germany, India, Indonesia, Italy, Japan, South Korea, Mexico, Russian Federation, Saudi Arabia, South Africa, Turkey, United Kingdom, United States and the European Union**

**European Union (see Appendix II): Austria, Belgium, Bulgaria, Cyprus, Czech Rep., Denmark, Estonia, Finland, France, Germany, Greece, Hungary, Ireland, Italy, Latvia, Lithuania, Luxembourg, Malta, Netherlands, Poland, Portugal, Romania, Slovakia, Slovenia, Spain, Sweden and the United Kingdom

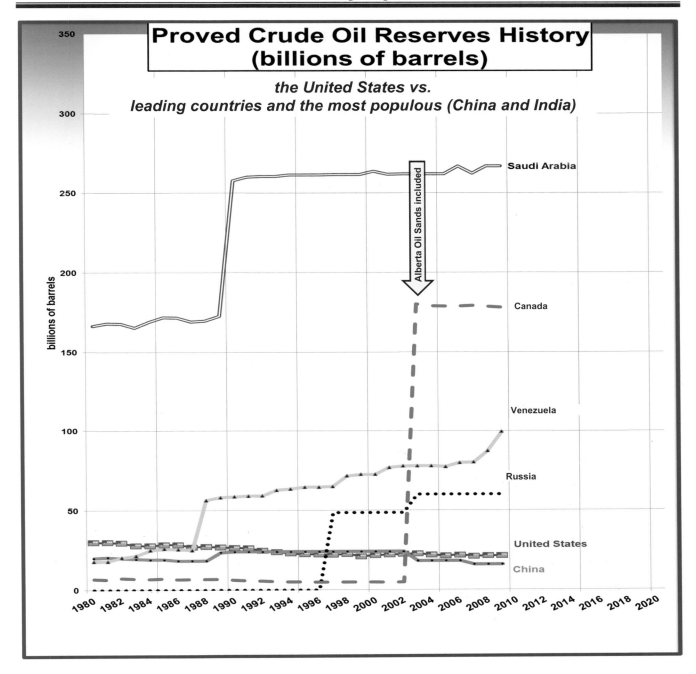

Proved Crude Oil Reserves History (billions of barrels)

the United States vs.
leading countries and the most populous (China and India)

Proved crude oil reserves, including Canda's Alberta oil sands; stock of proved reserves of crude oil where proved reserves are those quantities of petroleum that, by analysis of geological and engineering data, can be estimated with a high degree of confidence to be commercially recoverable from a given date forward, from known reservoirs and under current economic conditions.

SOURCE: U.S. Energy Information Administration

http://www.eia.doe.gov/pub/international/iealf/crudeoilreserves.xls

http://www.eia.gov/dnav/pet/hist/leafhandler.ashx?n=PET&s=RCRR01NUS_1&f=A

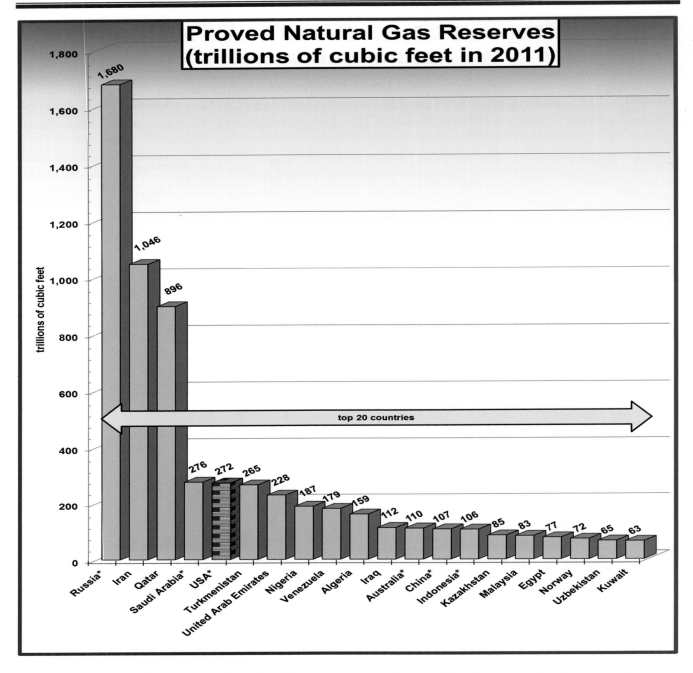

Proved Natural Gas Reserves (trillions of cubic feet in 2011)

trillions of cubic feet

top 20 countries

- Russia*: 1,680
- Iran: 1,046
- Qatar: 896
- Saudi Arabia*: 276
- USA*: 272
- Turkmenistan: 265
- United Arab Emirates: 228
- Nigeria: 187
- Venezuela: 179
- Algeria: 159
- Iraq: 112
- Australia*: 110
- China*: 107
- Indonesia*: 106
- Kazakhstan: 85
- Malaysia: 83
- Egypt: 77
- Norway: 72
- Uzbekistan: 65
- Kuwait: 63

Stock of proved reserves of natural gas in trillions of cu ft. Proved reserves are those quantities of natural gas, that, by analysis of geological and engineering data, can be estimated with a high degree of confidence to be commercially recoverable from a given date forward, from known reservoirs and under current economic conditions. Note: data converted: (1 cubic meter = 35.31 cubic feet).

SOURCE: CIA, 2011 database accessed in October 2011

https://www.cia.gov/library/publications/the-world-factbook/rankorder/rankorderguide.html

*G20 Members (see Appendix I): Argentina, Australia, Brazil, Canada, China, France, Germany, India, Indonesia, Italy, Japan, South Korea, Mexico, Russian Federation, Saudi Arabia, South Africa, Turkey, United Kingdom, United States and the European Union**

**European Union (see Appendix II): Austria, Belgium, Bulgaria, Cyprus, Czech Rep., Denmark, Estonia, Finland, France, Germany, Greece, Hungary, Ireland, Italy, Latvia, Lithuania, Luxembourg, Malta, Netherlands, Poland, Portugal, Romania, Slovakia, Slovenia, Spain, Sweden and the United Kingdom

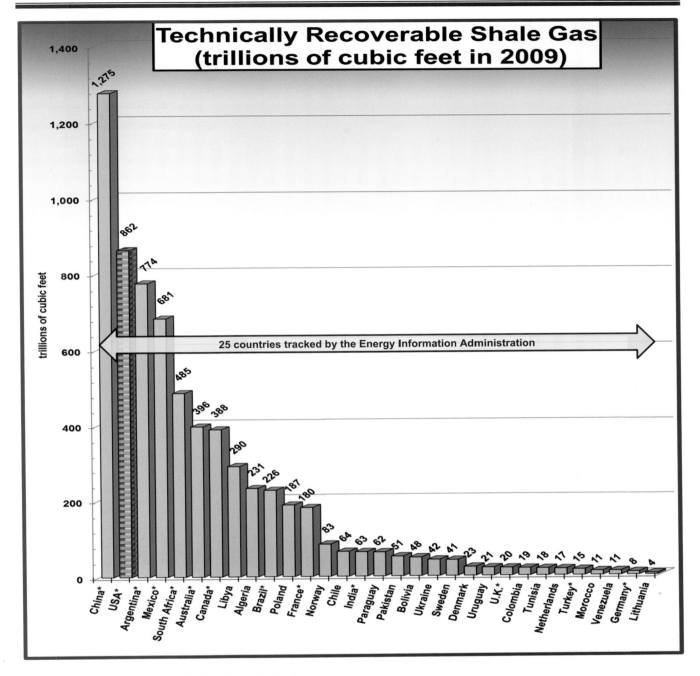

Technically Recoverable Shale Gas (trillions of cubic feet in 2009)

trillions of cubic feet

25 countries tracked by the Energy Information Administration

China* 1,275
USA* 862
Argentina* 774
Mexico* 681
South Africa* 485
Australia* 396
Canada* 388
Libya 290
Algeria 231
Brazil* 226
Poland 187
France* 180
Norway 83
Chile 64
India* 63
Paraguay 62
Pakistan 51
Bolivia 48
Ukraine 42
Sweden 41
Denmark 23
Uruguay 21
U.K.* 20
Colombia 19
Tunisia 18
Netherlands 17
Turkey* 15
Morocco 11
Venezuela 11
Germany* 8
Lithuania 4

Technically recoverable shale gas 2009, trillions of cubic feet.

SOURCE: U.S. Energy Information Administration

http://www.eia.gov/analysis/studies/worldshalegas/

*G20 Members (see Appendix I): Argentina, Australia, Brazil, Canada, China, France, Germany, India, Indonesia, Italy, Japan, South Korea, Mexico, Russian Federation, Saudi Arabia, South Africa, Turkey, United Kingdom, United States and the European Union**

**European Union (see Appendix II): Austria, Belgium, Bulgaria, Cyprus, Czech Rep., Denmark, Estonia, Finland, France, Germany, Greece, Hungary, Ireland, Italy, Latvia, Lithuania, Luxembourg, Malta, Netherlands, Poland, Portugal, Romania, Slovakia, Slovenia, Spain, Sweden and the United Kingdom

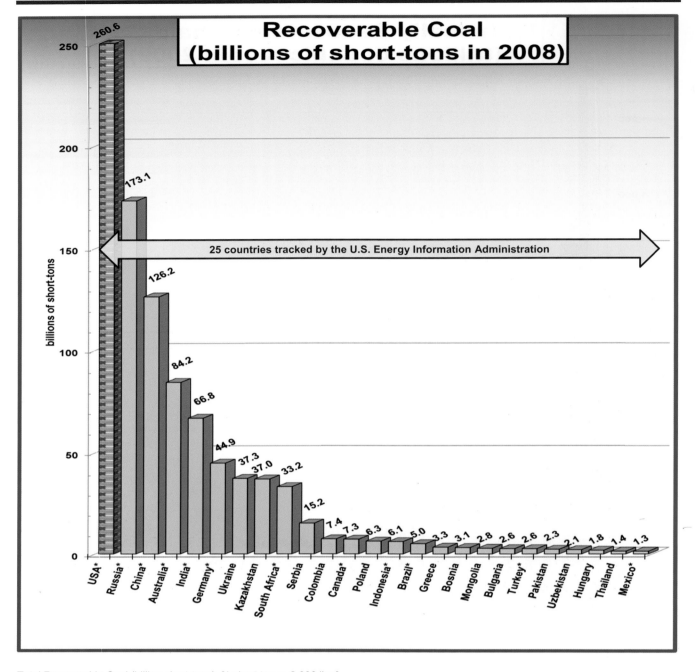

Recoverable Coal
(billions of short-tons in 2008)

25 countries tracked by the U.S. Energy Information Administration

billions of short-tons

- USA* — 260.6
- Russia* — 173.1
- China* — 126.2
- Australia* — 84.2
- India* — 66.8
- Germany* — 44.9
- Ukraine — 37.3
- Kazakhstan — 37.0
- South Africa* — 33.2
- Serbia — 15.2
- Colombia — 7.4
- Canada* — 7.3
- Poland — 6.3
- Indonesia* — 6.1
- Brazil* — 5.0
- Greece — 3.3
- Bosnia — 3.1
- Mongolia — 2.8
- Bulgaria — 2.6
- Turkey* — 2.6
- Pakistan — 2.3
- Uzbekistan — 2.1
- Hungary — 1.8
- Thailand — 1.4
- Mexico* — 1.3

Total Recoverable Coal (billion short-tons) [1 short-ton = 2,000 lbs.]

SOURCE: U.S. Energy Information Administration

http://www.eia.gov/cfapps/ipdbproject/IEDIndex3.cfm?tid=1&pid=7&aid=6

*G20 Members (see Appendix I): Argentina, Australia, Brazil, Canada, China, France, Germany, India, Indonesia, Italy, Japan, South Korea, Mexico, Russian Federation, Saudi Arabia, South Africa, Turkey, United Kingdom, United States and the European Union**

**European Union (see Appendix II): Austria, Belgium, Bulgaria, Cyprus, Czech Rep., Denmark, Estonia, Finland, France, Germany, Greece, Hungary, Ireland, Italy, Latvia, Lithuania, Luxembourg, Malta, Netherlands, Poland, Portugal, Romania, Slovakia, Slovenia, Spain, Sweden and the United Kingdom

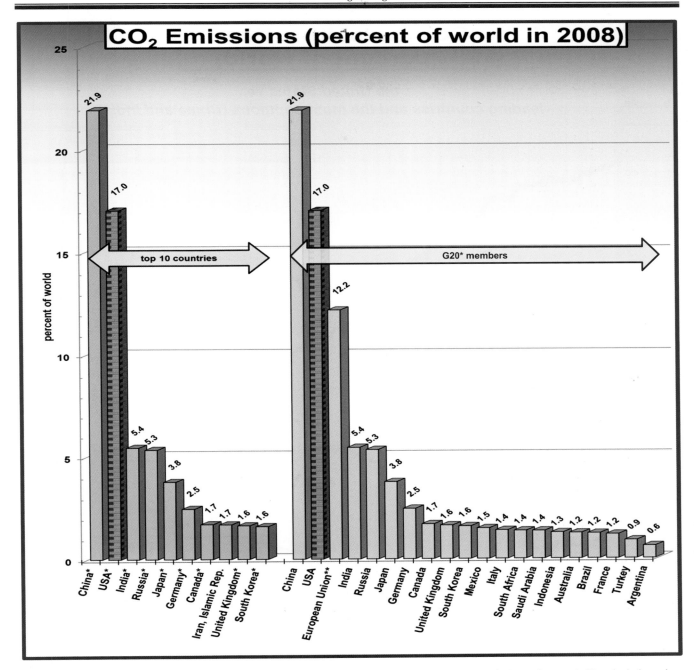

CO₂ Emissions (percent of world in 2008)

CO₂ (Carbon dioxide) emissions are those stemming from the burning of fossil fuels and the manufacture of cement. They include carbon dioxide produced during consumption of solid, liquid, and gas fuels and gas flaring.

SOURCE: World Bank. Carbon Dioxide Information Analysis Center, Environmental Sciences Division, Oak Ridge National Laboratory, Tennessee, United States; 2008 database accessed in January 2012

http://data.worldbank.org/data-catalog/world-development-indicators?cid=GPD_WDI

*G20 Members (see Appendix I): Argentina, Australia, Brazil, Canada, China, France, Germany, India, Indonesia, Italy, Japan, South Korea, Mexico, Russian Federation, Saudi Arabia, South Africa, Turkey, United Kingdom, United States and the European Union**

**European Union (see Appendix II): Austria, Belgium, Bulgaria, Cyprus, Czech Rep., Denmark, Estonia, Finland, France, Germany, Greece, Hungary, Ireland, Italy, Latvia, Lithuania, Luxembourg, Malta, Netherlands, Poland, Portugal, Romania, Slovakia, Slovenia, Spain, Sweden and the United Kingdom

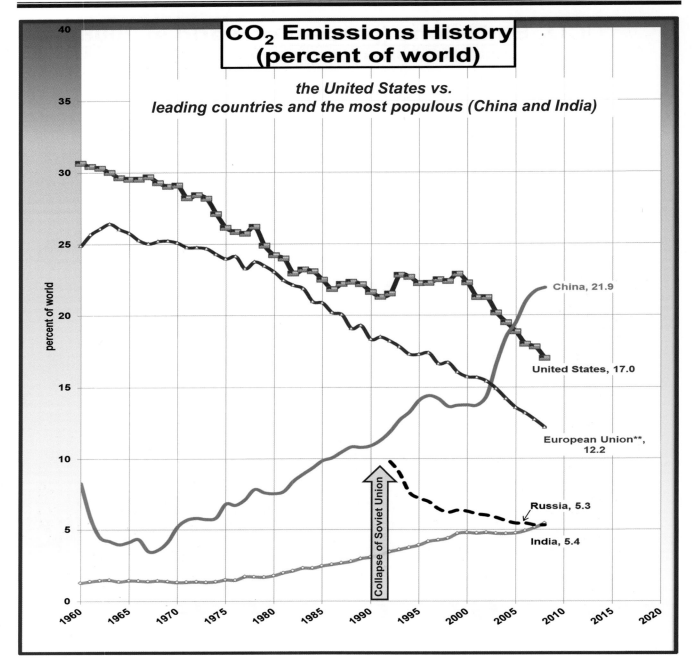

CO₂ Emissions History (percent of world)

the United States vs. leading countries and the most populous (China and India)

China, 21.9

United States, 17.0

European Union**, 12.2

Russia, 5.3

India, 5.4

Collapse of Soviet Union

percent of world

Carbon dioxide emissions are those stemming from the burning of fossil fuels and the manufacture of cement. They include carbon dioxide produced during consumption of solid, liquid, and gas fuels and gas flaring.

SOURCE: World Bank. Carbon Dioxide Information Analysis Center, Environmental Sciences Division, Oak Ridge National Laboratory, Tennessee, United States; 2008 database accessed in January 2012

http://data.worldbank.org/data-catalog/world-development-indicators?cid=GPD_WDI

**European Union (see Appendix II): Austria, Belgium, Bulgaria, Cyprus, Czech Rep., Denmark, Estonia, Finland, France, Germany, Greece, Hungary, Ireland, Italy, Latvia, Lithuania, Luxembourg, Malta, Netherlands, Poland, Portugal, Romania, Slovakia, Slovenia, Spain, Sweden and the United Kingdom

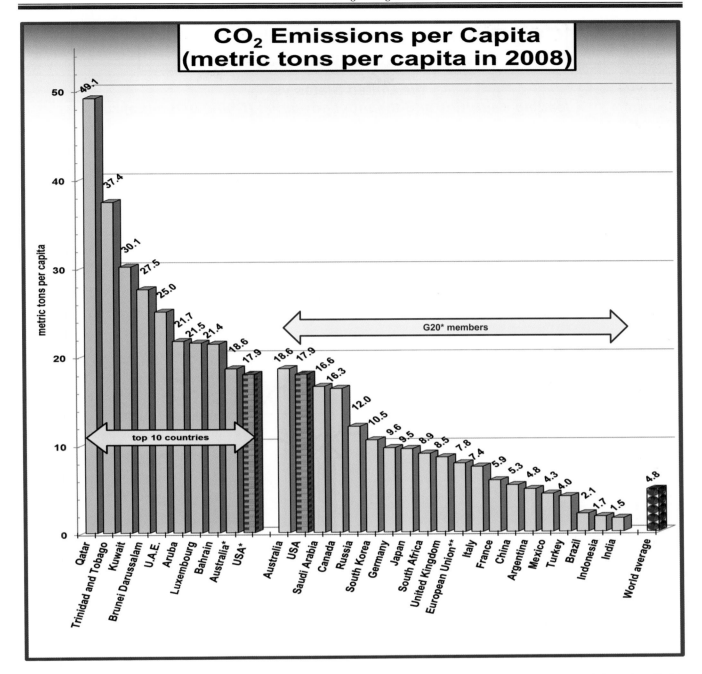

CO₂ Emissions per Capita
(metric tons per capita in 2008)

Carbon dioxide emissions are those stemming from the burning of fossil fuels and the manufacture of cement. They include carbon dioxide produced during consumption of solid, liquid, and gas fuels and gas flaring.

SOURCE: World Bank. Carbon Dioxide Information Analysis Center, Environmental Sciences Division, Oak Ridge National Laboratory, Tennessee, United States; 2008 database accessed in April 2012

http://data.worldbank.org/data-catalog/world-development-indicators?cid=GPD_WDI

*G20 Members (see Appendix I): Argentina, Australia, Brazil, Canada, China, France, Germany, India, Indonesia, Italy, Japan, South Korea, Mexico, Russian Federation, Saudi Arabia, South Africa, Turkey, United Kingdom, United States and the European Union**

**European Union (see Appendix II): Austria, Belgium, Bulgaria, Cyprus, Czech Rep., Denmark, Estonia, Finland, France, Germany, Greece, Hungary, Ireland, Italy, Latvia, Lithuania, Luxembourg, Malta, Netherlands, Poland, Portugal, Romania, Slovakia, Slovenia, Spain, Sweden and the United Kingdom

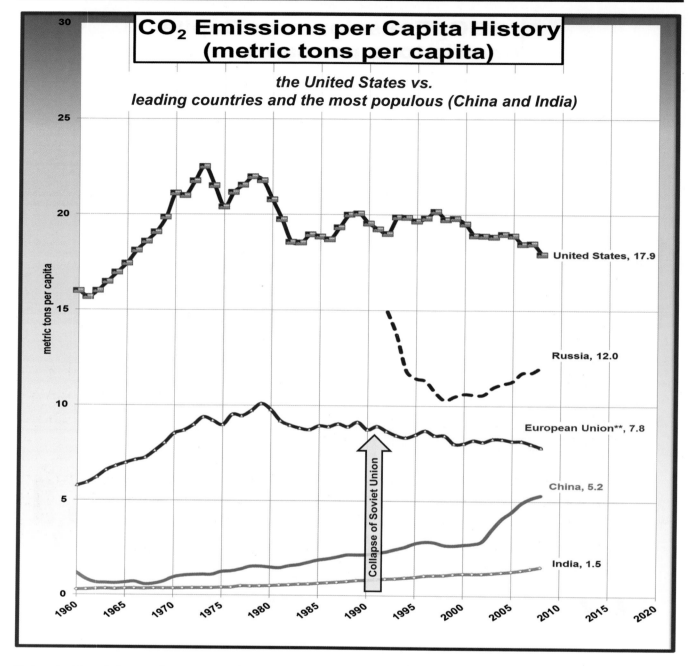

CO$_2$ Emissions per Capita History (metric tons per capita)

the United States vs.
leading countries and the most populous (China and India)

metric tons per capita

United States, 17.9

Russia, 12.0

European Union**, 7.8

China, 5.2

India, 1.5

Collapse of Soviet Union

Carbon dioxide emissions are those stemming from the burning of fossil fuels and the manufacture of cement. They include carbon dioxide produced during consumption of solid, liquid, and gas fuels and gas flaring.

SOURCE: World Bank. Carbon Dioxide Information Analysis Center, Environmental Sciences Division, Oak Ridge National Laboratory, Tennessee, United States; 2008 database accessed in April 2012

http://data.worldbank.org/data-catalog/world-development-indicators?cid=GPD_WDI

**European Union (see Appendix II): Austria, Belgium, Bulgaria, Cyprus, Czech Rep., Denmark, Estonia, Finland, France, Germany, Greece, Hungary, Ireland, Italy, Latvia, Lithuania, Luxembourg, Malta, Netherlands, Poland, Portugal, Romania, Slovakia, Slovenia, Spain, Sweden and the United Kingdom

Chapter 11: U.S. Energy

Overview

In 2010, 23 percent of all energy consumed by the U.S. was imported and 83 percent of total consumption was from fossil fuel.

U.S. proved reserves of oil were equivalent to 4 years of consumption, versus 56 years for natural gas (including shale gas), versus 248 years for coal. U.S. "proved" oil reserves peaked in 1970 and by 2009 had declined by 47 percent.

U.S. oil consumption increased 18 percent between 1981 and 2011. During this period, production decreased 31 percent and imports increased 180 percent.

The U.S. produced 92 percent of the natural gas it consumed in 2011, an increase from the 86 percent level in 2001. The U.S. had the second largest amount of "technically recoverable" shale gas in the world which could supply 47 years at 2011 U.S. natural gas consumption rates.

Coal supplied 21 percent of U.S. energy in 2010 and U.S. proved reserves were equivalent to 248 years at 2010 U.S. consumption rates. The U.S. produced 3.5 percent more coal in 2010 than it consumed.

~

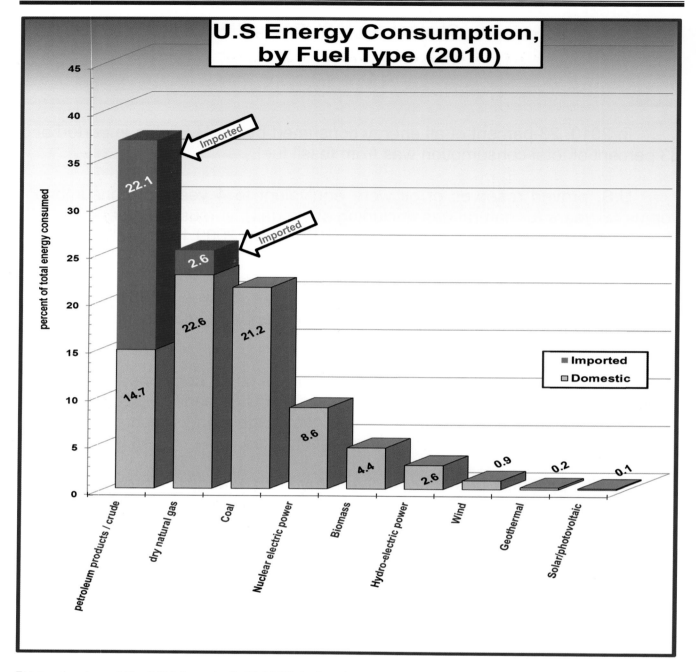

U.S Energy Consumption, by Fuel Type (2010)

percent of total energy consumed

Imported

Imported

Imported
Domestic

- Petroleum products / crude: 22.1, 14.7
- dry natural gas: 2.6, 22.6
- Coal: 21.2
- Nuclear electric power: 8.6
- Biomass: 4.4
- Hydro-electric power: 2.6
- Wind: 0.9
- Geothermal: 0.2
- Solar/photovoltaic: 0.1

Energy values in quadrillion British thermal units (Btu) 2010 database from Energy Supply and Disposition by Type of Fuel.

SOURCE: U.S. Census Bureau

http://www.census.gov/compendia/statab/cats/energy_utilities.html

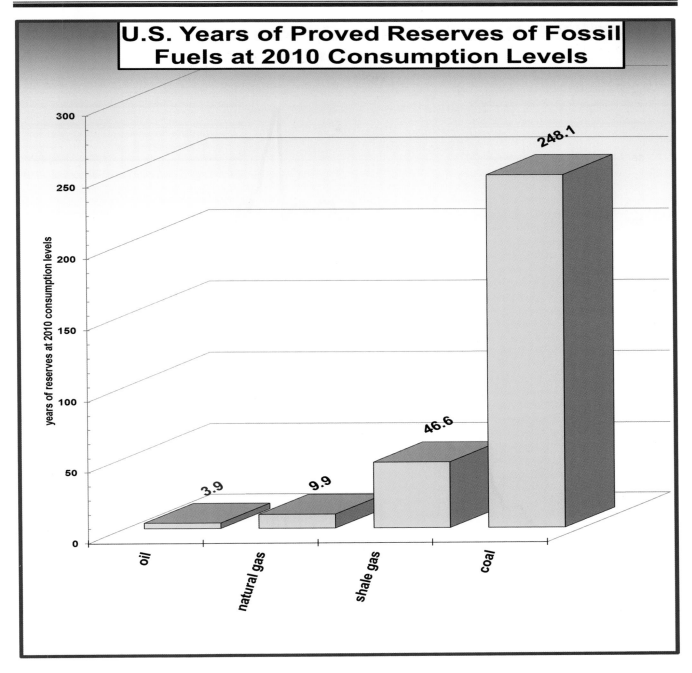

U.S. Years of Proved Reserves of Fossil Fuels at 2010 Consumption Levels

Years of reserves are calculated based on:

(1) oil consumption at 5.3 billion barrels per year and 20.68 billion barrels of proved reserves,
(2) natural gas consumption at 27.36 trillion cu. ft. per year and 272 trillion cu. ft. in reserves + 1,547 trillion cu. ft. of technically recoverable shale gas, and
(3) coal consumption at 1.048 billion tons per year and 260 billion tons of proved reserves; 2010 database from Energy Supply and Disposition by Type of Fuel.

SOURCE: U.S. Census Bureau

http://www.census.gov/compendia/statab/cats/energy_utilities.html

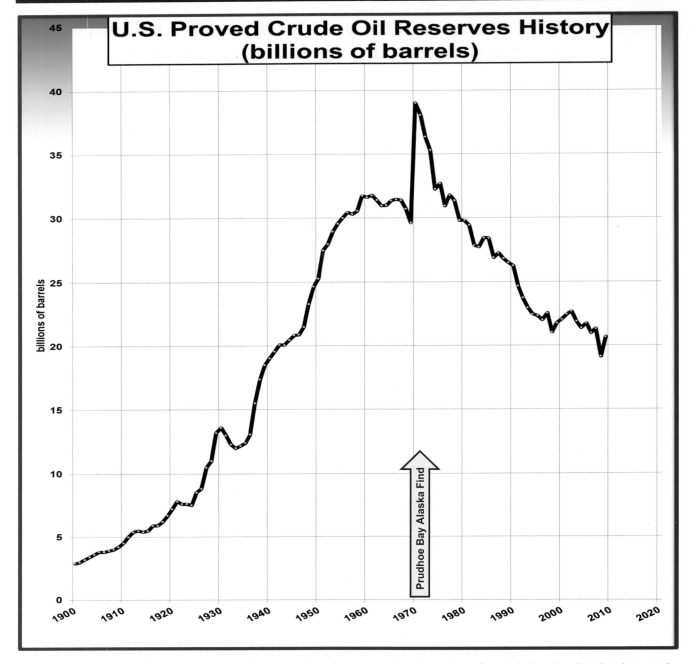

U.S. Proved Crude Oil Reserves History (billions of barrels)

y-axis: billions of barrels

Prudhoe Bay Alaska Find

Proved crude oil reserves. Proved reserves are those quantities of petroleum that, by analysis of geological and engineering data, can be estimated with a high degree of confidence to be commercially recoverable from a given date forward, from known reservoirs and under current economic conditions. Estimates of proved crude oil reserves do not include (1) oil, the recovery of which is subject to reasonable doubt because of uncertainty as to geology, reservoir characteristics, or economic factors; (2) oil that may occur in undrilled prospects; and (3) oil that may be recovered from oil shales, coal, gilsonite, and other such sources. It is necessary that production, gathering or transportation facilities be installed or operative for a reservoir to be considered proved. Because most shale gas and shale oil wells are only a few years old, their long-term productivity is untested. Consequently, the long-term production profiles of shale wells and their estimated ultimate recovery of oil and natural gas are uncertain.

SOURCE: U.S. Energy Information Administration

http://www.eia.doe.gov/pub/international/iealf/crudeoilreserves.xls

http://www.eia.gov/dnav/pet/hist/leafhandler.ashx?n=PET&s=RCRR01NUS_1&f=A

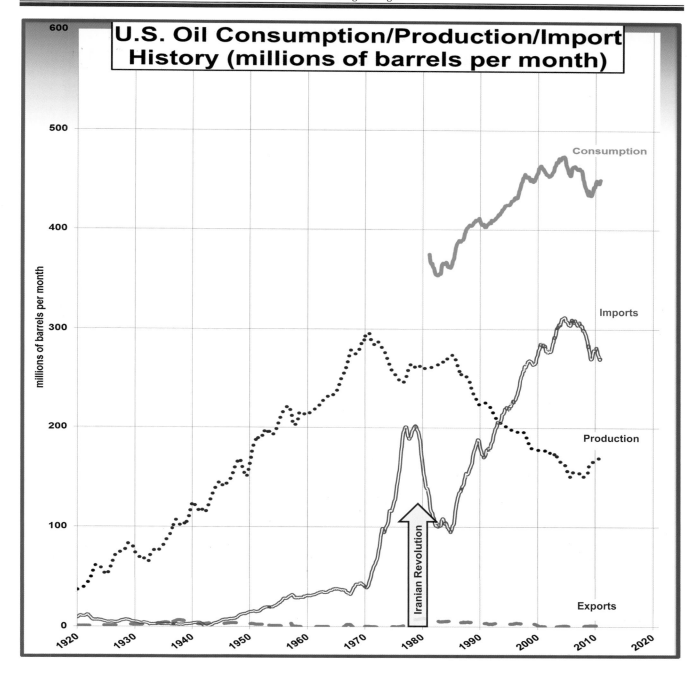

U.S. Field Production of Crude Oil, U.S. Refinery and Blender Net Input of Crude Oil, U.S. Imports of Crude Oil, U.S. Exports of Crude Oil.

SOURCE: U.S. Energy Information Administration

http://www.eia.gov/dnav/pet/pet_move_impcus_a2_nus_ep00_im0_mbbl_m.htm

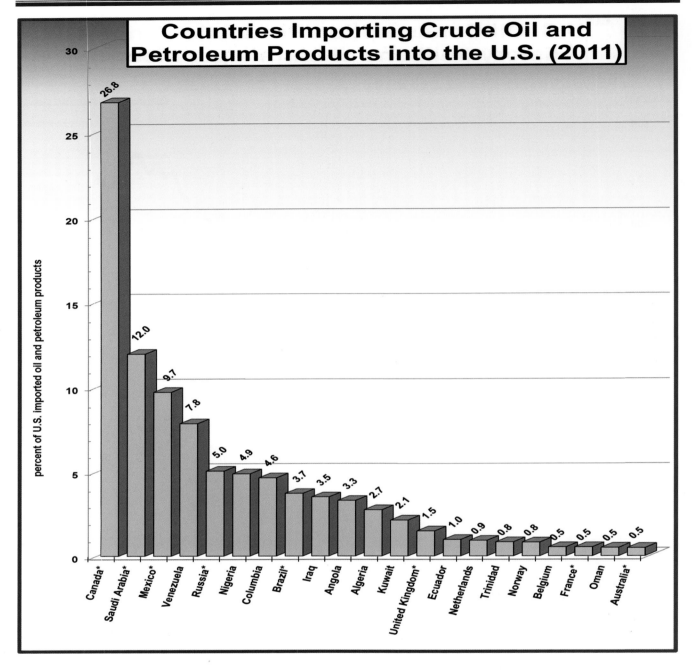

Countries Importing Crude Oil and Petroleum Products into the U.S. (2011)

percent of U.S. imported oil and petroleum products

- Canada*: 26.8
- Saudi Arabia*: 12.0
- Mexico*: 9.7
- Venezuela: 7.8
- Russia*: 5.0
- Nigeria: 4.9
- Columbia: 4.6
- Brazil*: 3.7
- Iraq: 3.5
- Angola: 3.3
- Algeria: 2.7
- Kuwait: 2.1
- United Kingdom*: 1.5
- Ecuador: 1.0
- Netherlands: 0.9
- Trinidad: 0.8
- Norway: 0.8
- Belgium: 0.5
- France*: 0.5
- Oman: 0.5
- Australia*: 0.5

Import country data are barrels/day as of October 2011.

SOURCE: U.S. Energy Information Administration

http://www.eia.gov/dnav/pet/pet_move_impcus_a2_nus_ep00_im0_mbbl_m.htm

*G20 Members (see Appendix I): Argentina, Australia, Brazil, Canada, China, France, Germany, India, Indonesia, Italy, Japan, South Korea, Mexico, Russian Federation, Saudi Arabia, South Africa, Turkey, United Kingdom, United States and the European Union**

**European Union (see Appendix II): Austria, Belgium, Bulgaria, Cyprus, Czech Rep., Denmark, Estonia, Finland, France, Germany, Greece, Hungary, Ireland, Italy, Latvia, Lithuania, Luxembourg, Malta, Netherlands, Poland, Portugal, Romania, Slovakia, Slovenia, Spain, Sweden and the United Kingdom

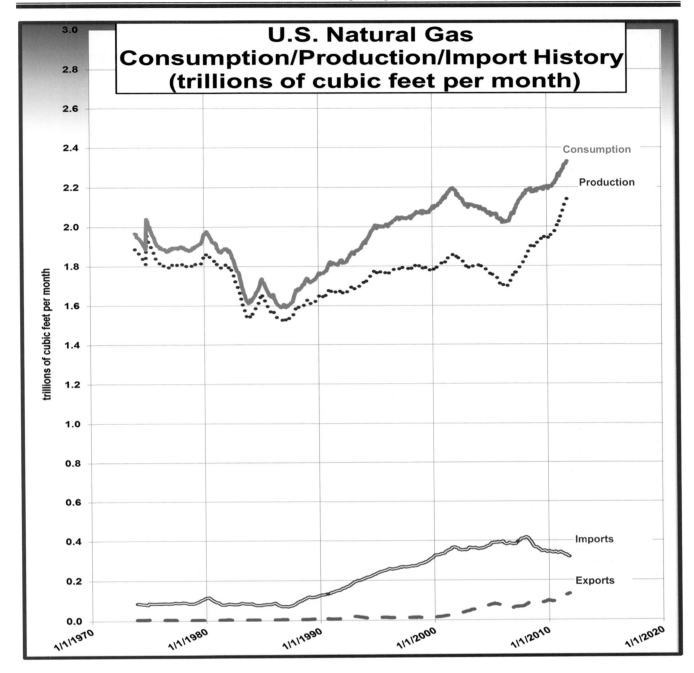

U.S. Natural Gas (trillions of cu feet per month).

SOURCE: U.S. Energy Information Administration

http://www.eia.gov/dnav/ng/hist/n9130us2m.htm

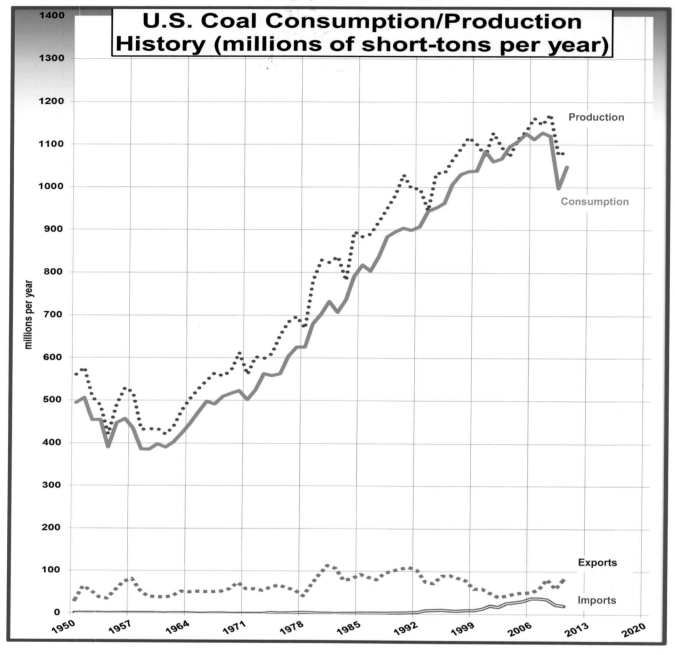

U.S. Coal Consumption/Production History (millions of short-tons per year)

Millions of short-tons of coal produced per year. The U.S. short-ton is 2,000 pounds.

SOURCE: U.S. Energy Information Administration

http://www.eia.gov/coal/

Chapter 12: U.S. Health in Relation to the World

Overview

The U.S. spent $7,410 per capita on public and private health care expenditures in 2009, double the amount spent in 1995 and placed number one among the G20* members, spending twice as much as Japan.

U.S. life expectancy at birth in 2009 was 78.1 years, which ranked thirty-ninth in the world, 4.8 years less than babies born in Japan and 5 years more than babies born in China. The infant mortality rate ranked forty-sixth in the world and although the rates for Japan and the U.S. were the same in 1962, by 2010 Japan's rate had declined to just one-third of the U.S. rate.

One-third of U.S. adults are obese, ranking the United States sixth in the world, versus Japan's 3 percent obesity rate, whereas only 26 percent of U.S. males smoke, versus 42 percent of males in Japan.

The U.S. suicide rate is approximately at world average and one-half of Japan's rate.

~

*G20 Members (see Appendix I): Argentina, Australia, Brazil, Canada, China, France, Germany, India, Indonesia, Italy, Japan, South Korea, Mexico, Russian Federation, Saudi Arabia, South Africa, Turkey, United Kingdom, United States and the European Union**

**European Union (see Appendix II): Austria, Belgium, Bulgaria, Cyprus, Czech Rep., Denmark, Estonia, Finland, France, Germany, Greece, Hungary, Ireland, Italy, Latvia, Lithuania, Luxembourg, Malta, Netherlands, Poland, Portugal, Romania, Slovakia, Slovenia, Spain, Sweden and the United Kingdom

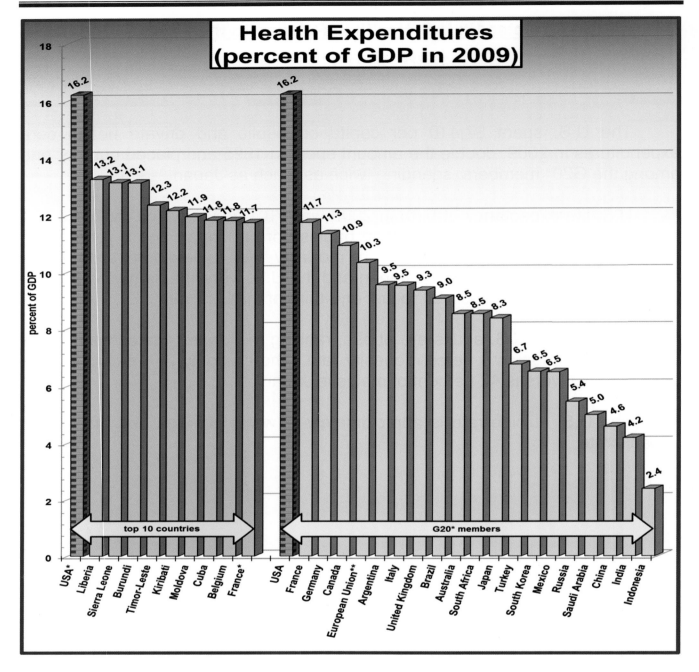

Health Expenditures (percent of GDP in 2009)

top 10 countries: USA* 16.2, Liberia 13.2, Sierra Leone 13.1, Burundi 13.1, Timor-Leste 12.3, Kiribati 12.2, Moldova 11.9, Cuba 11.8, Belgium 11.8, France* 11.7

G20 members:* USA 16.2, France 11.7, Germany 11.3, Canada 10.9, European Union** 10.3, Argentina 9.5, Italy 9.5, United Kingdom 9.3, Brazil 9.0, Australia 8.5, South Africa 8.5, Japan 8.3, Turkey 6.7, South Korea 6.5, Mexico 6.5, Russia 5.4, Saudi Arabia 5.0, China 4.6, India 4.2, Indonesia 2.4

Total health expenditure is the sum of public and private health expenditure. It covers the provision of health services (preventive and curative), family planning activities, nutrition activities, and emergency aid designated for health but does not include provision of water and sanitation.

GDP = private consumption + gross investment + government consumption (exclusive of transfer payments such as Social Security) + [exports − imports].

SOURCE: World Bank. World Health Organization National Health Account database (www.who.int/nha/en) supplemented by country data.

http://data.worldbank.org/data-catalog/world-development-indicators?cid=GPD_WDI

*G20 Members (see Appendix I): Argentina, Australia, Brazil, Canada, China, France, Germany, India, Indonesia, Italy, Japan, South Korea, Mexico, Russian Federation, Saudi Arabia, South Africa, Turkey, United Kingdom, United States and the European Union**

**European Union (see Appendix II): Austria, Belgium, Bulgaria, Cyprus, Czech Rep., Denmark, Estonia, Finland, France, Germany, Greece, Hungary, Ireland, Italy, Latvia, Lithuania, Luxembourg, Malta, Netherlands, Poland, Portugal, Romania, Slovakia, Slovenia, Spain, Sweden and the United Kingdom

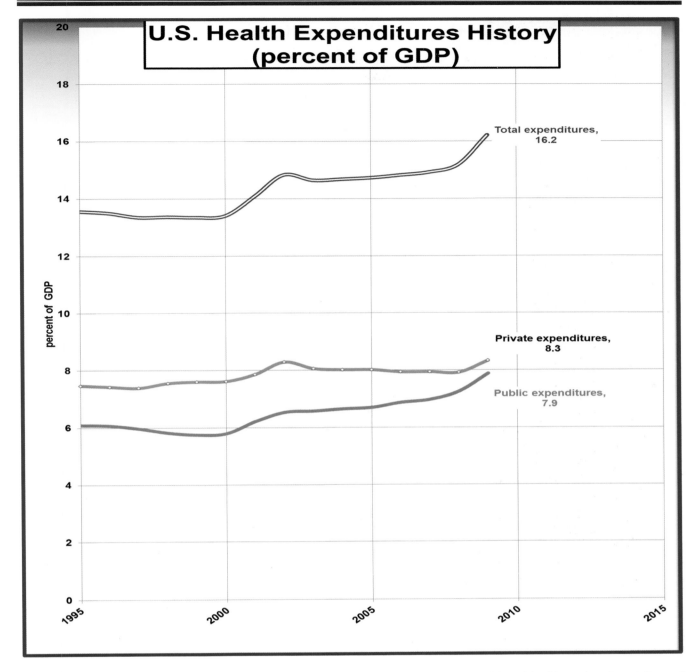

U.S. Health Expenditures History (percent of GDP)

Total health expenditure is the sum of public and private health expenditure. It covers the provision of health services (preventive and curative), family planning activities, nutrition activities, and emergency aid designated for health but does not include provision of water and sanitation.

GDP = private consumption + gross investment + government consumption (exclusive of transfer payments such as Social Security) + [exports − imports]

SOURCE: World Bank. World Health Organization National Health Account database (www.who.int/nha/en) supplemented by country data.

http://data.worldbank.org/data-catalog/world-development-indicators?cid=GPD_WDI

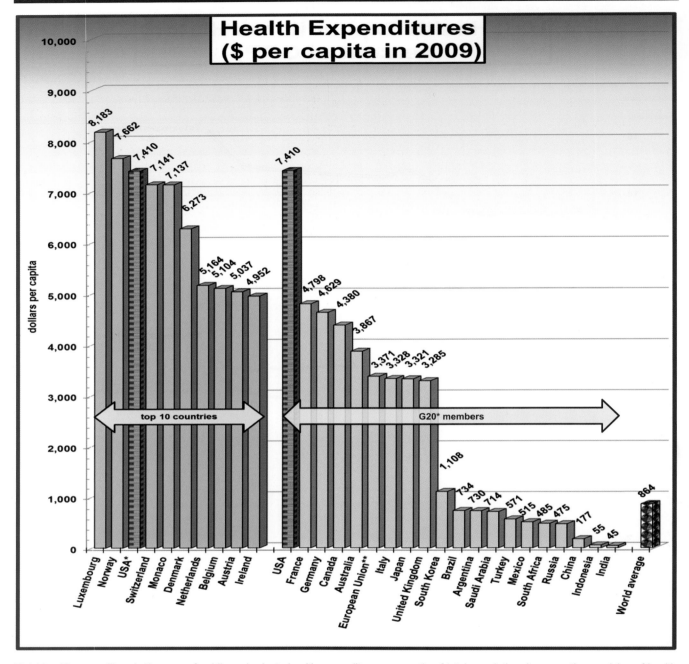

Health Expenditures ($ per capita in 2009)

dollars per capita

top 10 countries

G20* members

Luxembourg 8,183
Norway 7,662
USA* 7,410
Switzerland 7,410
Monaco 7,141
Denmark 7,137
Netherlands 6,273
Belgium 5,164
Austria 5,104
Ireland 5,037
4,952

USA 7,410
France 4,798
Germany 4,629
Canada 4,380
Australia 3,867
European Union** 3,371
Italy 3,328
Japan 3,321
United Kingdom 3,285
South Korea 1,108
Brazil 734
Argentina 730
Saudi Arabia 714
Turkey 571
Mexico 515
South Africa 485
Russia 475
China 177
Indonesia 55
India 45
World average 864

Total health expenditure is the sum of public and private health expenditures as a ratio of total population. It covers the provision of health services (preventive and curative), family planning activities, nutrition activities, and emergency aid designated for health but does not include provision of water and sanitation. Data for time series are 2005 U.S. dollars at PPP (Purchasing Power Parities).

SOURCE: World Bank. World Health Organization National Health Account database (www.who.int/nha/en) supplemented by country data; 2009 database accessed in April 2012

http://data.worldbank.org/data-catalog/world-development-indicators?cid=GPD_WDI

*G20 Members (see Appendix I): Argentina, Australia, Brazil, Canada, China, France, Germany, India, Indonesia, Italy, Japan, South Korea, Mexico, Russian Federation, Saudi Arabia, South Africa, Turkey, United Kingdom, United States and the European Union**

**European Union (see Appendix II): Austria, Belgium, Bulgaria, Cyprus, Czech Rep., Denmark, Estonia, Finland, France, Germany, Greece, Hungary, Ireland, Italy, Latvia, Lithuania, Luxembourg, Malta, Netherlands, Poland, Portugal, Romania, Slovakia, Slovenia, Spain, Sweden and the United Kingdom

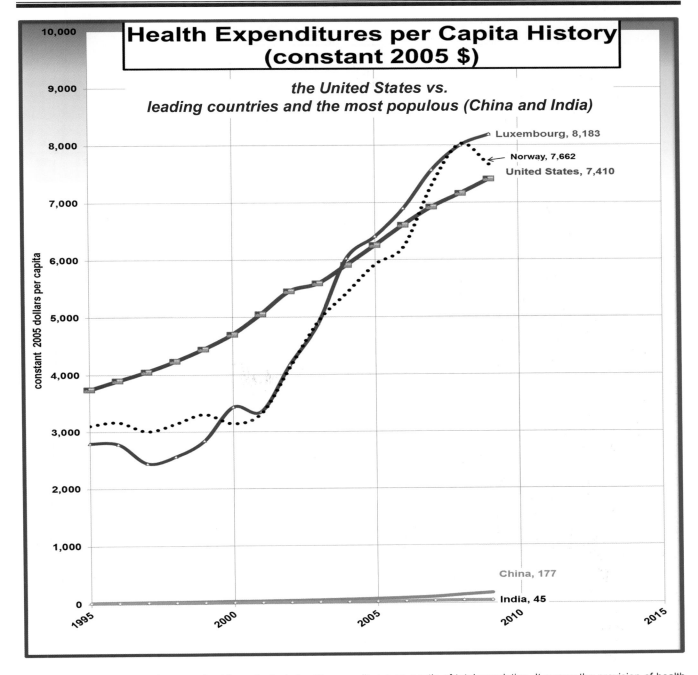

Health Expenditures per Capita History (constant 2005 $)

the United States vs.
leading countries and the most populous (China and India)

Luxembourg, 8,183
Norway, 7,662
United States, 7,410
China, 177
India, 45

Total health expenditure is the sum of public and private health expenditures as a ratio of total population. It covers the provision of health services (preventive and curative), family planning activities, nutrition activities, and emergency aid designated for health but does not include provision of water and sanitation.

SOURCE: World Bank. World Health Organization National Health Account database (www.who.int/nha/en) supplemented by country data; 2009 database accessed in January 2012

http://data.worldbank.org/data-catalog/world-development-indicators?cid=GPD_WDI

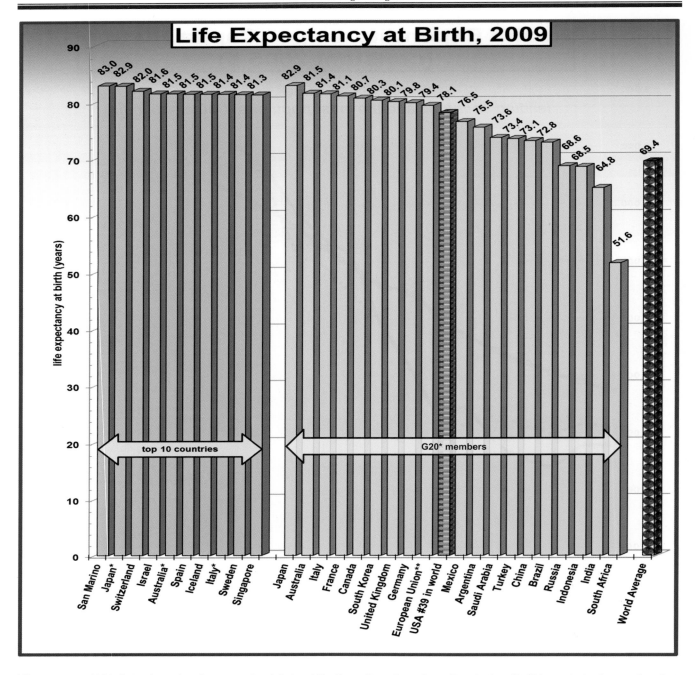

Life Expectancy at Birth, 2009

life expectancy at birth (years)

top 10 countries

G20* members

San Marino 83.0, Japan* 82.9, Switzerland 82.0, Israel 81.6, Australia* 81.5, Spain 81.5, Iceland 81.5, Italy* 81.4, Sweden 81.4, Singapore 81.3

Japan 82.9, Australia 81.5, Italy 81.4, France 81.1, Canada 80.7, South Korea 80.3, United Kingdom 80.1, Germany 79.8, European Union** 79.4, USA #39 in world 78.1, Mexico 76.5, Argentina 75.5, Saudi Arabia 73.6, Turkey 73.4, China 73.1, Brazil 72.8, Russia 68.6, Indonesia 68.5, India 64.8, South Africa 51.6

World Average 69.4

Life expectancy at birth indicates the number of years a newborn infant would live if prevailing patterns of mortality at the time of its birth were to stay the same throughout its life.

SOURCE: World Bank. Derived from male and female life expectancy at birth. Male and female life expectancy source: (1) United Nations Population Division; 2009. World Population Prospects: New York, United Nations, Department of Economic and Social Affairs (advanced Excel tables), (2) Census reports and other statistical publications from national statistical offices, (3) Eurostat: Demographic Statistics, (4) Secretariat of the Pacific Community: Statistics and Demography Programme, and (5) U.S. Census Bureau: International Database; 2009 database accessed in January 2012

http://data.worldbank.org/data-catalog/world-development-indicators?cid=GPD_WDI

*G20 Members (see Appendix I): Argentina, Australia, Brazil, Canada, China, France, Germany, India, Indonesia, Italy, Japan, South Korea, Mexico, Russian Federation, Saudi Arabia, South Africa, Turkey, United Kingdom, United States and the European Union**

**European Union (see Appendix II): Austria, Belgium, Bulgaria, Cyprus, Czech Rep., Denmark, Estonia, Finland, France, Germany, Greece, Hungary, Ireland, Italy, Latvia, Lithuania, Luxembourg, Malta, Netherlands, Poland, Portugal, Romania, Slovakia, Slovenia, Spain, Sweden and the United Kingdom

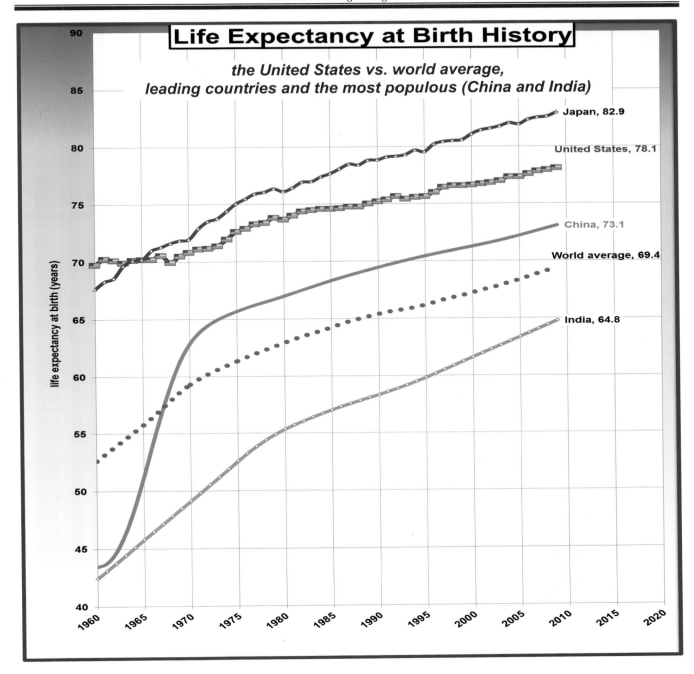

Life Expectancy at Birth History

the United States vs. world average, leading countries and the most populous (China and India)

Japan, 82.9

United States, 78.1

China, 73.1

World average, 69.4

India, 64.8

life expectancy at birth (years)

Life expectancy at birth indicates the number of years a newborn infant would live if prevailing patterns of mortality at the time of its birth were to stay the same throughout its life.

SOURCE: World Bank. Derived from male and female life expectancy at birth. Male and female life expectancy source: (1) United Nations Population Division; 2009. World Population Prospects: New York, United Nations, Department of Economic and Social Affairs (advanced Excel tables), (2) Census reports and other statistical publications from national statistical offices, (3) Eurostat: Demographic Statistics, (4) Secretariat of the Pacific Community: Statistics and Demography Programme; and (5) U.S. Census Bureau: International Database; 2009 database accessed in January 2012

http://data.worldbank.org/data-catalog/world-development-indicators?cid=GPD_WDI

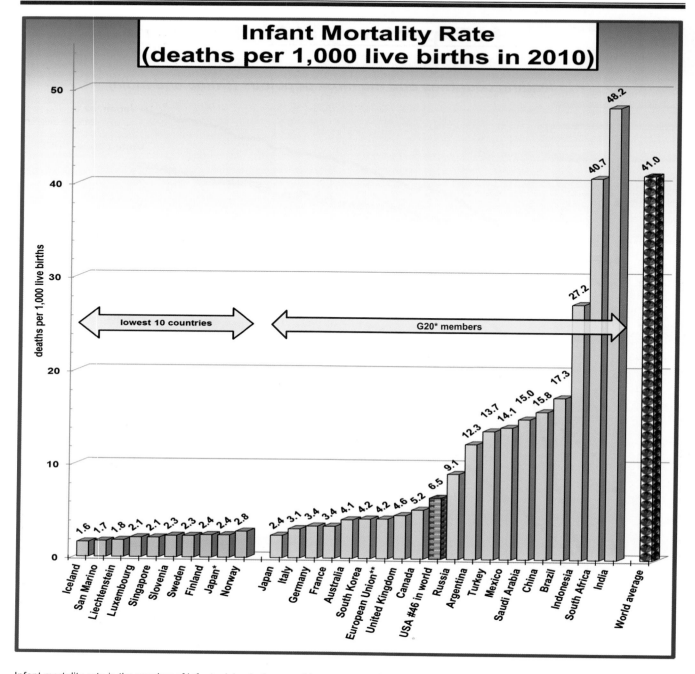

Infant mortality rate is the number of infants dying before reaching one year of age, per 1,000 live births in a given year.

SOURCE: World Bank. Level and Trends in Child Mortality. Report 2011. Estimates Developed by the UN Inter-agency Group for Child Mortality Estimation (UNICEF, WHO, World Bank, UN DESA, UNPD); 2010 database accessed in April 2012

http://data.worldbank.org/data-catalog/world-development-indicators?cid=GPD_WDI

*G20 Members (see Appendix I): Argentina, Australia, Brazil, Canada, China, France, Germany, India, Indonesia, Italy, Japan, South Korea, Mexico, Russian Federation, Saudi Arabia, South Africa, Turkey, United Kingdom, United States and the European Union**

**European Union (see Appendix II): Austria, Belgium, Bulgaria, Cyprus, Czech Rep., Denmark, Estonia, Finland, France, Germany, Greece, Hungary, Ireland, Italy, Latvia, Lithuania, Luxembourg, Malta, Netherlands, Poland, Portugal, Romania, Slovakia, Slovenia, Spain, Sweden and the United Kingdom

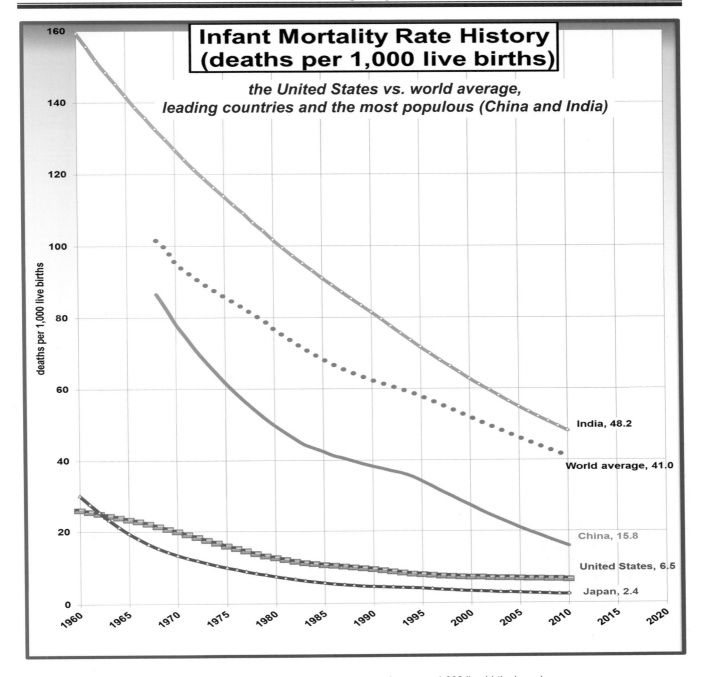

Infant Mortality Rate History (deaths per 1,000 live births)

the United States vs. world average, leading countries and the most populous (China and India)

India, 48.2

World average, 41.0

China, 15.8

United States, 6.5

Japan, 2.4

Infant mortality rate is the number of infants dying before reaching one year of age, per 1,000 live births in a given year.

SOURCE: World Bank. Level and Trends in Child Mortality. Report 2011. Estimates Developed by the UN Inter-agency Group for Child Mortality Estimation (UNICEF, WHO, World Bank, UN DESA, UNPD); 2010 database accessed in April 2012

http://data.worldbank.org/data-catalog/world-development-indicators?cid=GPD_WDI

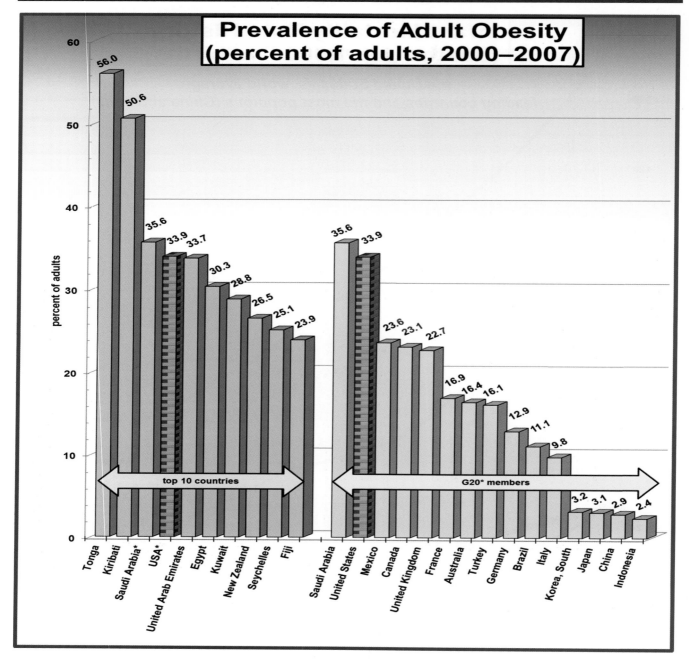

**Prevalence of Adult Obesity
(percent of adults, 2000–2007)**

Obesity is defined as an adult having a Body Mass Index (BMI) greater than or equal to 30.0. BMI is calculated by taking a person's weight in kg and dividing it by the person's squared height in meters.

SOURCE: CIA, 2000–2007 databases accessed in October 2011.

https://www.cia.gov/library/publications/the-world-factbook/rankorder/rankorderguide.html

*G20 Members (see Appendix I): Argentina, Australia, Brazil, Canada, China, France, Germany, India, Indonesia, Italy, Japan, South Korea, Mexico, Russian Federation, Saudi Arabia, South Africa, Turkey, United Kingdom, United States and the European Union**

**European Union (see Appendix II): Austria, Belgium, Bulgaria, Cyprus, Czech Rep., Denmark, Estonia, Finland, France, Germany, Greece, Hungary, Ireland, Italy, Latvia, Lithuania, Luxembourg, Malta, Netherlands, Poland, Portugal, Romania, Slovakia, Slovenia, Spain, Sweden and the United Kingdom

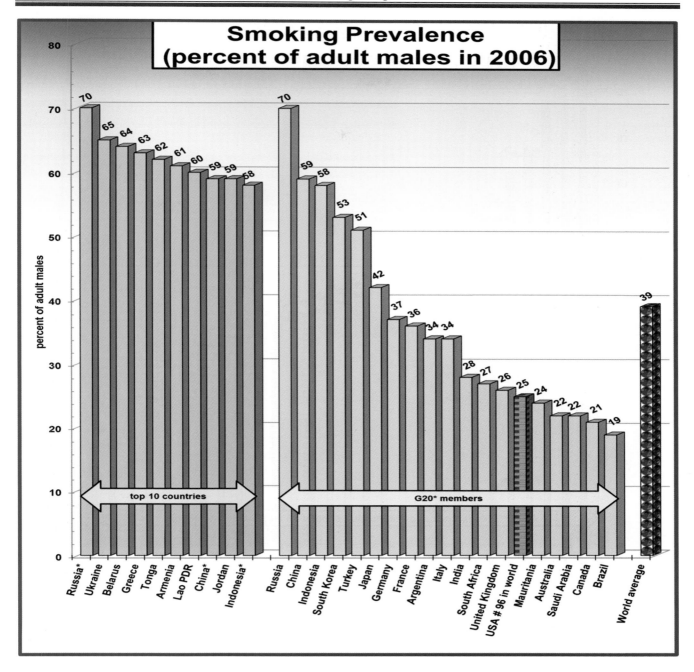

Smoking Prevalence (percent of adult males in 2006)

Prevalence of males who smoke is the percentage of men ages 15 and over who smoke any form of tobacco, including cigarettes, cigars, and pipes, and excluding smokeless tobacco. Data include daily and non-daily smoking.

SOURCE: World Bank. WHO Report on the Global Tobacco Epidemic; 2006 database accessed April 2012

http://data.worldbank.org/data-catalog/world-development-indicators?cid=GPD_WDI and http://data.worldbank.org/indicator/all

*G20 Members (see Appendix I): Argentina, Australia, Brazil, Canada, China, France, Germany, India, Indonesia, Italy, Japan, South Korea, Mexico, Russian Federation, Saudi Arabia, South Africa, Turkey, United Kingdom, United States and the European Union**

**European Union (see Appendix II): Austria, Belgium, Bulgaria, Cyprus, Czech Rep., Denmark, Estonia, Finland, France, Germany, Greece, Hungary, Ireland, Italy, Latvia, Lithuania, Luxembourg, Malta, Netherlands, Poland, Portugal, Romania, Slovakia, Slovenia, Spain, Sweden and the United Kingdom

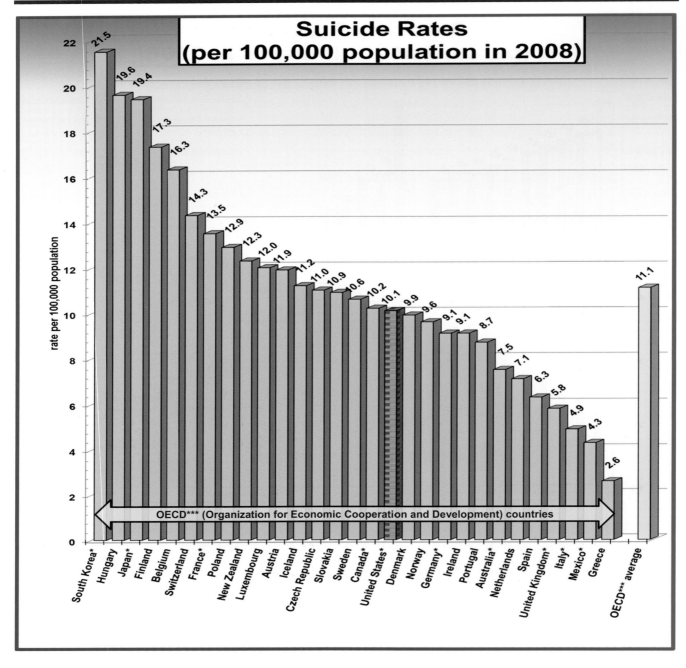

Suicide Rates
(per 100,000 population in 2008)

rate per 100,000 population

South Korea* 21.5, Hungary 19.6, Japan* 19.4, Finland 17.3, Belgium 16.3, Switzerland 14.3, France* 13.5, Poland 12.9, New Zealand 12.3, Luxembourg 12.0, Austria 11.9, Iceland 11.2, Czech Republic 11.0, Slovakia 10.9, Sweden 10.6, Canada* 10.2, United States* 10.1, Denmark 9.9, Norway 9.6, Germany* 9.1, Ireland 9.1, Portugal 8.7, Australia* 7.5, Netherlands 7.1, Spain 6.3, United Kingdom* 5.8, Italy* 4.9, Mexico* 4.3, Greece 2.6, OECD*** average 11.1

OECD*** (Organization for Economic Cooperation and Development) countries

Suicides per 100,000 persons; data are for 2008.

SOURCE: U.S. Census Bureau. Organization for Economic Cooperation and Development (OECD***), 2011, "OECD Health Data," OECD Health Statistics database (copyright), http://dx.doi.org/10.1787data-00350-en

http://www.census.gov/econ/susb/methodology.html

*G20 Members (see Appendix I): Argentina, Australia, Brazil, Canada, China, France, Germany, India, Indonesia, Italy, Japan, South Korea, Mexico, Russian Federation, Saudi Arabia, South Africa, Turkey, United Kingdom, United States and the European Union**

**European Union (see Appendix II): Austria, Belgium, Bulgaria, Cyprus, Czech Rep., Denmark, Estonia, Finland, France, Germany, Greece, Hungary, Ireland, Italy, Latvia, Lithuania, Luxembourg, Malta, Netherlands, Poland, Portugal, Romania, Slovakia, Slovenia, Spain, Sweden and the United Kingdom

***OECD (see appendix III for members)

Chapter 13: U.S. Innovation in Relation to the World

Overview

In 2007, the U.S. government spent 2.7 percent of GDP* on R&D (research and development) and ranked seventh in the world, compared with Sweden that ranked number one at 3.6 percent and China which ranked twentieth at 1.5 percent.

In 2010, the U.S. published 28 percent of the world's scientific and technical journal articles, a decline from 40 percent in 1982. During that same period China's portion grew from zero to 8 percent. In 2010 the U.S. was number one in the number of patent applications filed, however 50 percent were filed by foreigners, whereas the U.S. and China both had the same number of resident filings. In China, 794,000 trademark applications were filed, three times as many as in the United States.

In 2010, 79 percent of the U.S. population had access to the Internet compared with 96 percent in Iceland and 34 percent in China. There were also 90 mobile cellular subscriptions per 100 persons in the United States, half as many as Saudi Arabia and Russia. These subscriptions include all mobile cellular devices.

In 1997, the United States launched 38 rockets, the largest number of commercial and non-commercial space launches, and by 2010 the number declined to 15, trailing Russia's 31 and China's 16.

~

*GDP (Gross Domestic Product) is the primary measure of a country's economic size, equal to private consumption + gross investment + government consumption (exclusive of transfer payments such as Social Security) + net trade [exports − imports]

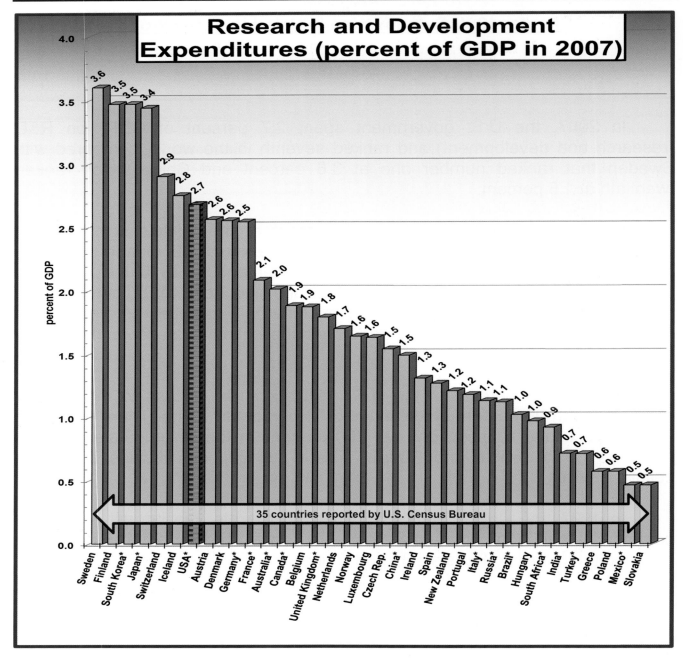

Research and Development Expenditures (percent of GDP in 2007)

percent of GDP

35 countries reported by U.S. Census Bureau

Sweden 3.6, Finland 3.5, South Korea* 3.5, Japan* 3.4, Switzerland 2.9, Iceland 2.8, USA* 2.7, Austria 2.6, Denmark 2.6, Germany* 2.5, France* 2.5, Australia* 2.1, Canada* 2.0, Belgium 1.9, United Kingdom* 1.9, Netherlands 1.8, Norway 1.7, Luxembourg 1.6, Czech Rep. 1.6, China* 1.5, Ireland 1.5, Spain 1.3, New Zealand 1.3, Portugal 1.2, Italy* 1.2, Russia* 1.1, Brazil* 1.1, Hungary 1.0, South Africa* 1.0, India* 0.9, Turkey* 0.7, Greece 0.7, Poland 0.6, Mexico* 0.6, Slovakia 0.5, 0.5

Research and Development (R&D) Expenditures by country for select countries; figures are for 2007. [U.S. percentage refers to expenditures funded by government].

GDP (Gross Domestic Product) is the sum of all domestic purchases of final products and services + private domestic investment + government consumption + net trade (exports - imports). Government includes federal + state + local.

SOURCE: U.S. Census Bureau. Organization for Economic Cooperation and Development (OECD), 2010, "Main Science and Technology Indicators," OECD Science, Technology and R&D Statistics database (copyright)

http://www.census.gov/econ/susb/methodology.html

*G20 Members (see Appendix I): Argentina, Australia, Brazil, Canada, China, France, Germany, India, Indonesia, Italy, Japan, South Korea, Mexico, Russian Federation, Saudi Arabia, South Africa, Turkey, United Kingdom, United States and the European Union**

**European Union (see Appendix II): Austria, Belgium, Bulgaria, Cyprus, Czech Rep., Denmark, Estonia, Finland, France, Germany, Greece, Hungary, Ireland, Italy, Latvia, Lithuania, Luxembourg, Malta, Netherlands, Poland, Portugal, Romania, Slovakia, Slovenia, Spain, Sweden and the United Kingdom

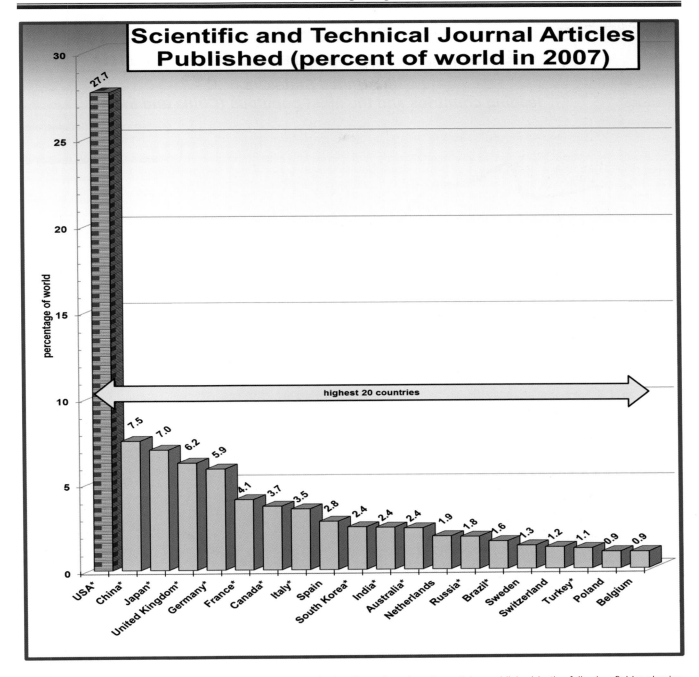

Scientific and technical journal articles refer to the number of scientific and engineering articles published in the following fields: physics, biology, chemistry, mathematics, clinical medicine, biomedical research, engineering and technology, and earth and space sciences.

SOURCE: World Bank. National Science Foundation, Science and Engineering Indicators. 2007 database accessed in April 2012

http://data.worldbank.org/data-catalog/world-development-indicators?cid=GPD_WDI

*G20 Members (see Appendix I): Argentina, Australia, Brazil, Canada, China, France, Germany, India, Indonesia, Italy, Japan, South Korea, Mexico, Russian Federation, Saudi Arabia, South Africa, Turkey, United Kingdom, United States and the European Union**

**European Union (see Appendix II): Austria, Belgium, Bulgaria, Cyprus, Czech Rep., Denmark, Estonia, Finland, France, Germany, Greece, Hungary, Ireland, Italy, Latvia, Lithuania, Luxembourg, Malta, Netherlands, Poland, Portugal, Romania, Slovakia, Slovenia, Spain, Sweden and the United Kingdom

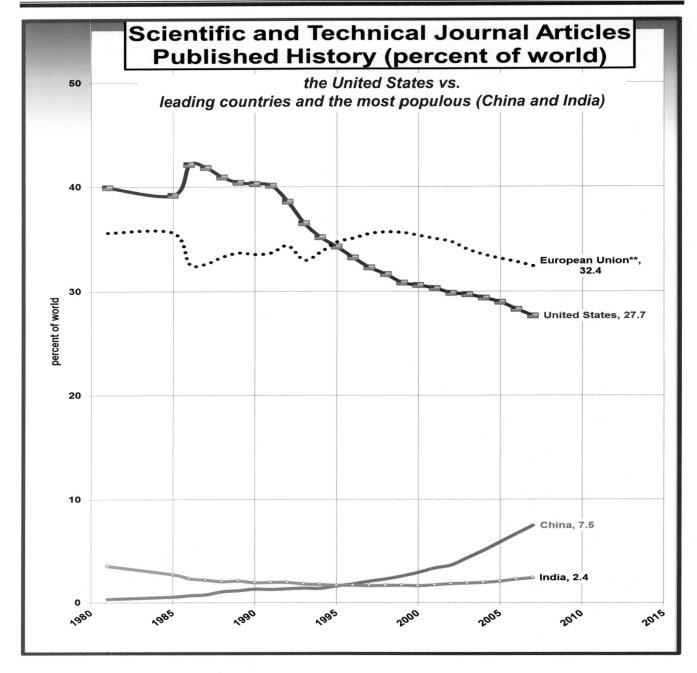

Scientific and Technical Journal Articles Published History (percent of world)

the United States vs.
leading countries and the most populous (China and India)

Scientific and technical journal articles refer to the number of scientific and engineering articles published in the following fields: physics, biology, chemistry, mathematics, clinical medicine, biomedical research, engineering and technology, and earth and space sciences.

SOURCE: World Bank. National Science Foundation, Science and Engineering Indicators. 2007 database accessed in April 2012

http://data.worldbank.org/data-catalog/world-development-indicators?cid=GPD_WDI

**European Union (see Appendix II): Austria, Belgium, Bulgaria, Cyprus, Czech Rep., Denmark, Estonia, Finland, France, Germany, Greece, Hungary, Ireland, Italy, Latvia, Lithuania, Luxembourg, Malta, Netherlands, Poland, Portugal, Romania, Slovakia, Slovenia, Spain, Sweden and the United Kingdom

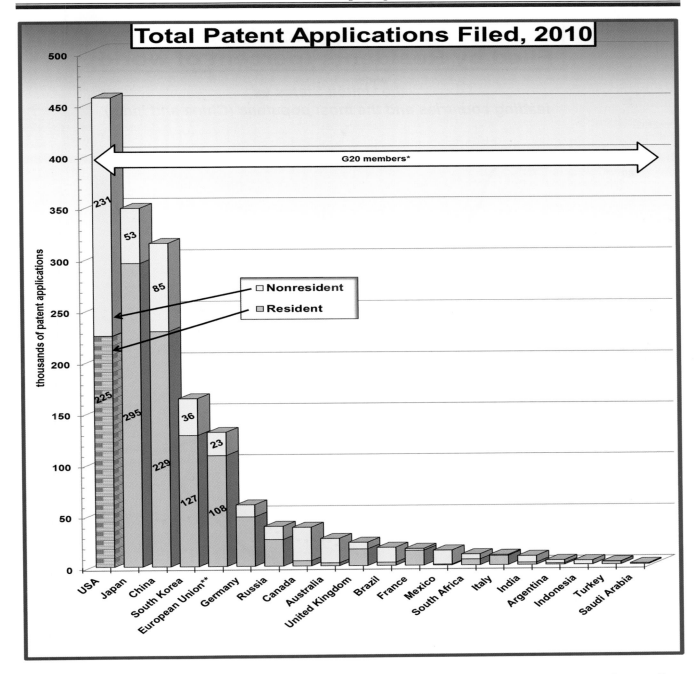

Total Patent Applications Filed, 2010

thousands of patent applications

- □ Nonresident
- ▣ Resident

G20 members*

USA: 231, 225
Japan: 53, 295
China: 85, 229
South Korea: 36, 127
European Union**: 23, 108

USA, Japan, China, South Korea, European Union**, Germany, Russia, Canada, Australia, United Kingdom, Brazil, France, Mexico, South Africa, Italy, India, Argentina, Indonesia, Turkey, Saudi Arabia

Patent applications are worldwide patent applications filed through the Patent Cooperation Treaty procedure or with a national patent office.

SOURCE: World Bank. World Intellectual Property Organization (WIPO), World Intellectual Property Indicators and www.wipo.int/econ_stat. The International Bureau of WIPO assumes no responsibility with respect to the transformation of these data; 2010 database accessed in April 2012

http://data.worldbank.org/data-catalog/world-development-indicators?cid=GPD_WDI

*G20 Members (see Appendix I): Argentina, Australia, Brazil, Canada, China, France, Germany, India, Indonesia, Italy, Japan, South Korea, Mexico, Russian Federation, Saudi Arabia, South Africa, Turkey, United Kingdom, United States and the European Union**

**European Union (see Appendix II): Austria, Belgium, Bulgaria, Cyprus, Czech Rep., Denmark, Estonia, Finland, France, Germany, Greece, Hungary, Ireland, Italy, Latvia, Lithuania, Luxembourg, Malta, Netherlands, Poland, Portugal, Romania, Slovakia, Slovenia, Spain, Sweden and the United Kingdom

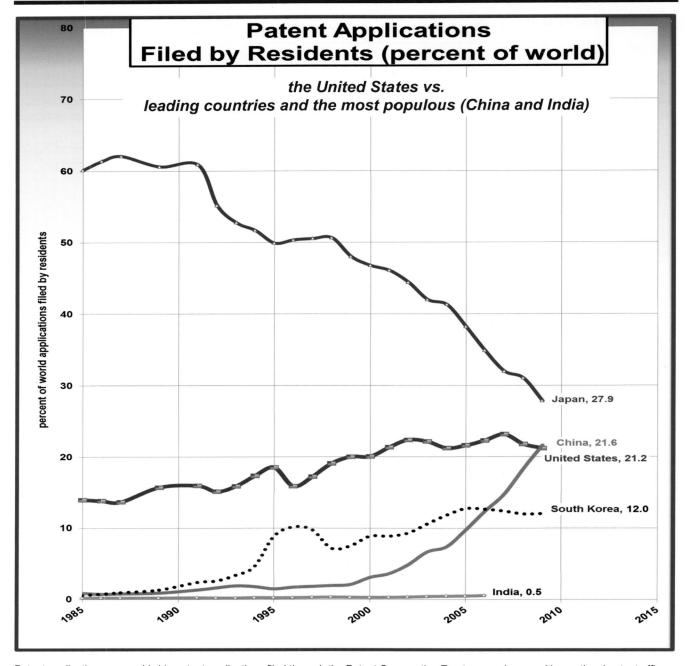

**Patent Applications
Filed by Residents (percent of world)**

*the United States vs.
leading countries and the most populous (China and India)*

Patent applications are worldwide patent applications filed through the Patent Cooperation Treaty procedure or with a national patent office.

SOURCE: World Bank. World Intellectual Property Organization (WIPO), World Intellectual Property Indicators and www.wipo.int/econ_stat. The International Bureau of WIPO assumes no responsibility with respect to the transformation of these data; 2010 database accessed in January 2012

http://data.worldbank.org/data-catalog/world-development-indicators?cid=GPD_WDI

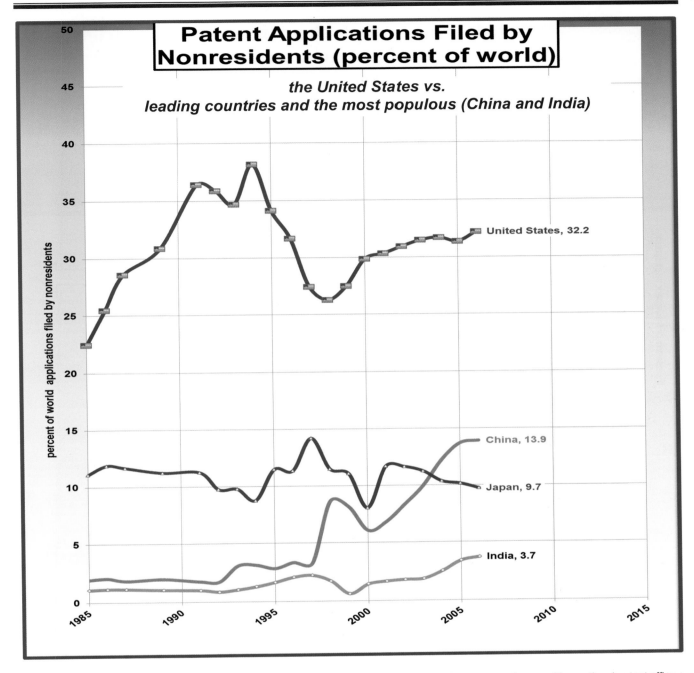

Patent Applications Filed by Nonresidents (percent of world)

the United States vs.
leading countries and the most populous (China and India)

percent of world applications filed by nonresidents

United States, 32.2

China, 13.9

Japan, 9.7

India, 3.7

Patent applications are worldwide patent applications filed through the Patent Cooperation Treaty procedure or with a national patent office.

SOURCE: World Bank. World Intellectual Property Organization (WIPO), World Intellectual Property Indicators and www.wipo.int/econ_stat. The International Bureau of WIPO assumes no responsibility with respect to the transformation of these data; 2010 database accessed in April 2012

http://data.worldbank.org/data-catalog/world-development-indicators?cid=GPD_WDI

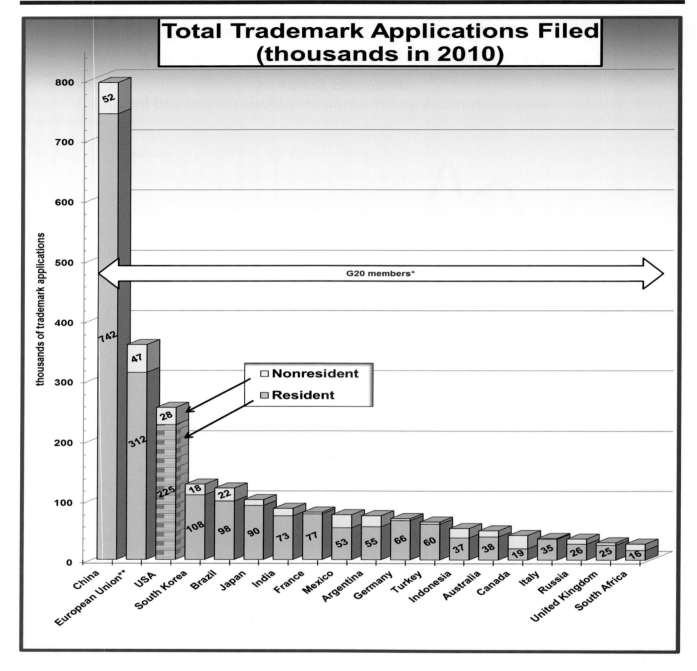

Total Trademark Applications Filed (thousands in 2010)

Trademark applications filed are applications to register a trademark with a national or regional Intellectual Property (IP) office.

SOURCE: World Bank. World Intellectual Property Organization (WIPO), World Intellectual Property Indicators and www.wipo.int/econ_stat. The International Bureau of WIPO assumes no responsibility with respect to the transformation of these data; 2010 database accessed in April 2012

http://data.worldbank.org/data-catalog/world-development-indicators?cid=GPD_WDI

*G20 Members (see Appendix I): Argentina, Australia, Brazil, Canada, China, France, Germany, India, Indonesia, Italy, Japan, South Korea, Mexico, Russian Federation, Saudi Arabia, South Africa, Turkey, United Kingdom, United States and the European Union**

**European Union (see Appendix II): Austria, Belgium, Bulgaria, Cyprus, Czech Rep., Denmark, Estonia, Finland, France, Germany, Greece, Hungary, Ireland, Italy, Latvia, Lithuania, Luxembourg, Malta, Netherlands, Poland, Portugal, Romania, Slovakia, Slovenia, Spain, Sweden and the United Kingdom

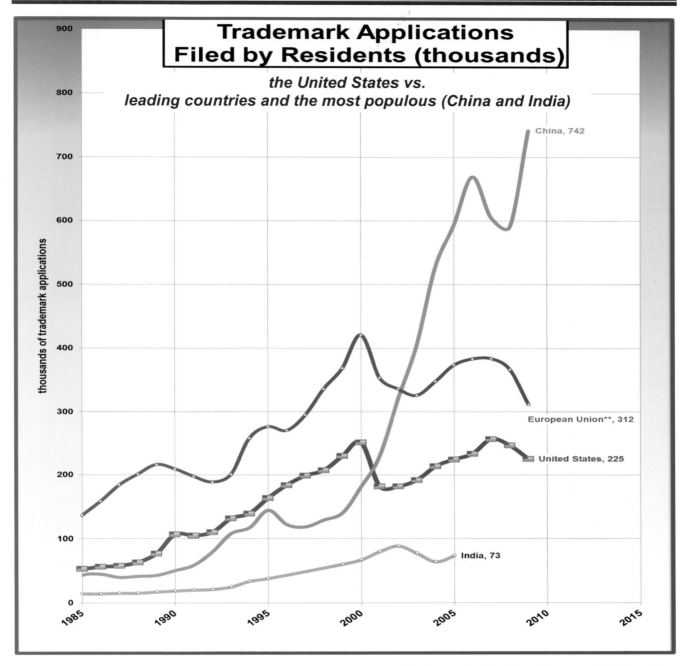

Trademark Applications Filed by Residents (thousands)

the United States vs. leading countries and the most populous (China and India)

China, 742

European Union**, 312

United States, 225

India, 73

thousands of trademark applications

Trademark applications filed are applications to register a trademark with a national or regional Intellectual Property (IP) office. Direct nonresident trademark applications are those filed by applicants from abroad directly at a given national IP office.

SOURCE: World Bank. World Intellectual Property Organization (WIPO), World Intellectual Property Indicators and www.wipo.int/econ_stat. The International Bureau of WIPO assumes no responsibility with respect to the transformation of these data.

http://data.worldbank.org/data-catalog/world-development-indicators?cid=GPD_WDI.

**European Union (see Appendix II): Austria, Belgium, Bulgaria, Cyprus, Czech Rep., Denmark, Estonia, Finland, France, Germany, Greece, Hungary, Ireland, Italy, Latvia, Lithuania, Luxembourg, Malta, Netherlands, Poland, Portugal, Romania, Slovakia, Slovenia, Spain, Sweden and the United Kingdom

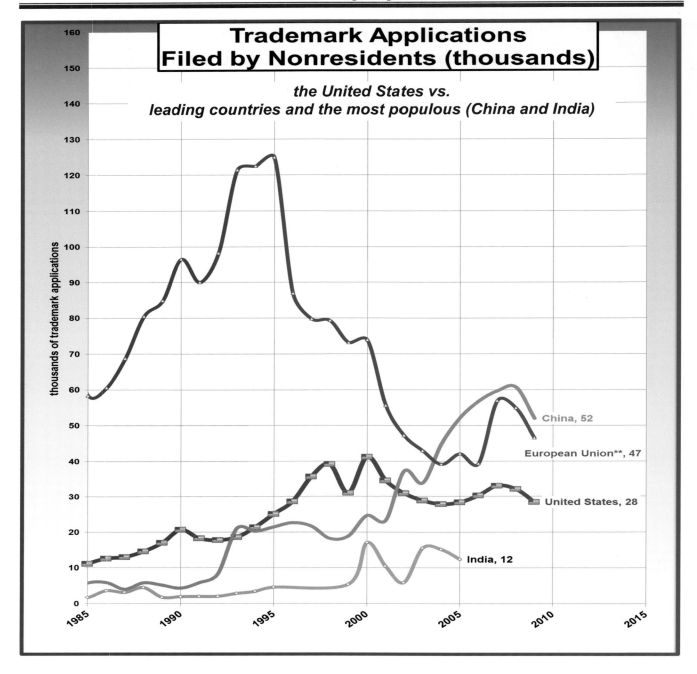

Trademark Applications Filed by Nonresidents (thousands)

the United States vs. leading countries and the most populous (China and India)

China, 52
European Union**, 47
United States, 28
India, 12

Trademark applications filed are applications to register a trademark with a national or regional Intellectual Property (IP) office. Direct nonresident trademark applications are those filed by applicants from abroad directly at a given national IP office.

SOURCE: World Bank. World Intellectual Property Organization (WIPO), World Intellectual Property Indicators and www.wipo.int/econ_stat. The International Bureau of WIPO assumes no responsibility with respect to the transformation of these data.

http://data.worldbank.org/data-catalog/world-development-indicators?cid=GPD_WDI

**European Union (see Appendix II): Austria, Belgium, Bulgaria, Cyprus, Czech Rep., Denmark, Estonia, Finland, France, Germany, Greece, Hungary, Ireland, Italy, Latvia, Lithuania, Luxembourg, Malta, Netherlands, Poland, Portugal, Romania, Slovakia, Slovenia, Spain, Sweden and the United Kingdom

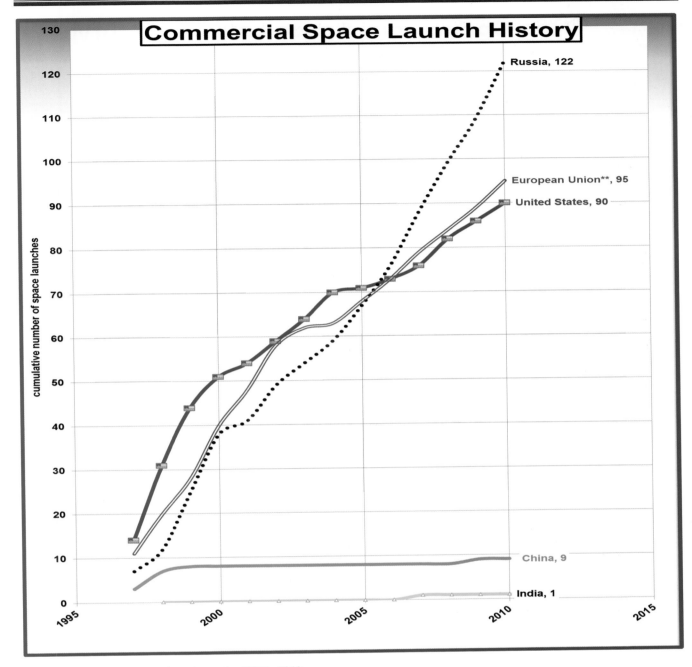

Commercial Space Launch History

- Russia, 122
- European Union**, 95
- United States, 90
- China, 9
- India, 1

cumulative number of space launches

Commercial world-wide space launch events: 1997 to 2010

SOURCE: U.S. Census Bureau, accessed in January 2012.

http://www.census.gov/compendia/statab/cats/international_statistics/vital_statistics_health_education.html

**European Union (see Appendix II): Austria, Belgium, Bulgaria, Cyprus, Czech Rep., Denmark, Estonia, Finland, France, Germany, Greece, Hungary, Ireland, Italy, Latvia, Lithuania, Luxembourg, Malta, Netherlands, Poland, Portugal, Romania, Slovakia, Slovenia, Spain, Sweden and the United Kingdom

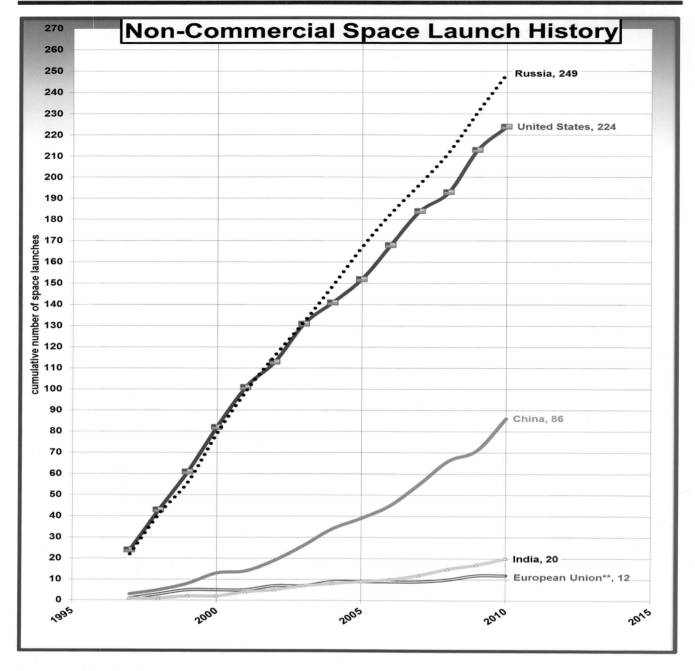

Non-Commercial Space Launch History

cumulative number of space launches

Russia, 249

United States, 224

China, 86

India, 20

European Union**, 12

1995 2000 2005 2010 2015

Non-commercial world-wide space launch events: 1997 to 2010.

SOURCE: U.S. Census Bureau, accessed in January 2012

http://www.census.gov/compendia/statab/cats/international_statistics/vital_statistics_health_education.html

**European Union (see Appendix II): Austria, Belgium, Bulgaria, Cyprus, Czech Rep., Denmark, Estonia, Finland, France, Germany, Greece, Hungary, Ireland, Italy, Latvia, Lithuania, Luxembourg, Malta, Netherlands, Poland, Portugal, Romania, Slovakia, Slovenia, Spain, Sweden and the United Kingdom

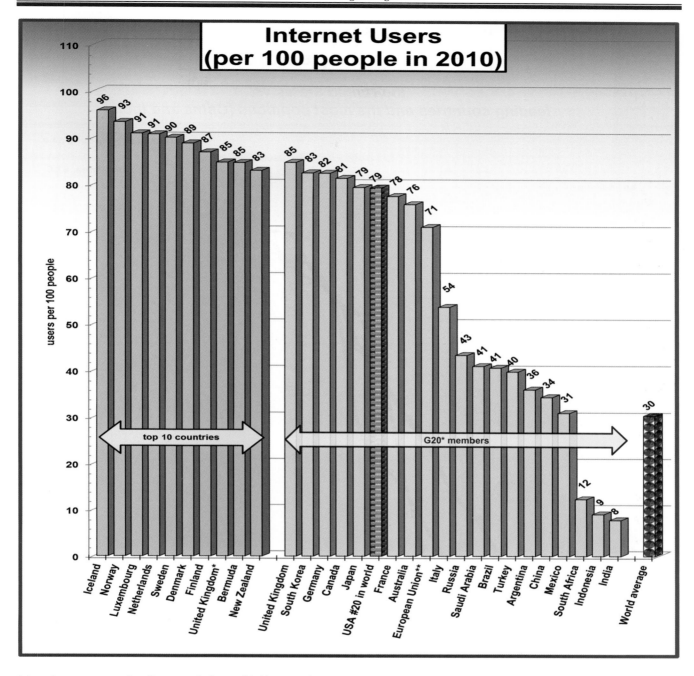

Internet Users
(per 100 people in 2010)

users per 100 people

top 10 countries

G20* members

Iceland 96, Norway 93, Luxembourg 91, Netherlands 91, Sweden 90, Denmark 89, Finland 87, United Kingdom* 85, Bermuda 85, New Zealand 83

United Kingdom 85, South Korea 83, Germany 82, Canada 81, Japan 79, USA #20 in world 79, France 78, Australia 76, European Union** 71, Italy 54, Russia 43, Saudi Arabia 41, Brazil 41, Turkey 40, Argentina 36, China 34, Mexico 31, South Africa 12, Indonesia 9, India 8

World average 30

Internet users are people with access to the worldwide network.

SOURCE: World Bank. International Telecommunication Union, World Telecommunication/ICT Development Report and database, and World Bank estimates; 2010 database accessed in April 2012

http://data.worldbank.org/data-catalog/world-development-indicators?cid=GPD_WDI

*G20 Members (see Appendix I): Argentina, Australia, Brazil, Canada, China, France, Germany, India, Indonesia, Italy, Japan, South Korea, Mexico, Russian Federation, Saudi Arabia, South Africa, Turkey, United Kingdom, United States and the European Union**

**European Union (see Appendix II): Austria, Belgium, Bulgaria, Cyprus, Czech Rep., Denmark, Estonia, Finland, France, Germany, Greece, Hungary, Ireland, Italy, Latvia, Lithuania, Luxembourg, Malta, Netherlands, Poland, Portugal, Romania, Slovakia, Slovenia, Spain, Sweden and the United Kingdom

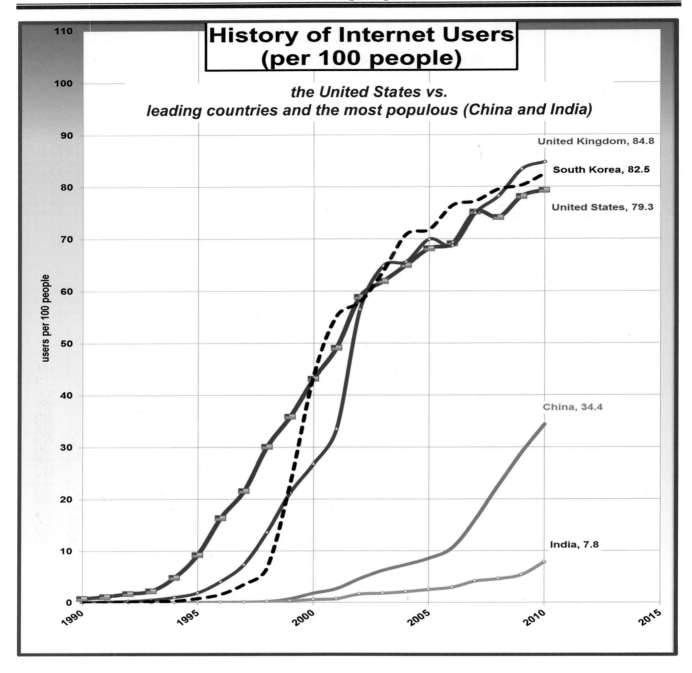

History of Internet Users (per 100 people)

*the United States vs.
leading countries and the most populous (China and India)*

- United Kingdom, 84.8
- South Korea, 82.5
- United States, 79.3
- China, 34.4
- India, 7.8

Internet users are people with access to the worldwide network.

SOURCE: World Bank. International Telecommunication Union, World Telecommunication/ICT Development Report and database, and World Bank estimates; 2010 database accessed in April 2012

http://data.worldbank.org/data-catalog/world-development-indicators?cid=GPD_WDI

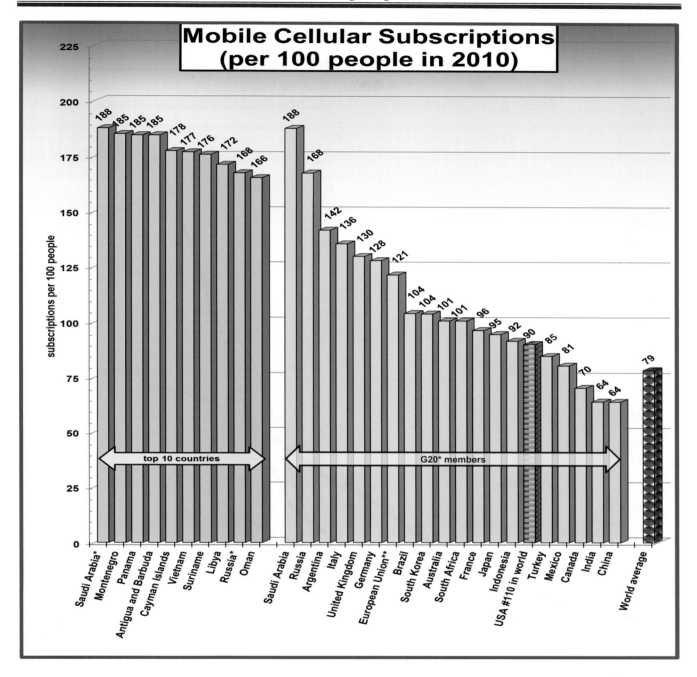

Mobile Cellular Subscriptions (per 100 people in 2010)

Mobile cellular telephone subscriptions are subscriptions to a public mobile telephone service using cellular technology, that provide access to the public switched telephone network. Post-paid and prepaid subscriptions are included. Mobile cellular subscriptions may include data card accounts for devices such as laptop computers and tablets as well as mobile telephones.

SOURCE: World Bank. International Telecommunication Union, World Telecommunication/ICT Development Report and database, and World Bank estimates; 2010 database accessed in April, 2012

http://data.worldbank.org/data-catalog/world-development-indicators?cid=GPD_WDI

*G20 Members (see Appendix I): Argentina, Australia, Brazil, Canada, China, France, Germany, India, Indonesia, Italy, Japan, South Korea, Mexico, Russian Federation, Saudi Arabia, South Africa, Turkey, United Kingdom, United States and the European Union**

**European Union (see Appendix II): Austria, Belgium, Bulgaria, Cyprus, Czech Rep., Denmark, Estonia, Finland, France, Germany, Greece, Hungary, Ireland, Italy, Latvia, Lithuania, Luxembourg, Malta, Netherlands, Poland, Portugal, Romania, Slovakia, Slovenia, Spain, Sweden and the United Kingdom

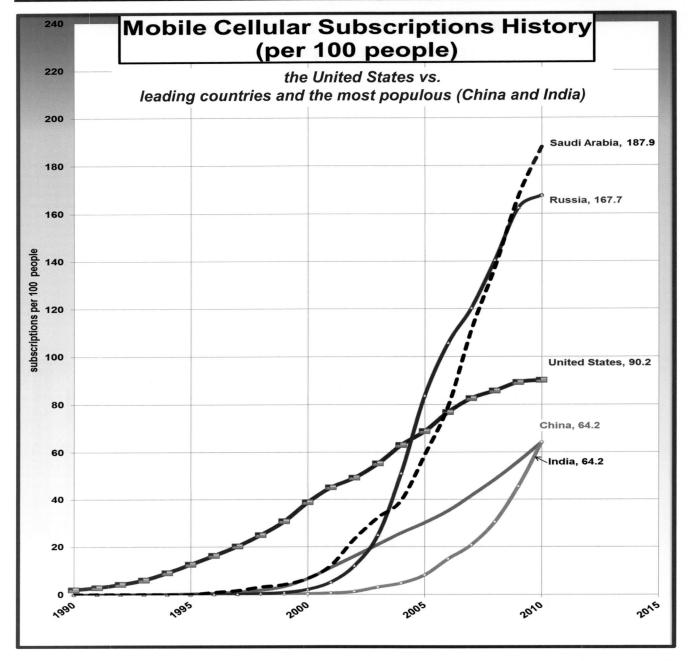

Mobile Cellular Subscriptions History (per 100 people)

the United States vs.
leading countries and the most populous (China and India)

Mobile cellular telephone subscriptions are subscriptions to a public mobile telephone service using cellular technology, which provide access to the public switched telephone network. Post-paid and prepaid subscriptions are included. Mobile cellular subscriptions may include data card accounts for devices such as laptop computers and tablets as well as mobile telephones.

SOURCE: World Bank. International Telecommunication Union, World Telecommunication/ICT Development Report and database, and World Bank estimates; 2010 database accessed in January 2012

http://data.worldbank.org/data-catalog/world-development-indicators?cid=GPD_WDI

*G20 Members (see Appendix I): Argentina, Australia, Brazil, Canada, China, France, Germany, India, Indonesia, Italy, Japan, South Korea, Mexico, Russian Federation, Saudi Arabia, South Africa, Turkey, United Kingdom, United States and the European Union**

**European Union (see Appendix II): Austria, Belgium, Bulgaria, Cyprus, Czech Rep., Denmark, Estonia, Finland, France, Germany, Greece, Hungary, Ireland, Italy, Latvia, Lithuania, Luxembourg, Malta, Netherlands, Poland, Portugal, Romania, Slovakia, Slovenia, Spain, Sweden and the United Kingdom

Chapter 14: U.S. National Defense in Relation to the World

Overview

In 2010, the United States spent 4.8 percent of GDP on defense, the sixth highest level in the world, equivalent to 41 percent of the world's total military expenditure of $1.71 trillion. These levels were approximately the same in 1991. The U.S. also exported 35 percent of the world's arms versus Russia's 24 percent, whereas in 1961 the U.S. exported 65 percent of the world's arms.

In 2009, the United States had 1.6 million armed forces personnel, the third largest military in the world, behind China's 2.9 million and India's 2.6 million. This was a decline in U.S. personnel from 2.1 million in 1991. There were 300,000 U.S. military personnel stationed in foreign countries, including 54,000 in Germany, 34,000 in Japan and 25,000 in South Korea.

In 2008, the United States distributed $45 billion in foreign aid, including $480 million to Russia.

~

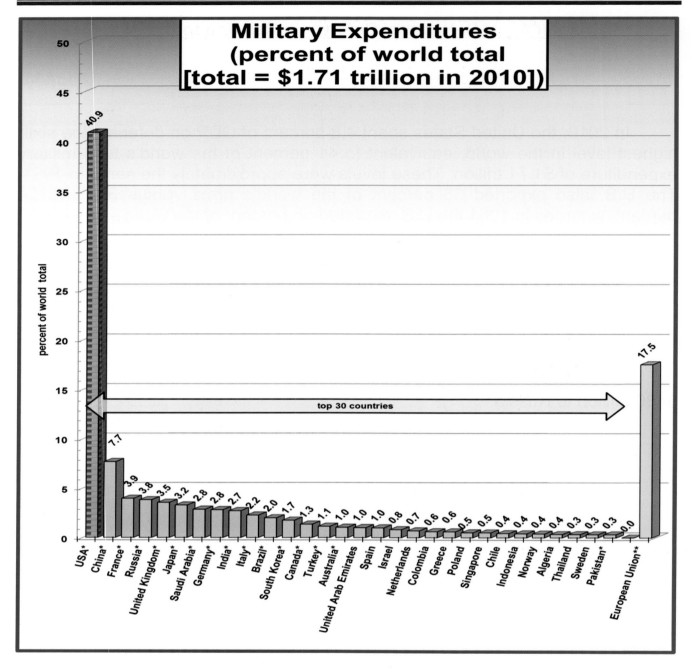

Military expenditures data from SIPRI (Stockholm International Peace Research Institute) are derived from the NATO definition, which includes all current and capital expenditures on the armed forces, including peacekeeping forces; defense ministries, and other government agencies engaged in defense projects; paramilitary forces, if these are judged to be trained and equipped for military operations; and military space activities. Such expenditures include military and civil personnel, including retirement pensions of military personnel and social services for personnel; operation and maintenance; procurement; military research and development; and military aid.

SOURCE: World Bank. Stockholm International Peace Research Institute (SIPRI), Yearbook: Armaments, Disarmament and International Security. Calculated based on 2010 GDP and military expenditures as percent of GDP from databases accessed in September 2012

http://data.worldbank.org/data-catalog/world-development-indicators?cid=GPD_WDI

*G20 Members (see Appendix I): Argentina, Australia, Brazil, Canada, China, France, Germany, India, Indonesia, Italy, Japan, South Korea, Mexico, Russian Federation, Saudi Arabia, South Africa, Turkey, United Kingdom, United States and the European Union**

**European Union (see Appendix II): Austria, Belgium, Bulgaria, Cyprus, Czech Rep., Denmark, Estonia, Finland, France, Germany, Greece, Hungary, Ireland, Italy, Latvia, Lithuania, Luxembourg, Malta, Netherlands, Poland, Portugal, Romania, Slovakia, Slovenia, Spain, Sweden and the United Kingdom

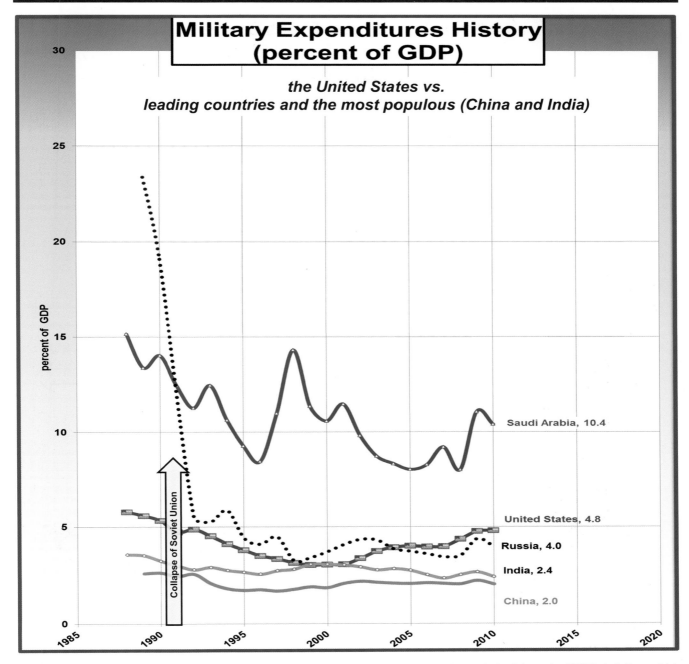

Military Expenditures History (percent of GDP)

the United States vs.
leading countries and the most populous (China and India)

percent of GDP

Collapse of Soviet Union

Saudi Arabia, 10.4

United States, 4.8

Russia, 4.0

India, 2.4

China, 2.0

Military expenditures data from SIPRI (Stockholm International Peace Research Institute) are derived from the NATO definition, which includes all current and capital expenditures on the armed forces, including peacekeeping forces; defense ministries and other government agencies engaged in defense projects; paramilitary forces, if these are judged to be trained and equipped for military operations; and military space activities. Such expenditures include military and civil personnel, including retirement pensions of military personnel and social services for personnel; operation and maintenance; procurement; military research and development; and military aid (in the military expenditures of the donor country). GDP = private consumption + gross investment + government consumption (exclusive of transfer payments such as Social Security) + [exports − imports].

SOURCE: World Bank. Stockholm International Peace Research Institute (SIPRI), Yearbook: Armaments, Disarmament and International Security; 2010 database accessed in April 2012

http://data.worldbank.org/data-catalog/world-development-indicators?cid=GPD_WDI

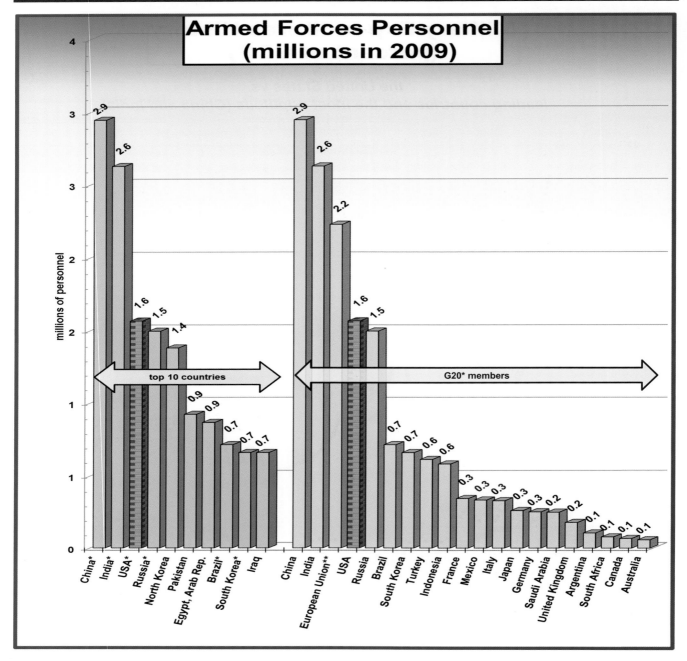

Armed Forces Personnel (millions in 2009)

Armed forces personnel are active duty military personnel, including paramilitary forces if the training, organization, equipment, and control suggest they may be used to support or replace regular military forces.

SOURCE: World Bank. International Institute for Strategic Studies, The Military Balance; 2009 database accessed in April 2012

http://data.worldbank.org/data-catalog/world-development-indicators?cid=GPD_WDI

*G20 Members (see Appendix I): Argentina, Australia, Brazil, Canada, China, France, Germany, India, Indonesia, Italy, Japan, South Korea, Mexico, Russian Federation, Saudi Arabia, South Africa, Turkey, United Kingdom, United States and the European Union**

**European Union (see Appendix II): Austria, Belgium, Bulgaria, Cyprus, Czech Rep., Denmark, Estonia, Finland, France, Germany, Greece, Hungary, Ireland, Italy, Latvia, Lithuania, Luxembourg, Malta, Netherlands, Poland, Portugal, Romania, Slovakia, Slovenia, Spain, Sweden and the United Kingdom

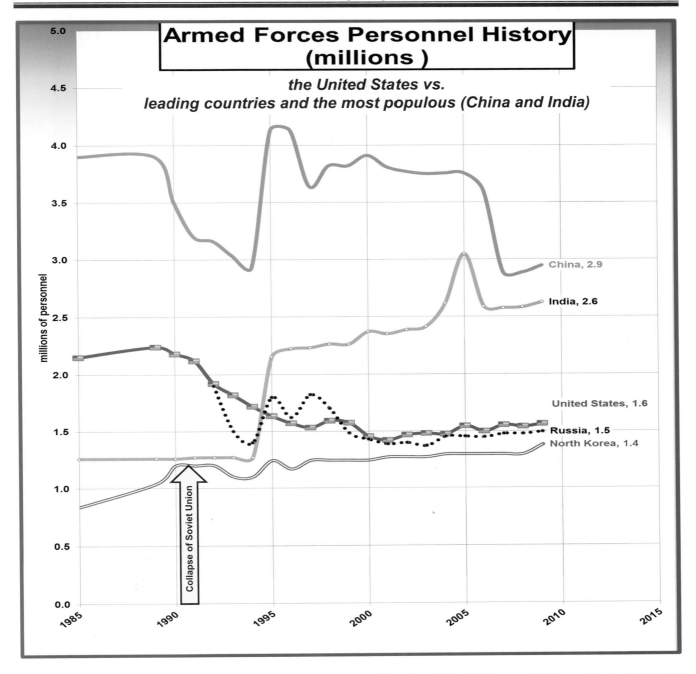

Armed Forces Personnel History (millions)

the United States vs.
leading countries and the most populous (China and India)

millions of personnel

Collapse of Soviet Union

China, 2.9

India, 2.6

United States, 1.6

Russia, 1.5

North Korea, 1.4

Armed forces personnel are active duty military personnel, including paramilitary forces if the training, organization, equipment, and control suggest they may be used to support or replace regular military forces.

SOURCE: World Bank. International Institute for Strategic Studies, The Military Balance; 2009 database accessed in April 2012

http://data.worldbank.org/data-catalog/world-development-indicators?cid=GPD_WDI

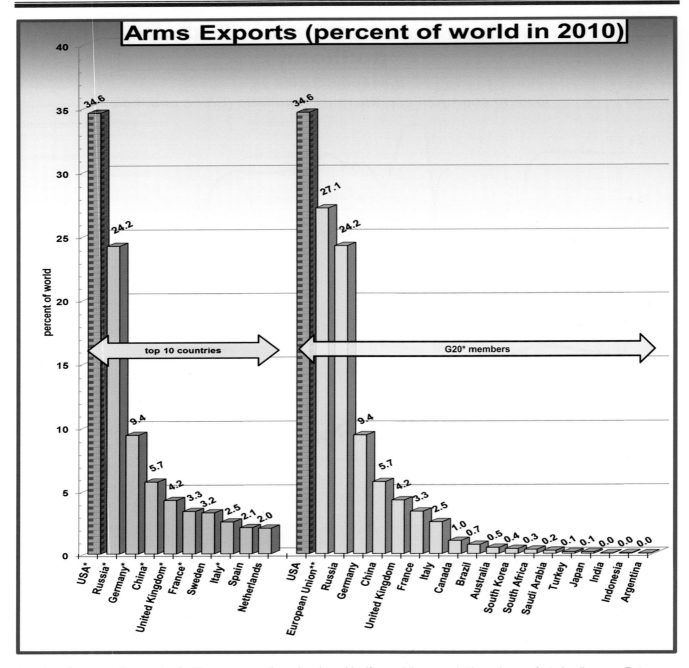

Arms transfers cover the supply of military weapons through sales, aid, gifts, and those made through manufacturing licenses. Data cover major conventional weapons such as aircraft, armored vehicles, artillery, radar systems, missiles, and ships designed for military use. Excluded are transfers of other military equipment such as small arms and light weapons, trucks, small artillery, ammunition, support equipment, technology transfers, and other services.

SOURCE: World Bank. Stockholm International Peace Research Institute (SIPRI), Yearbook: Armaments, Disarmament and International Security; 2010 database accessed in April 2012

http://data.worldbank.org/data-catalog/world-development-indicators?cid=GPD_WDI

*G20 Members (see Appendix I): Argentina, Australia, Brazil, Canada, China, France, Germany, India, Indonesia, Italy, Japan, South Korea, Mexico, Russian Federation, Saudi Arabia, South Africa, Turkey, United Kingdom, United States and the European Union**

**European Union (see Appendix II): Austria, Belgium, Bulgaria, Cyprus, Czech Rep., Denmark, Estonia, Finland, France, Germany, Greece, Hungary, Ireland, Italy, Latvia, Lithuania, Luxembourg, Malta, Netherlands, Poland, Portugal, Romania, Slovakia, Slovenia, Spain, Sweden and the United Kingdom

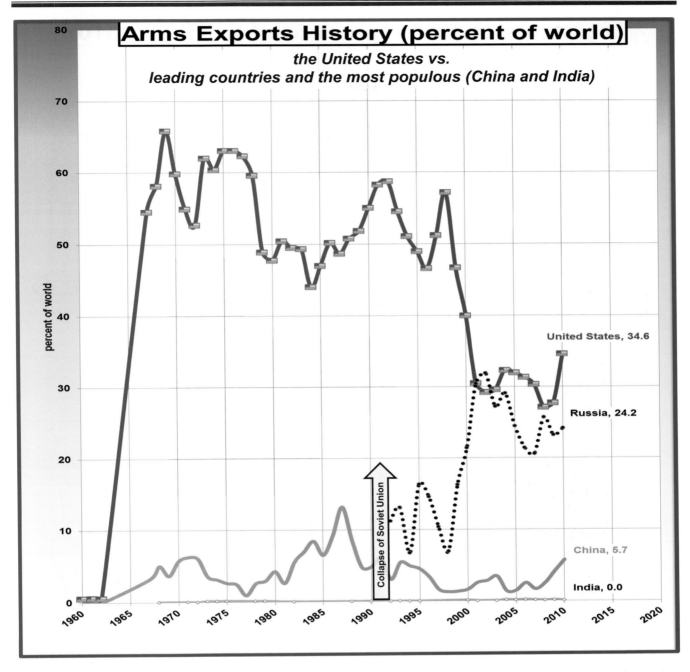

Arms Exports History (percent of world)

the United States vs.
leading countries and the most populous (China and India)

Collapse of Soviet Union

United States, 34.6

Russia, 24.2

China, 5.7

India, 0.0

Arms transfers cover the supply of military weapons through sales, aid, gifts, and those made through manufacturing licenses. Data cover major conventional weapons such as aircraft, armored vehicles, artillery, radar systems, missiles, and ships designed for military use. Excluded are transfers of other military equipment such as small arms and light weapons, trucks, small artillery, ammunition, support equipment, technology transfers, and other services.

SOURCE: World Bank. Stockholm International Peace Research Institute (SIPRI), Yearbook: Armaments, Disarmament and International Security; 2010 database accessed in April 2012

http://data.worldbank.org/data-catalog/world-development-indicators?cid=GPD_WDI

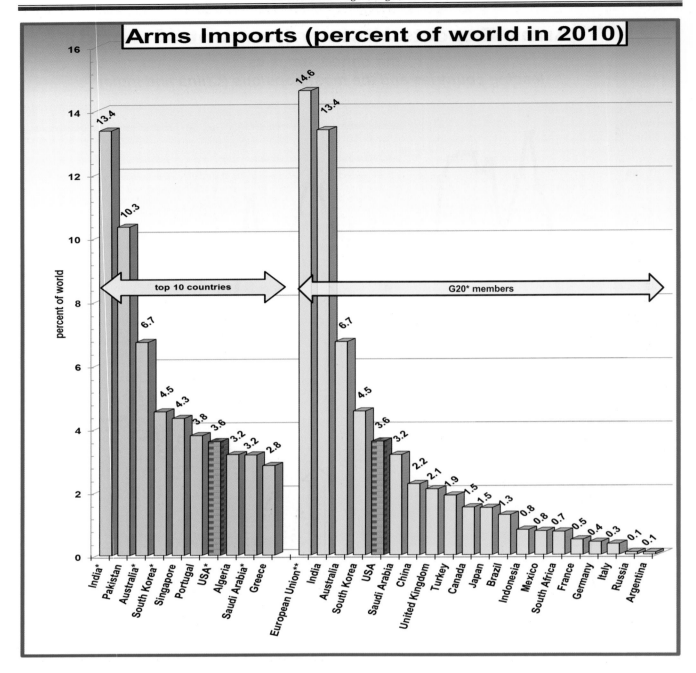

Arms Imports (percent of world in 2010)

Arms transfers cover the supply of military weapons through sales, aid, gifts, and those made through manufacturing licenses. Data cover major conventional weapons such as aircraft, armored vehicles, artillery, radar systems, missiles, and ships designed for military use. Excluded are transfers of other military equipment such as small arms and light weapons, trucks, small artillery, ammunition, support equipment, technology transfers, and other services.

SOURCE: World Bank. Stockholm International Peace Research Institute (SIPRI), Yearbook: Armaments, Disarmament and International Security; 2010 database accessed in April 2012

http://data.worldbank.org/data-catalog/world-development-indicators?cid=GPD_WDI

*G20 Members (see Appendix I): Argentina, Australia, Brazil, Canada, China, France, Germany, India, Indonesia, Italy, Japan, South Korea, Mexico, Russian Federation, Saudi Arabia, South Africa, Turkey, United Kingdom, United States and the European Union**

**European Union (see Appendix II): Austria, Belgium, Bulgaria, Cyprus, Czech Rep., Denmark, Estonia, Finland, France, Germany, Greece, Hungary, Ireland, Italy, Latvia, Lithuania, Luxembourg, Malta, Netherlands, Poland, Portugal, Romania, Slovakia, Slovenia, Spain, Sweden and the United Kingdom

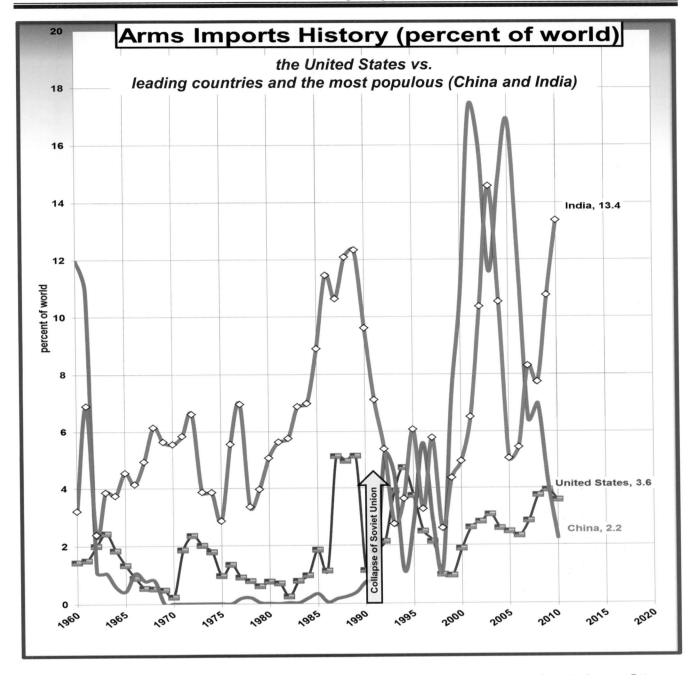

Arms Imports History (percent of world)

the United States vs.
leading countries and the most populous (China and India)

India, 13.4

United States, 3.6

China, 2.2

Collapse of Soviet Union

percent of world

Arms transfers cover the supply of military weapons through sales, aid, gifts, and those made through manufacturing licenses. Data cover major conventional weapons such as aircraft, armored vehicles, artillery, radar systems, missiles, and ships designed for military use. Excluded are transfers of other military equipment such as small arms and light weapons, trucks, small artillery, ammunition, support equipment, technology transfers, and other services.

SOURCE: World Bank. Stockholm International Peace Research Institute (SIPRI), Yearbook: Armaments, Disarmament and International Security; 2010 database accessed in April 2012

http://data.worldbank.org/data-catalog/world-development-indicators?cid=GPD_WDI

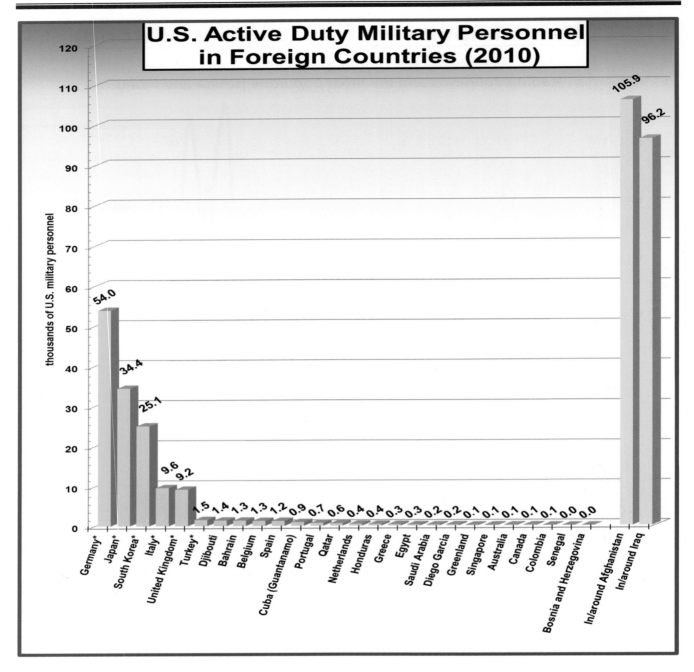

U.S. Active Duty Military Personnel in Foreign Countries (2010)

thousands of U.S. military personnel

Germany*: 54.0
Japan*: 34.4
South Korea*: 25.1
Italy*: 9.6
United Kingdom*: 9.2
Turkey*: 1.5
Djibouti: 1.4
Bahrain: 1.3
Belgium: 1.3
Spain: 1.2
Cuba (Guantanamo): 0.9
Portugal: 0.7
Qatar: 0.6
Netherlands: 0.4
Honduras: 0.4
Greece: 0.3
Egypt: 0.3
Saudi Arabia: 0.2
Diego Garcia: 0.2
Greenland: 0.1
Singapore: 0.1
Australia: 0.1
Canada: 0.1
Colombia: 0.1
Senegal: 0.0
Bosnia and Herzegovina: 0.0
In/around Afghanistan: 105.9
In/around Iraq: 96.2

U.S. military personnel on selected active duty in foreign countries. per U.S. Department of Defense, Defense Manpower Data Center. 2010 data (except Japan is 2008). U.S. foreign economic and military aid in 2008.

SOURCE: U.S. Census Bureau http://www.census.gov/compendia/statab/cats/international_statistics/vital_statistics_health_education.html; U.S. Agency for International Development; U.S. overseas loans and grants, obligations and loan authorizations

http://siadapp.dmdc.osd.mil/personnel/

*G20 Members (see Appendix I): Argentina, Australia, Brazil, Canada, China, France, Germany, India, Indonesia, Italy, Japan, South Korea, Mexico, Russian Federation, Saudi Arabia, South Africa, Turkey, United Kingdom, United States and the European Union**

**European Union (see Appendix II): Austria, Belgium, Bulgaria, Cyprus, Czech Rep., Denmark, Estonia, Finland, France, Germany, Greece, Hungary, Ireland, Italy, Latvia, Lithuania, Luxembourg, Malta, Netherlands, Poland, Portugal, Romania, Slovakia, Slovenia, Spain, Sweden and the United Kingdom

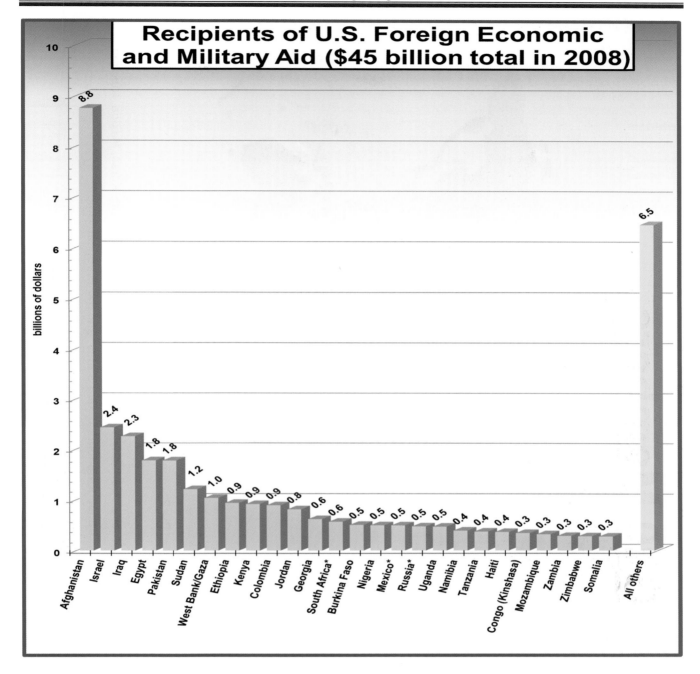

U.S. foreign economic and military aid by major recipient country: For 2008, ending September 30. Annual figures are in obligations.

SOURCE: U.S. Census Bureau [http://www.census.gov/compendia/statab/cats/international_statistics/vital_statistics_health_education.html]

http://data.worldbank.org/data-catalog/world-development-indicators?cid=GPD_WDI

*G20 Members (see Appendix I): Argentina, Australia, Brazil, Canada, China, France, Germany, India, Indonesia, Italy, Japan, South Korea, Mexico, Russian Federation, Saudi Arabia, South Africa, Turkey, United Kingdom, United States and the European Union**

**European Union (see Appendix II): Austria, Belgium, Bulgaria, Cyprus, Czech Rep., Denmark, Estonia, Finland, France, Germany, Greece, Hungary, Ireland, Italy, Latvia, Lithuania, Luxembourg, Malta, Netherlands, Poland, Portugal, Romania, Slovakia, Slovenia, Spain, Sweden and the United Kingdom

G20 Members

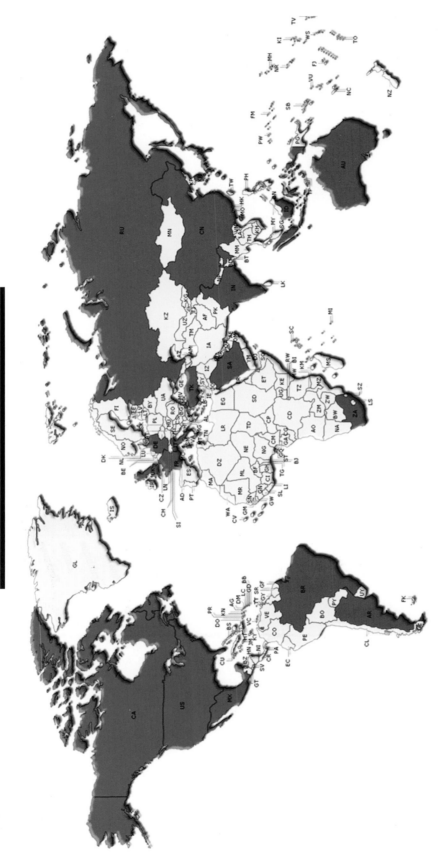

In 2012 there were 19 G20 Member Countries and the European Union**

Argentina, Australia, Brazil*, Canada*, China*, France*, Germany*, India*, Indonesia, Italy*, Japan*, South Korea, Mexico, Russian Federation*, Saudi Arabia, South Africa, Turkey, United Kingdom*, United States* and the European Union**

* One of ten largest economies in the world based on Gross Domestic Product (see page 46)

** see Appendix II for definition of European Union

European Union

In 2012 there were 27 <u>European Union</u> Members

Austria, Belgium, Bulgaria, Cyprus, Czech Republic, Denmark, Estonia, Finland, France*, Germany*, Greece, Hungary, Ireland, Italy*, Latvia, Lithuania, Luxembourg, Malta, Netherlands, Poland, Portugal, Romania, Slovakia, Slovenia, Spain, Sweden, and the United Kingdom*

* One of the ten largest economies in the world based on Gross Domestic Product (see page 46)

OECD* Members

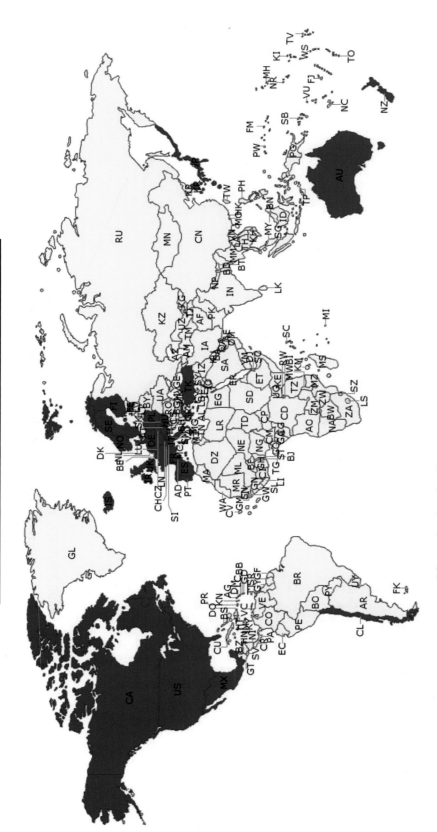

*Organization for Economic Cooperation and Development

In May 2012 there were 34 <u>OECD</u> Member Countries:

Australia, Austria, Belgium, Canada, Chile, China, Czech Republic, Denmark, Estonia, Finland, France, Germany, Greece, Hungary, Iceland, Ireland, Israel, Italy, Japan, South Korea, Luxembourg, Mexico, Netherlands, New Zealand, Norway, Poland, Slovak Republic, Slovenia, Spain, Sweden, Switzerland, Turkey, the United Kingdom, and the United States

* One of the world's 10 largest economies based on Gross Domestic Product (see page 46).

**see Appendix II for definition of European Union

OPEC* Members

*Organization of Petroleum Exporting Countries

In 2012 there were 12 OPEC member countries:

Algeria, Angola, Ecuador, Iran, Iraq, Kuwait, Libya, Niger, Qatar, Saudi Arabia, United Arab Emirates and Venezuela

~ <u>Resources</u> ~

The following sources were selected for data mining used to create the charts in this book. The author judges these sources to be unbiased and apolitical; however all data should be viewed with some skepticism, especially when pertaining to matters sensitive to national status or when obtained from closed societies, e.g., China. Updates to these databases occur at varying intervals ranging from weekly to multiple years, depending on the source and the parameter. Generally, demographic-type databases that compare all the world's countries tend to be updated in one-to-five year intervals, whereas data limited to the United States, especially economic data, may be updated daily.

<u>Database Resources</u>   <u>Website Portals</u>

Database Resources	Website Portals
National Archive of Criminal Justice Data	http://www.icpsr.umich.edu/icpsrweb/NACJD
National Science Foundation	http://www.nsf.gov/statistics/
Organization for Economic Cooperation and Development	http://www.oecd.org/edu
U.S. Bureau of Economic Analysis	http://www.bea.gov/
U.S. Bureau of Labor Statistics	http://www.bls.gov/
U.S. Bureau of Justice Statistics	http://bjs.ojp.usdoj.gov/
U.S. Census Bureau	http://www.treasury.gov/resource-center/Pages/default.aspx
U.S. Central Intelligence Agency	https://www.cia.gov/library/publications/the-world-factbook/index.html
U.S. Congressional Budget Office	http://www.cbo.gov/
U.S. Department of Agriculture	http://www.fns.usda.gov/fns/
U.S. Energy Information Administration	http://www.eia.gov/
U.S. Federal Reserve Economic Data	http://research.stlouisfed.org/
U.S. Internal Revenue Service	http://www.irs.gov/taxstats/indtaxstats/
U.S. Office of Policy and Management	http://www.opm.gov/feddata/HistoricalTables/
U.S. Treasury	http://www.treasury.gov/resource-center/data-chart-center/
World Bank	http://data.worldbank.org/data-catalog/

~ <u>Index</u> ~

B

C

D

F

G

H

I

N

O

P

Q

R

S

U